DOWN
TO
THE
BONE

ALSO BY CAITLIN ROTHER

Poisoned Love

Twisted Triangle (by Caitlin Rother with John Hess)

Body Parts

Where Hope Begins/Deadly Devotion
(by Alysia Sofios with Caitlin Rother)

My Life, Deleted (by Scott and Joan Bolzan and Caitlin Rother)

Lost Girls

I'll Take Care of You

Then No One Can Have Her

Hunting Charles Manson (by Lis Wiehl with Caitlin Rother)

Naked Addiction

Love Gone Wrong

Secrets, Lies, and Shoelaces

Dead Reckoning

Death on Ocean Boulevard

DOWN
TO
THE
BONE

A MISSING FAMILY'S MURDER AND THE ELUSIVE QUEST FOR JUSTICE

Caitlin Rother

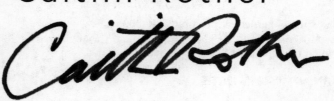

CITADEL PRESS
Kensington Publishing Corp.
kensingtonbooks.com

10 9 8 7 6 5 4 3 2 1

First Citadel hardcover printing: July 2025

Printed in the United States of America

ISBN: 978-0-8065-4262-1

ISBN: 978-0-8065-4264-5 (e-book)

Library of Congress Control Number: 2023944268

The authorized representative in the EU for product safety and compliance
is eucomply OU, Parnu mnt 139b-14, Apt 123,
Tallinn, Berlin 11317; hello@eucompliancepartner.com

Prologue

Motorcyclist John Bluth was off-roading in the Mojave Desert, looking for a trail one November morning, when a curved white object on a pile of rocks caught his eye.

At first, he thought it was a turtle shell. But after dismounting his bike, he turned it over with a stick, and realized it looked more like a piece of bone. Possibly a human bone.

Marking the spot so he could find it again amongst the greasewoods, he rode his bike across the wash until he found a road south of the landfill, where he called 911.

"I found what looks like part of a human skull," he told the dispatcher.

A deputy drove out from the San Bernardino County Sheriff's Department (SBCSD) station in Victorville and followed Bluth back to the bone. Recognizing the bridge of a small child's nose and upper eye sockets, the deputy sent a photo to his sergeant. A coroner's investigator and forensic anthropologist were promptly dispatched to examine it more closely.

After confirming it was, in fact, a child's partial skull, they walked across the beige ripples of desert sand until they came across several child-sized ribs and part of a leg bone, bleached and weathered by the sun and wind.

Surveying the surrounding area, they found two sunken patches of dirt about fifty yards east of where Bluth had found the skull fragment, as if someone had dug two holes, then dumped the earth back in.

Carefully brushing away the dirt, they uncovered a set of rib bones and stopped to take pause. These were not just holes, they were two shallow graves—six feet long, two feet wide, eighteen inches deep, and about twenty feet apart—where animals had been digging around and dragging the bones across the wash.

Leading to each grave was a set of tire tracks, as if two large vehicles had turned left from the gas-line road and backed in. Although they'd been eroded by the elements, the tracks were still deep and distinct enough to measure seventy-three and seventy-six inches, respectively, as if they were made when the ground was soft and wet.

As the sun went down and dusk descended, it became too hard to see, so they quit for the day, leaving a couple of patrol deputies to keep watch until the homicide team arrived first thing the next morning.

The investigators soon determined that these skeletal remains belonged to a man, a woman, and two young children. Because it was so unusual for an entire family to go missing, it didn't take long to link possible names to the bones they had carefully curated.

The two adults were quickly identified through dental records as Joseph and Summer McStay, who had been reported missing along with their three- and four-year-old sons, on February 15, 2010—nearly four years earlier.

The boys, Gianni and Joseph Jr., were identified a week later through a DNA match with their placentas, which Summer had stored in the freezer to bury under a tree she wanted to plant at their new house in Fallbrook.

But the unraveling of the family's sudden disappearance had only just begun.

Chapter 1

As Deputy Michael Tingley walked into the McStay family's house on Avocado Vista Lane, a mix of odors and uncertainty hung in the air.

Half a carton of eggs, a bowl of overripe bananas and oranges, and some dirty dishes were sitting on the counter. Soiled diapers were fermenting in the trash bin. A bag of popping corn kernels was open near the microwave, with two corresponding kid-sized bowls of popcorn on the futon couch. Mold was floating in the coffee maker, and an apple, with a child's bite taken out of it, lay on the carpeted staircase.

It looked as if time had stopped for Summer and Joseph's family, who had been reported missing to the San Diego County Sheriff's Department (SDSD) that morning by Joseph's brother, Michael. No one had seen or talked to them for eleven days, which was highly unusual, because Joseph had an online waterfall manufacturing business to run and several major projects in the works.

Someone had been painting the kitchen, but it appeared they'd been interrupted. The roller was stuck to the metal tray, caked with dried paint, and cabinet doors and drawers were stacked on sheets of newspaper on the floor. Boxes of hardwood flooring were piled up near the front door, awaiting installation.

Were the McStays a messy bunch, apathetic about housekeeping in the midst of remodeling their new home? Or had something—or someone—caused them to drop what they were doing and flee?

The front door to the two-story, five-bedroom house was locked, so Tingley stood outside while Michael climbed through the same rear office window he'd entered two days earlier. Then the two of them walked from room to room, searching for clues to the family's whereabouts.

Thankfully, Tingley had the foresight to snap a few photos, which became the only surviving images to illustrate the state of the McStays' house that day, presumably as they'd left it. By the time sheriff's investigators executed a search warrant four days later, the scene had been irrevocably altered.

Tingley noted some disarray upstairs, where a pole lamp had toppled onto some bedding on the master bedroom floor, where the family had been sleeping on two air mattresses. Mounds of clothes spilled out of suitcases, covering the closet floor.

The family's green Dodge truck was parked in the driveway, with a newspaper, dated February 5, 2010, lodged under a tire. But a registration check showed that their second vehicle, a 1996 white Isuzu Trooper, had been towed on February 8 from a San Ysidro shopping mall, half a mile from the Mexican border. How did they get to their destination if both vehicles were accounted for?

None of Joseph's extended family lived nearby—Michael and their mother, Susan Blake, were in different counties, and their father, Patrick McStay, was in Texas. And as close as they all said they were to Joseph, none of them were very concerned, at least initially.

Joseph liked to take the occasional break from answering his phone. He'd also taken his wife and kids on unannounced weekend trips or vacations before. So, Susan and Michael thought Joseph might have taken them somewhere special for Valentine's Day, like the previous summer, when they took off to a

Christian camp in Yucaipa without telling anyone. But they'd boarded their dog, Bear, before they went, and this time, he and their new puppy, Digger, were outside, barking, in the backyard.

More importantly, Joseph always stayed in touch by phone and email with two of his business associates: Charles "Chase" Merritt, a welder who built custom fountains, lived about seventy miles north in Rancho Cucamonga, and Dan Kavanaugh, who had built and maintained the company's website, lived in San Diego, but had recently gone surfing in Hawaii with his girlfriend.

So, after five days of being unable to reach Joseph, Merritt drove to Susan's house in Corona to ask if she'd seen him, and Kavanaugh tried to contact Joseph's father. Susan, Michael, Merritt, and Kavanaugh had been checking in with one another ever since.

Setting his clipboard on the dining room table, Tingley didn't find any leads, such as vacation brochures, for where the family might be. Neither had Michael, who had already walked through the house with Merritt.

It was unclear what time of day they'd left. Although coffee and breakfast food were left out on the counter, the lamp in Joseph's home office was still on. He routinely kept that light on overnight so the boys didn't fall when they came downstairs to the kitchen for a drink of water.

Although Tingley didn't see any blood, broken glass, or obvious signs of a struggle—other than possibly the toppled lamp upstairs—his gut told him something wasn't right.

Every year, an average of 600,000 people go missing in the United States. While it's not uncommon for a single child or an adult to do so, it's quite rare for a family of four, especially with two young children.

"It appeared that whoever was there, in my mind, had just got up and left," which "raised suspicions, didn't seem normal," Tingley testified later.

The SDSD had no dedicated missing persons unit, so area deputies handled the initial reports. After talking to the family and checking hospitals and jails, the deputy would forward the report to homicide if the missing party hadn't turned up within ten days. Because no one had seen or heard from the McStays since February 4th, they were now at eleven days.

"To cover my bases, to make sure we cross our *I*s and dot our *T*s," Tingley alerted the on-call homicide sergeant.

"We'll be right out," the sergeant said.

With his 2004 bankruptcy in the rearview mirror, Joseph boasted that he'd gotten "a smokin' deal at 316K" on the house, which they'd bought in foreclosure, filing the deed on November 17, 2009. Joseph, who had better credit than Summer, financed the home in his name with a $330,000 loan that would also help finance the remodel. The goal was to flip the property in two years, then move back to the coast with a pile of profit.

"He was really proud," Susan recalled. "It was their first home, and it was the first time Joey bought a home."

After eight years of living in a cramped duplex apartment in San Clemente, the McStay family loved having extra space in which to roam around. In addition to nearly 2,800 square feet indoors, the house had two side yards and a fenced backyard with fruit trees, a cement patio, and a lawn, where the boys wore themselves out chasing after their new Labrador rescue puppy and their eight-year-old black German shepherd/rottweiler mix.

But that raised a troubling question: why would Joseph and Summer leave their dogs outside without food or water? Summer always brought them indoors at night and put the puppy in the laundry room to sleep.

The McStays hadn't met all their neighbors yet, but the quiet Lake Rancho Viejo subdivision was full of middle-class families like theirs. Joseph worked from home, so he was free to join Summer in family activities he videotaped and uploaded to his YouTube channel. His tour of the new house featured a view of the camel-humped mountain across the street, peppered with tan boulders and clusters of green avocado trees.

Joseph and Summer would rather have bought a place closer to the beach, but they couldn't afford it. So they settled for this one in the rural unincorporated community of Fallbrook, known for its small-town feel, open space, and annual Avocado Festival.

With convenient access to Interstates 15 and 76, Fallbrook was a straight, thirty-minute shot west to Oceanside, where Joseph could still catch some waves. It was also a drivable distance to his Friday night soccer games in Orange County and the sheet-metal workshop in Los Angeles County where Merritt built their fountains.

Although Joseph made a decent living from his business, Earth Inspired Products (EIP), the McStays maintained a minimalist lifestyle while the renovations were underway. The home office was up and running, and his mother had lent them furniture for the dining and family rooms, but they were living out of suitcases for the time being.

The garage was stacked with boxes they'd unloaded from a PODS storage unit. They were waiting to finish painting and installing the flooring downstairs before unloading two other units, which were in Anaheim.

Remodeling was stressful enough, but Joseph had also been experiencing a mysterious illness for the past eight months, which caused nausea, breathing problems, and severe vertigo that often kept him in bed, working on his laptop. None of his doctors or holistic health practitioners could identify what was wrong.

Before they left San Clemente, a bout of dizziness landed him in the ER one Saturday night in August 2009. "I'm really sick . . . Asthma & head all messed up . . . Tough time breahtn [sic] since," he emailed a friend afterward.

The illness kept him from playing soccer for a while. He thought he felt well enough to start up again in late January, but the symptoms returned.

When he last talked to his mother, he said he'd felt so dizzy while driving, he had to pull over. Later, she wondered if he'd taken ill on the way home from his lunch meeting with Merritt on February 4 in Rancho Cucamonga, which was a ninety-minute drive at that time of day.

Susan and Summer weren't close, but Susan was in the home-building business, so they'd been chatting more often lately about designs and materials for the remodel. Summer got along better with Joseph's father, Patrick.

When Joseph talked to Patrick for the last time on February 3, he was excited about the deal he'd gotten on granite countertops for the kitchen and three bathrooms. Patrick couldn't see him taking off in the middle of the project, though he remembered Summer jumping in on a call in January to say that if anything happened to Joseph, she would bring the boys to Texas so Patrick could help raise them. Joseph reiterated that sentiment on a Skype call a week later, as Summer nodded affirmingly.

Was this due to Joseph's illness, or were they expecting something bad to come down the pike?

Chapter 2

The week before they went missing, Summer's first priority was the painting project. After a handyman she found on Craigslist fell through in late January, the couple's friend and DIY guy, Jeffrey "McGyver" McCargar, offered to help them out for a little gas money.

He removed the cabinet doors and drawers and lined edges and baseboards with blue tape. But after painting some areas in a beige Joseph had chosen, Summer said she wanted them to redo it in a lighter color before the floor installers came. Summer was so stressed, she reamed out McCargar, who cancelled last minute, saying he'd forgotten his pregnant girlfriend had an ultrasound appointment.

Luckily, the floor crew rescheduled due to a rain forecast, so McCargar had a little more time. He came back for half-days on February 2 and 3, but when he called and texted Summer and Joseph on February 5 to schedule his next visit, he got no response. After trying again unsuccessfully on February 6, he didn't press it. Summer had been more difficult than usual lately.

Chase Merritt, who had been working for Joseph for several years, showed up unannounced at Susan Blake's house on February 9. He wasn't a complete stranger to her, because he'd been at Joseph's wedding, and he'd also come by with her son in December.

With several waterfall jobs pending, Merritt said he was concerned he hadn't been able to reach Joseph for five days. They'd gotten to be close friends and normally talked many times throughout the day.

"Do you have any idea where Joseph is?" he asked, saying he'd gone by the house, but no one was home. "I can't reach him, and I can't find him."

"No, I don't," she said. "I haven't heard from him either, but that's not unusual. I'll try to get a hold of him."

"If you do, could you please let him know that Chase is looking for him?"

Susan tried calling Joseph herself, but it went straight to voicemail. She also called Michael to see if he could meet Merritt at Joseph's house, but he said he was too busy installing fire sprinklers in Huntington Beach.

The next day, Patrick called Michael, too, because he hadn't been able to reach Joseph in several days, either.

"Can you go down there and check on your brother?" he asked. "Something's wrong."

"I don't have time," Michael said.

Michael hadn't talked to his brother in a week, but that was typical these days. If Joseph hadn't turned up by Saturday, February 13, Michael said he would drive down then.

Patrick told Michael he'd gotten a weird email from someone named Dan Kavanaugh and then a call from a "D. Kavanaugh" with the 619 area code in San Diego. He didn't answer either one, because he didn't recognize the name.

"Dad, you know who that is. That's Dan the Hacker," Michael said, reminding his dad that he'd met the kid when he was building Joseph's website in 2005. Patrick asked Michael to call him and see what he wanted.

Kavanaugh was the first to announce on Joseph's Facebook page that he'd gone AWOL: has anyone seen joe in the last 5 days?

he wrote on February 9. His phone has been off since Saturday and hes not reading his emails???

Kavanaugh also called the San Diego Police Department (SDPD) and the SDSD, requesting a welfare check at the house in Fallbrook on February 10: *Does online business with him and for five days he's getting no response. Very unusual behavior for subject. Works 9-5 Monday thru Friday,* the sheriff's dispatcher wrote in the log after Kavanaugh's call.

But when a deputy showed up that afternoon, he reported back that no one was home: *No answer at door. Large dog in backyard, green Dodge parked in front yard.*

Kavanaugh didn't mention to the authorities that he'd had a falling-out with Joseph, who had been buying him out of the business after he sent Joseph a series of instant messages in January 2009, threatening to shut down the website and destroy the business:

it will be about 30 days from today that your site is gone from the search engines, Kavanaugh wrote. i will make my own fountain site . . . you and i had a business . . . don't burn fools.

Joseph replied: do you see the 'contradiction'? You wish the best for me & my family, but have no problem destroying our livelihood?

Kavanaugh offered Joseph a way to avert disaster: you can disregard my offer to buy me out and continue thinking your site is permanent, or you can simply do it, and keep your site.

Joseph tried guilting Kavanaugh into retracting his ultimatum: Now, I, Summer & Kids know the 'Real You' and what you would potentially do to harm me and my family. Your [sic] a great guy Dan . . . FK'n Sad.

Kavanaugh gave Joseph a day to sleep on it and come back with a "fair" dollar figure. He could even do it over time with a payment plan: so now that you know how serious I am, and what im capable of you can make a better decision how to end this.

But Joseph didn't seem hopeful. Clearly, Kavanaugh couldn't

be trusted: you would take the $$$ and still do those malicious things. What's the point?

Joseph told his parents and close friends that he had no choice but to comply with the threats. However, he was recalibrating and planning to expand—without Kavanaugh—by adding more welders and fabricators, and consolidating his manufacturing, shipping, and IT operations, all in one warehouse.

Nonetheless, Susan didn't question Kavanaugh's offer to go through Joseph's financial accounts and emails to help track down the family, nor did she question how or why he had access to those accounts.

On Saturday, February 13, Michael met Merritt at a gas station and followed him to the house. Although he told Deputy Tingley he'd been by there February 4 or 6, Michael later said this Saturday trip with Merritt was his first. He and his wife had never been invited over due to a spat with Summer. But because Merritt had already updated him by phone after a couple of visits, Michael said he felt he'd "had eyeballs" on the house.

Summer and Michael didn't get along. As she'd complained to her mother, Blanche Almanza, Joseph often gave his brother money for bills and rent, and that was on top of the $2,000 in seed money to start Michael's fire-sprinkler company.

The final rift came in July 2009, when Summer told Michael's wife Erin her daughters were "dirty" during a breakfast at IHOP. Michael called out Summer for being disrespectful to his wife, and Summer disinvited them to Gianni's birthday party. When they showed up to drop off a gift anyway, Summer was furious.

Michael had also upset Summer by describing her as a "beaner," a derogatory slur against Hispanics, and calling her "Heather," the name of Joseph's ex-wife. Michael said the latter incident was accidental, but Summer put it on the mental list of wrongs she kept.

"Refer to the list," she would say.

Summer didn't care for Heather, either, claiming she left Joseph's teenage son, Elijah, with Summer to watch for extended periods of time, and had walked in unannounced to talk with Joseph while he was showering, which Heather denied.

Since Summer's spat with Michael, Joseph usually talked to his brother by phone on the way to his weekly soccer games. The one time Michael and Erin came to the apartment to pray with Joseph while he was sick in bed with vertigo, Summer left abruptly.

After Merritt and Michael arrived at the house that Saturday, Michael was leery about trying to enter, because the doors were locked.

"Just go in," Merritt said, leading him through the side gate to the backyard.

He said Joseph usually brought the dogs inside in the evening, but they saw that someone had ripped open a bag of dry food for them in the shed and moved their water dish under a slow-dripping faucet. That made Michael and Susan think the family had arranged for someone to feed the animals while they were gone.

Merritt showed Michael that Joseph's office window was unlocked, but didn't offer to help him get inside. So Michael held the blinds aside, climbed up on his belly, slid one leg through, and hopped in.

After opening the sliding glass door in back, he looked around while Merritt unlocked the front door for Erin and the kids, who needed to use the restroom.

Merritt said he suggested they call the police. "What if Joseph did go to the mountains and he drove off a cliff, and he's in a ravine two hundred feet down and nobody sees the car down there for two or three weeks?"

But Michael wanted to wait a couple more days. In the meantime, he went door to door, asking neighbors if they'd seen his brother's family. They all said no, although one said he'd seen a work truck parked outside.

Michael locked the house back up and left his phone number on the front door, asking anyone with information to call him. He also posted a message on Joseph's Facebook page: All of Joeys friends. Hit me back once you read this. Does anyone know where he's at? He's been MIA for 8 days and his family is concerned. Call me.

He said Joseph hadn't answered calls or emails since February 4, and now his phone was dead: My Mom, Dad, Dan, Chase are very worried. It's not like him to not return emails . . . phone calls, maybe . . . but not all his business stuff.

The next day, a neighbor, frustrated by ten days and nights of incessant barking, called the county to report the McStays' dogs as abandoned, which triggered a visit by animal control.

It was dark when Officer Kathleen Conwell arrived at 7:40 p.m. Hearing barking in the backyard, she opened, then promptly closed, the gate after seeing a mature rottweiler in a protective guarding stance. With three of her own, she knew the breed could get aggressive.

Seeing the dogs had blankets and food in the shed, Conwell went next door to talk to a neighbor. She didn't know where the McStays had gone, but she'd been feeding their animals.

Conwell called Michael and got his voicemail, so she called the sheriff's dispatcher to request that a deputy do a welfare check inside the house. She was posting an "abandoned animal" warning when Michael called back to say he was planning to file a missing person's report and collect the dogs the next day. After he told her the SDSD had already done a welfare check, Conwell cancelled her request.

Chapter 3

The next morning at nine o'clock, Michael McStay called to report Joseph and his family missing, as promised.

When Deputy Tingley called him back, Michael said he was heading to the house that afternoon with his wife and kids.

"Can you meet me at the station?" Tingley asked.

As the deputy asked background questions for his report, Michael seemed genuinely concerned about his brother and family.

Michael said growing up "three years, two months, three days" younger than Joseph made him feel he was living in his brother's shadow. But they'd always hung out together—racing motorcycles, fishing or camping on weekends at Fort Hood in Dallas, and surfing after moving to Southern California as teenagers.

"He was really good at a lot of things, so I always looked up to him," Michael said. "He was a hard worker. He could just outwork anybody. He was organized. He was a good communicator. He put in the time."

Joseph was also a giving man, a good listener, and "a very hands-on father." With his kind brown eyes, gentle voice, and sun-bleached curly brown hair, some people said he looked like Jesus. His right shoulder was tattooed with a kangaroo holding a cross next to the word and symbol for Scorpio. His left shoulder was tattooed with his firstborn son's name.

Although Joseph's height and weight were average, he had a distinctive laugh and duck-like gait. Friendly, easygoing, and forgiving, Joseph was loved by most everyone, a stark contrast to Summer, who had only a few close friends. She could get emotional and argumentative, going for months or years without talking to her own family members.

A few inches shorter than Joseph, Summer weighed 115 pounds, and wore prescription glasses. She was good with the witty one-liners and liked to laugh. It was a mix of a giggle and a coo as she played with her kids, whom she cherished. Because she had brown eyes and long straight dark hair, people thought her looks were passed down from her Colombian great-grandmother.

Joseph was smitten with her from the start. He took her moods and occasional sharp tone in stride, calling her "my little Colombian," and let her call him Giuseppe, because she loved all things Italian. He even gave the same nickname to his new Dell laptop.

When Tingley asked Michael for Summer's age and ethnicity, he said she was approximately thirty-two, and described her as "Colombian-Italian."

The boys, Gianni and Joey Jr., also known as Baby J, were miniature versions of Joseph, other than a strawberry birthmark on Joey Jr.'s forehead.

Gianni Giuseppe Martelli-McStay came first on July 9, 2005. Smart and inquisitive, he enjoyed reading and talking about books and animals, dinosaurs in particular. But he also liked using his hands to play with toys, chugging the train around the track with a remote control.

After Joseph Mateo Martelli-McStay was born eighteen months later, the boys grew close, giggling together in their knit beanies, which Summer had them both wear to hide Joey Jr.'s birthmark.

Nicknamed "Chubba" for his "thunder thighs," Joey Jr. thought he could keep up with Gianni, jumping like a deer as he ran after Gianni until he got tuckered out and fell asleep while Joseph rocked the boy against his chest.

As Tingley later testified, Michael wasn't "rock solid on dates" for when he'd gone to the house looking for Joseph. Tingley's report also quoted Michael as saying, "I am not supposed to tell you this, but my brother's best friend and chief engineer for the company hacked into Joseph's email and PayPal account." This friend said Joseph hadn't checked his bank account since February 4, and his "PayPal account has not been touched," either.

Those facts seem to have gotten jumbled in translation, however, because Kavanaugh was the one who had offered to go through Joseph's emails and business records, though Michael's "best friend and chief engineer" description referred to Merritt. Neither Michael nor Merritt had access to Joseph's email, and Kavanaugh was the only one Joseph paid via PayPal.

The company that towed the family's Trooper on February 8 told Tingley that a blanket and child car seats were visible in the back, so he asked them not to release the vehicle without a detective's permission.

With all that squared away, he and Michael drove separately to Avocado Vista Lane.

Even police officers have been known to miss a body during a walk-through, so Tingley did a protective sweep, double-checking that no one was dead, hurt, or hiding in a closet Michael might have missed.

"You didn't knock the lamp over, right?" he asked Michael, referring to the toppled pole-light upstairs. "Or touch anything?"

"Nope."

Agreeing with Michael that "something was not jibing," Tingley called for additional deputies to help canvass the neighborhood, search for surveillance cameras, and ensure no one entered the house until the homicide detectives arrived.

Until then, Michael was told to wait by his car, where he called his mother. Susan Blake immediately got in the car and started driving south from her job in Oxnard, three counties north in Ventura County, to talk to detectives herself.

Chapter 4

Detective Troy DuGal, who had been in the homicide detail for almost two years, showed up around 7 p.m.

While Tingley was briefing DuGal, he remembered he'd forgotten to clear the garage, which allowed them to take another walk through the house without a search warrant, looking for probable cause that a crime had occurred. After that, they had no right to be inside without a warrant, nor could they technically "secure" it with yellow tape or prevent family members from entering.

DuGal noticed the same rotting food, dirty dishes, and paint job underway. As he later testified, he didn't see any sign of blood or foul play, but it was hard to say for sure with so little furniture, because major renovations can make for a messy house. He did note, however, the absence of a ladies' purse.

Once DuGal was finished, he closed the door and walked into the cold, drizzly night air to interview Michael, leaving it to him to lock up afterward.

Joined by his partner, Suzanne Fiske, DuGal didn't tell Michael he suspected or feared this was a homicide—or that he was planning to get a search warrant—because he didn't "want to scare the family to death."

But because the McStays had been missing for eleven days,

he testified later, "I found that suspicious without a doubt. I needed to talk to a family member. Was this unusual? Had this ever happened before? What level of concern are we at?"

Michael said Joseph had taken the family camping one weekend, and no one could get hold of him, so DuGal thought this eleven-day no-contact period "seemed out of the ordinary, but it wasn't crazy suspicious."

As far as they knew, Chase Merritt was the last person to see Joseph, so DuGal knew they needed to talk to him. DuGal asked for contact information for Summer's family, but Michael didn't have any, and neither did Susan.

At this point, DuGal knew he had a missing persons case, "and I'm more than concerned, because the children are gone, and I don't have a good story for why they're gone," he testified. "I even reached out to find out if the adults are fighting." Domestic violence cases often involve one parent running off with the kids and the other parent running after them, leaving the rest of the family in the dark.

Due to Michael's "Colombian-Italian" description of Summer, DuGal honed in on her. Although Michael said neither she nor Joseph were involved with drugs, DuGal said her heritage could still be important. If she had family in Colombia, "and somebody wants a piece of what's happening in Colombia, they will go to the extremes sometimes of coming to the United States to deal with the person here," DuGal said. "So, is that possible?"

"I have no idea," Michael said. "That's way over my head."

But based on these questions, Michael jumped to conclusions, asking if Summer's father, whose last name he assumed was Martelli, was "a big, like, gang lord?"

"No, I don't know," DuGal said.

"Dude, should I go and register for a gun or something?"

"No, no, no."

"I think people watch too much TV, to be honest," Fiske, DuGal's partner, said.

"I'm just asking, man. Do I need to be looking over my shoulder like someone's coming after my girls, too?"

"No," DuGal said.

Recounting his spat with Summer, Michael said she'd driven wedges between Joseph and his friends, ex-wife, and even his oldest son. McGyver McCargar and a longtime friend and soccer buddy named Alan were the only two friends who "are not ousted [by Summer] right now," he said. "All I know is she's divided my whole family."

Asked about Joseph's relationship with his business associates, Michael said, "Web Dan was a partner," but Joseph had "paid him off, as far as ownership. He still pays him a monthly to do the internet stuff. Chase is contract labor, so he's paid upon whatever."

"What's the relationship between Chase and Joseph?"

"From what I hear, and because Chase seems like a very sweet individual, I trust that they've gotten really close. I mean, Chase helped them move," he said, relating Merritt's story of packing and repacking the PODS, because Summer was dissatisfied. "They got in an argument over it, my brother and Summer."

Merritt also said he'd built the backyard shed as a doghouse, because Joseph was too sick to do it. "My understanding is their relationship is pretty, pretty tight, and Chase thinks of him as a best friend."

As Michael described his previous trip to the house, he said Merritt stayed downstairs, close to the back door. He later speculated that Merritt didn't want to touch anything because of his prison record.

Asked what would be helpful for their investigation, DuGal and Fiske said they could use any credit card and ATM numbers Michael could find.

"Or just even dates, times, and locations to give us leads," Fiske said. "I think that would be a priority for us if you can somehow get those for us."

Michael said he would "hop on the computer" to look for

them. Later, in court, he cited this exchange as the rationale for taking home Joseph's computer and several other items that night.

"I asked if I would I be in trouble for taking anything," Michael testified, "and they said no, you're his brother." So, "I took the SIM card, I took the Maxtor external hard drive, and I took the [desktop] eMachine, of which I didn't have the power cord, so I couldn't power it up." In addition to looking for financial records, he wanted to download photos for a website and "missing" posters to help with the search.

However, DuGal disputed Michael's recollection that he'd given Michael permission to remove these items. "That would be inaccurate," DuGal testified.

Still, Michael seemed to think he'd been authorized to do so. Was this a nod-nod, wink-wink, in case the detectives couldn't get a search warrant? DuGal claimed he told Michael to return the devices before the search on February 19, but he actually conveyed that instruction to Susan Blake.

Susan arrived at the Fallbrook substation around nine o'clock, where she met with Detectives Dave Hillen and Dan Laibach.

She told them Summer was born and raised in California, not Colombia, but she insisted, mistakenly, that Summer spoke fluent Spanish. Informed that the Trooper was found near the border, Susan also insisted that Joseph would never have taken the kids into Mexico.

"To go down there would baffle me," she said.

Hillen said people often parked in San Ysidro to bring illegal narcotics back over the border. "Is that possible?" he asked.

No, she said, "they're very healthy eaters." They didn't even vaccinate their babies, because "they're so against it."

Hillen asked if they might have flown somewhere, like Hawaii, from Tijuana because it was cheaper.

"They would have sent an email," Susan said. "They would

never leave those dogs. That's her baby. She walks Bear every morning."

Susan racked her brain. "Have you talked to Dan in Hawaii?" She couldn't remember his last name, but he'd told her he had access to Joseph's business accounts, so she'd asked him to look for any activity, and he said he found none.

"I just don't have a clue," she said. "Did you check the airports?"

"We just got involved in this a couple of hours ago," Hillen said.

Susan asked if she or Kavanaugh could get into the family's computer to look for email contacts for Summer's brother or mother, although she noted they weren't at the wedding.

"I can't instruct you to go do that, but if you did, and find information, feel free to tell us," Hillen said.

Chapter 5

The next morning, Lieutenant Dennis Brugos issued a brief news release that the homicide detail was conducting a missing persons' investigation into the McStay family's disappearance. Tips started pouring in right away.

One of the standouts was the man who found a woman's head in a backpack, wrapped in grocery bags, while he was collecting cans in the desert of San Bernardino County, days after the McStays had gone missing. But it wasn't Summer.

Detective Hillen interviewed Joseph's father, Patrick McStay, by phone, asking about Joseph and Summer's earnings and savings.

Susan had said, "Joey's really generous. If one of his buddies needed a couple grand or whatever and they're really hurting, he would give it out," which was true. Three days before he disappeared, Joseph bought a $668 Acer laptop for Guy Joseph, his former business partner and surfing buddy of more than twenty years, whose computer had died.

"Because that's the type of guy he was," Guy said.

Patrick estimated that Joseph had anywhere from $30,000 to $150,000 in the bank, and Summer had some money after selling her house in Big Bear. It turned out that Joseph had only

$30,000 in his business account, and Summer had $20,000 in an out-of-state account.

He said Joseph had talked recently about taking a Mexican Riviera cruise out of Long Beach, stopping in Cabo San Lucas and Puerto Vallarta. "Could they have taken off? As far as I know, they could have got on a plane to Hawaii, and not told a person. But to neglect his business like this? I can't see that."

In their last conversation on February 3, Patrick said, he'd warned Joseph about a lawsuit, filed against Patrick in late 2009. To protect his son's assets from Patrick's debt collectors, he advised Joseph to change the name of the Earth Inspired Products bank account, because Patrick was the one who had originally set it up after Joseph's bankruptcy.

Although Joseph had put the business back in his own name as a sole proprietorship, Patrick was still worried, because it was a lawsuit that had torpedoed Joseph's previous fountain business with Michael. Joseph assured Patrick he would change the account name to EIP.

Years later, however, prosecutors ascribed a completely different motivation to the two calls Joseph made to Union Bank on February 4.

Susan Blake asked Joseph's friend, McGyver McCargar, to meet her at the house on February 16 so she didn't have to be there alone.

McCargar had met Joseph about ten years earlier, when they were both bartending at the St. Regis Bar in Monarch Beach. They also roomed together for several years. McCargar met Summer around the same time through some friends working in real estate.

He and Joseph were going out partying one night in the summer of 2004 when Summer happened to call, so he invited her along. Although she was still seeing her boyfriend, Vic Johansen, in Big Bear Lake, she and Joseph hit it off right away. One thing led to another.

When McCargar arrived at the house in Fallbrook, Susan was busy cleaning the kitchen, as if it gave her a way to expend her anxiety. It's not clear how she got in the house, which Michael said he'd locked the night before, because she didn't call a locksmith for two more weeks.

As McCargar saw her wiping down the counters, he was worried she was removing fingerprints or other evidence.

"Have the investigators completed their job here?" he asked. "You probably shouldn't be doing that if they haven't finished."

"They've already been here," she said.

She continued to clean, so he didn't push it any further. He simply rehung the cabinet doors and reinserted the drawers into the island.

Susan headed into Joseph's office, searching for clues and phone numbers to call Summer's family before they heard she was missing on the news. She apparently found the numbers, but hadn't called before they were informed, almost by accident, by an investigator the following day.

When she said, cryptically, "I've got to protect [Elijah]," McCargar had no idea what she meant and didn't ask her to elaborate.

Susan called Detective DuGal around 1 p.m. "I asked Mr. DuGal if I could clean this up some, because the smell was so bad," she testified later, describing the odor as "a rotten smell, mildew, dirty diapers, maggots."

DuGal testified that he never gave Susan permission to clean up. She'd given her first statement to two other detectives the night before, and she was in the middle of the job when she called and told DuGal about it.

"My homicide detective personality is going, 'You've got to be kidding me, don't do that,'" he testified. Trying not "to get in the family's face," he was firm but gentle. "I told her politely,

'Stop what you're doing and leave it alone, and have Michael return the computer,' because she didn't know I was working on a search warrant to get in that house. It was disheartening, but it wasn't her fault."

Because this was a missing persons case, he didn't feel he could tell the McStays what to do or not to do, especially when they didn't believe Joseph's family had been murdered. If there was a conflict or someone owed someone else money, they had to feel comfortable giving him that information.

Until then, he expected to hear only the good stuff: "'My family's great. Joey is great. Summer is great. The business is perfect. They're wealthy. The kids are a joy.' That's what you're going to get, and I know that."

By the time Susan had stopped "straightening up," she'd taken out the diaper-laden trash in the kitchen and downstairs bathroom, emptied the coffee pot, washed the plates and cups of partially eaten food and milk, cleared off and added chairs to the dining room table, threw the popcorn away, and returned the futon couch to a flat position. She'd also thrown away the newspapers on the floor and rearranged the paint cans and supplies.

Asked at trial in 2019 if she'd sprayed "Windex or bleach cleaner," dusted the house, or swept the floors, she said no, although she'd told detectives in 2014 that she'd wiped the windows with Windex. But she was sure she didn't see any blood on the dining table when she sat down to eat lunch.

As McCargar wandered through the house, he noticed a few oddities he later relayed to detectives as he outlined his last days with the family.

First, the cream-colored futon in the family room was missing its cover and several cushions.

I don't remember them taking off the futon cover, he thought.

Second, the metal paint pan and roller were covered with dried paint, tucked into a door-less slot in the island. He wondered why no one had washed the roller or removed the foil liner from the tray after he'd demonstrated that easy cleanup trick to Summer on his last day there. The old and new colors were too close to tell if someone had painted over some of the heavier trafficked areas since then, but the living room and family area looked the same.

Third, clothes were strewn all over the floor of the master-bedroom closet, and piled on the bathroom counters upstairs. When they were roommates, Joseph had put his clothes away. McCargar had never lived with Summer, but as he later testified, this seemed more "frantic" than messy.

Susan noticed the piles of clothes, too, but more importantly, she wondered why Summer's silk wedding dress was hanging, uncovered, in the corner of the closet, and not put away in the box where she'd last seen it. It seemed strange, so she wrapped it in a plastic bag and hung it back up. Because at that point, all of them wanted to believe Joseph's family was going to come back.

That afternoon, Detectives DuGal and Fiske drove to the San Ysidro Village mall, from which the Trooper had been towed.

Security guard David Jackson said his shift started at 2 p.m., but he didn't notice the vehicle parked in front of the Pink Zone clothing store until 9:18 p.m., when the lot was mostly empty because the stores had closed. The tow was authorized at 10:19 p.m., and the car was removed forty-five minutes later.

Jackson said he couldn't know when the car was originally parked, because it was in one of three contiguous lots, holding about eight hundred cars, he patrolled. But if he had to guess, the Trooper was parked around 7 p.m., and no earlier than 5 p.m. Although people often left their vehicles in the lot illegally to walk over the pedestrian bridge into Tijuana, the guards didn't mark tires or tow cars during the day unless the driver was a repeat offender.

DuGal had Jackson introduce him to managers at the Pink

Zone and surrounding businesses to get any available surveillance footage. Based on Jackson's estimate, he asked for video from 5 p.m. until midnight, hoping to catch sight of the driver parking the Trooper.

DuGal and Fiske also collected video from the more expansive Las Americas outlet mall across the boulevard, where surveillance cameras panned the overall area and entrances to both malls. But in the end, none of the footage proved useful.

The SDSD received a call that day from Jennifer Mitchley, who lived across the street from the McStays, and who said she had a motion-activated surveillance system that saved footage to her computer.

Mitchley had two exterior cameras, one on the front porch and one at the side gate, which picked up activity in her front yard, driveway, and her side of the street. As a result, they only captured the tires and lower portion of vehicles leaving the McStays' driveway.

Asked for footage from February 3 through February 8, Mitchley said she had video from February 3 and 4, but there was a gap from February 5 to the 14th because one camera had stopped working.

Detective Dan Laibach tried to take her computer to the Regional Computer Forensic Laboratory (RCFL) to download the relevant footage, but she said he would have to copy it onto a thumb drive at her house. Concerned about her family's safety after her neighbors' sudden disappearance, she didn't want to lose her ability to keep watch over the street.

"If they'd insisted on taking it, I would have given it to them," she said later, though she conceded that at some point, the computer would have "rewritten" over it.

On February 3 at 4:37 p.m., one camera recorded the McStay family's green truck pulling into their driveway. Then on February 4 at 7:47 p.m., it caught what detectives thought was "a white SUV pull out (as if backed in), and turn onto the street and drive away at a normal speed." The license plate wasn't visible, so they assumed the SUV was the McStays' Trooper, which Mitchley said the family typically backed into their driveway. But the grainy black-and-white footage didn't start until 7 p.m. and lasted less than an hour. Although a couple of other vehicles drove by that evening, none of them arrived or returned to the McStay house.

Mitchley slept in the master bedroom in the rear of the house, though if her neighbors were loud, she could hear them. She said she never heard any screams or other indications of violence or a struggle the night of February 4, only a noise that prompted her to turn on the porch light because she couldn't see anything on the cameras.

Chapter 6

When DuGal first spoke with Dan Kavanaugh by phone on February 16, the detective repeated what Susan Blake and Michael McStay had told him, not realizing they'd gotten their information from Kavanaugh. So, all of them assumed Kavanaugh had been in Hawaii for the past five weeks.

"You're in Hawaii right now?" DuGal asked.

"Yeah, I've been out here in Hawaii for over a month. I'm actually coming back in a couple days."

"I understand that you're probably, like, business partners of some sort with Joseph," DuGal asked somewhat rhetorically.

"Yeah," replied Kavanaugh, who had characterized himself in a voicemail to Summer ten days earlier as "Joseph's partner or ex-partner."

Asked if he shared profits from every sale or if he was contracted for "just the webmaster portion," Kavanaugh said, "No, I'm a half-owner of the site."

DuGal took this definitive statement at face value and used it to make additional assumptions. "Okay, good. All right, and that's why you have all this access to his account," he said. "When I talked to Michael, his brother, last night, he said that he thought that you were able to intercept emails to Joseph and you may also have financial records or access to his financial documents."

"Yeah," Kavanaugh said, adding that he didn't have access to Joseph's personal or business bank accounts. "I just have access to the PayPal, which we do monthly advertising off."

DuGal didn't question how Kavanaugh knew the state of Joseph's and Summer's cell phone battery power, either.

"It was on Saturday, and Joseph's phone had somehow run out of batteries by Saturday afternoon," Kavanaugh said. "I was calling it, and it was going straight to . . . the cell phone voice-mail."

"Uh-huh."

"So it just showed a small gap of cell phone power that, you know, what I'm sayin' at first, we were thinking maybe they went off a cliff in the car, and then their cell phones died, one after the other, after like twenty-four hours of sitting there, and they just weren't answering them."

DuGal also didn't question how or why Kavanaugh could access emails from Summer's personal Hotmail account, even after he basically admitted to hacking into it: "I just went in there, and I know their kids' names and stuff, so I got into her email address," he said.

Kavanaugh offered to give DuGal the same access, but DuGal said he'd rather Kavanaugh forward relevant data to him.

"Yeah, it's probably better if you do it, because if I do it, we get into legal stuff on searchable," DuGal said. "If you already have access, that's legal. It's not really legal for you to grant me access for law enforcement purposes."

Eager to help, Kavanaugh said Summer had exchanged emails with someone running a scam out of China, and suggested DuGal check into that, because it was "the last one in her outbox." He even offered to pull it for him.

When DuGal voiced his suspicions that Summer could be the cause of the disappearance, Kavanaugh promptly joined in, recalling her "money-hungry or gold-diggerish look" the first time they met and discussed how successful Joseph's business was. Kavanaugh also said Summer was involved in some shady mortgage-loan business, which he'd gathered from reading her emails.

"My favorite show is *Dexter,* so I know you guys are good," Kavanaugh said, referring to the TV crime series whose protagonist is a forensic crime tech who doubles as a vigilante serial killer.

From that point on, DuGal seemed to appreciate and even rely on Kavanaugh's help.

Chapter 7

Detectives DuGal and Fiske drove to Rancho Cucamonga to interview Joseph's custom builder, Chase Merritt, on the afternoon of February 17.

At his request, they met with him in his apartment complex clubhouse, while his partner, Cathy Jarvis, stayed behind with their three children. Although he and Jarvis weren't married, he called her his "wife."

Merritt had delayed meeting with detectives because he knew he had an outstanding arrest warrant. He'd served only half of a forty-six-day sentence for violating his probation on a prior commercial burglary, which the judge had allowed him to split into two stints so he could work to support his family in between. But as he explained to the detectives, he had to have heart surgery before he could report back, and had racked up a $107,000 hospital bill he was still negotiating. The doctors inserted two stents into his heart, for a total of three.

"My wife was taking me to the hospital, and I looked at her and said, 'I'm not going to make it to the hospital,'" so she made a U-turn and took them to a fire station three blocks away. "I tried to get out of the car, and I just fell on the pavement and was almost unconscious. She ran in and they came out. These guys were amazing. Had we not gone to the fire department, they told me there was no way I'd be alive. It was really close, so we took 'em a waterfall later."

After talking it over with his wife, Merritt decided to meet with the detectives, even if they might arrest him. "This is just too important to put off," he said. "Joseph's life is at stake. My little bullshit with this felony is a lot less important than Joseph and his family." If he put it off, then found out he could have helped, "I'm not prepared for that. Joseph was one of my best friends and obviously my business associate, and that's not something I want to live with."

The detectives said they knew about the warrant and assured him they weren't there to arrest him. They needed his help to try to locate the McStays. But they made him promise to take care of the warrant, emphasizing they would ensure that he did.

As they questioned Merritt about his role in Joseph's business, he handed them handwritten talking points about his last lunch meeting with Joseph, which DuGal read aloud as they talked: "Payments to Metro. Got checks and rent. Went over when to write the checks. QuickBooks online. Decide to delete and start QuickBooks Pro 2010. Credit card for purchasing QuickBooks."

Merritt said they met in person so Joseph could give him checks, some for him and two he passed on to Metro Sheet Metal (MSM) in Azusa, where Merritt assembled fountains for their customers.

He later explained that he'd printed and signed Joseph's name on these checks to buy materials for two pending fountain projects, one for a Paul Mitchell salon and one for a client in Saudi Arabia. The "when to write the checks" notation referred to the timing of the checks to make sure they would clear. Merritt said Dave Sequeida, MSM's owner, hadn't cashed his yet and was worried Joseph's account would be frozen because of his disappearance.

Merritt also gave DuGal a spreadsheet listing EIP's past custom jobs to show they were working off a separate ledger on QuickBooks. He said Joseph had given him a credit card number, which he'd since thrown away, to purchase the QuickBooks Pro software. Because Joseph often gave him one of his eight or ten card numbers to buy materials, he could only remember this one wasn't a VISA.

It was "two, three, or four days after February fourth that I actually bought the QuickBooks," he said.

Merritt said Joseph wanted to move the ledger to the Pro desktop program to keep his total income a secret from his wife, because "one of Summer's biggest problems is credit cards. I mean, she spends a lot of money. She goes to Ross all the time, so it had become a big thing with Joseph not letting her know exactly how much money he was making."

Merritt told them he'd contacted QuickBooks about transferring information from EIP's online accounts after he bought the new software.

"What do you think happened to these guys?" Fiske asked.

"I haven't been able to form any real explanation," Merritt said. "Joseph has no enemies whatsoever, that I know of."

"What about Summer?"

Merritt said he didn't think Summer "knows enough people to have enemies," but "most of the people that love Joseph dislike having her and him together. Everybody told Joseph, 'Don't marry her, don't marry her.'"

"Why?"

"Because she's a pain in the butt. She's very, very difficult. He always said, 'No, no. She's just Colombian.' Joseph is a super nice guy. He'll give you the shirt off his back, I mean, he'll do anything for you, and Summer is just the opposite."

For example, he and Joseph maintained a running tab of the lump sums they owed each other, which could range in the thousands for materials or supplies for different jobs, and they'd work it out every couple of months.

"Whatever it was, we got it done," he said, but "Summer never liked that."

So, that's part of what they discussed at lunch, because Joseph had sent him an email on February 1 with their current tab.

"Do I owe you money? Do you owe me money? This particular time, I owed him money," Merritt said, handing DuGal the email, which listed pending jobs and broke down the $42,845 Merritt owed Joseph.

The email also reflected their decision to split $27,000 in losses on two jobs—$19,000 on the "Provecho disaster," where a restaurant cancelled an order and pulled its deposit after Merritt had already installed a portion of a waterfall, and $8,000 on the "Levine" waterfall, which got damaged in shipping. The $15,045 balance reflected an overpayment to Merritt for jobs in 2009.

Merritt said Joseph called him a couple of times on his way home from their meeting, as they discussed where to install the electrical box on a particular waterfall. The last time they talked that day, Joseph was at his computer, working on drawings for that project.

"He had the drawings at home, so when he got there, he called me and we went over that fairly quickly," he said, guessing it was around 5:00 or 5:30 p.m. He could hear the kids in the background, shrieking as usual.

"He never said anything about going anywhere?"

"Never said."

DuGal's questions focused primarily on Merritt's business relationship with Joseph, and whether Merritt's company, IDesign4U, worked with or for Joseph's company. "Do you know if anyone has anything to gain by the loss of Joseph or Summer?"

"No," but without Joseph, "my business is done. I mean my, our entire business."

"You had nothing to do with, any, whether it was them going somewhere, you didn't help, participate, or—" DuGal asked.

"No, not even. Not in any way, shape, or form."

"—nothing to do with the disappearance, whether it's good or bad?"

"Absolutely not, no."

Merritt said he couldn't run the business or do what Joseph did—the drawings and talking to customers ten hours a day. "I don't know of anybody that can step into his shoes and know what he knows."

Dan Kavanaugh, whom he'd never met in person and had only talked to for the first time a week earlier, might be able to help, but "I have my doubts, because there's too much to do." At that point, he thought Kavanaugh lived in Hawaii year-round.

Merritt said he didn't all know the details, only that Joseph had been paying off Kavanaugh since their "spat" the previous year, when he threatened to shut down Joseph's online business.

"Joseph talked about that all the time," he said. "Joseph was always afraid that [Kavanaugh] was just going to push a button and the website would be gone, because that is what Dan said when they clashed. Apparently, Dan is extremely adept at website building, and he's a big hacker. When I talked to him over the last week, he said, 'Yeah, I'm not a person that you want to piss off on the web.'"

He said Joseph had decided he was only going to pay Kavanaugh to maintain the website each month "instead of them being partners" and "paying him a percentage of the sales," which had been their previous arrangement. Joseph had actually started the business with his dad, Patrick, because Joseph had credit problems. But Patrick eventually dropped back so Joseph could take it over with new bank accounts, a PayPal account, and credit cards of his own.

"Are you aware that either of them associated with anyone who used or sold drugs?" Fiske asked. "Did they use or sell drugs?"

"No, absolutely none," Merritt said, although Joseph had told him he used "E," meaning ecstasy, before they met, "in his drug days," and he still had some in the freezer. "He offered it to me seven, eight months ago. It was something he wasn't ever going to use."

"Any other drugs besides this 'E'?" Fiske asked.

Merritt shook his head as Fiske listed off marijuana, meth, and heroin. "No, he found religion," and had been "taking care of his health" lately because of some medical issues.

Asked if Joseph had been under any financial stress, Merritt said he was "fine financially, as far as I know."

"No other wheelin' and dealin', maybe helpin' transport drugs?"

"Joseph's not the type," Merritt said. "Personally, I've never done drugs. I've never smoked. I've never drank," other than half a cold beer before it got warm, and none since his heart attack.

Asked for other people to talk to, Merritt suggested Kavanaugh and some of Joseph's soccer buddies.

"He never even really talked to his brother except when his brother needed something. The only time Mikey ever really called him is to ask to borrow some money." Joseph was "a little tired of him, but I mean he was his brother, and Summer didn't like him."

Merritt told them about knocking on Susan Blake's door on February 9 and his subsequent visit to Joseph's house with Michael. But when he tried to walk them through his day on February 8, Presidents' Day, he drew a blank.

"Maybe you should call the wife," DuGal suggested.

Merritt called Jarvis on speakerphone a couple of times, but the reception was bad in the clubhouse, and the calls kept dropping. Once he got a better connection, she said they were at home during the day on February 8, then she went out.

"I got home at ten-twenty [p.m.] and you had already turned on the TV to a movie," she said.

Asked if he'd ever driven Joseph's Trooper, Merritt said no, but he'd been a passenger when they drove to play paintball at Camp Pendleton about six weeks before the family disappeared. Joseph typically drove the Trooper by himself and during family outings, while Summer drove the Dodge.

"Do you have any knowledge or information which indicates to you that they're dead?" Fiske asked.

"No."

"The reason I ask is because you have used the past tense about Joe a couple times. Typically, people don't do that when people are alive. Any explanation as to why you might have done that?"

"No, not really," he said.

"You said, 'Joe was my best friend.'"

"Oh, I did?"

"You did."

"Hmm. Yeah, well, I don't know why."

"Did you guys have any falling-out at all?"

"Never, no."

"So, it wouldn't be like, he was my best friend and now we're just—"

"No, absolutely not."

"How did you hurt your hand?" Fiske asked, in an abrupt change of topic.

"I just did it today on a piece of sheet metal. We deal in stainless-steel waterfalls, and I was at the shop today. I actually bled like a stuck pig."

Asked if he had any injuries on his stomach or back, he said no.

Although the Trooper was found near the border, Merritt said he didn't think the family went to Mexico, despite Susan Blake saying they might have gone there "and caught a plane to wherever." He said he'd encouraged Susan and Michael to call and report the family missing early on, but they kept putting it off.

"When was the last time you were down by the Mexican border?" Fiske asked.

"About a year ago," Merritt said.

After some prodding, Merritt acknowledged why he'd made that trip: "You can get Viagra over the counter."

"Have you been down to San Ysidro or Mexico since?"

"No."

As Merritt talked affectionately about his young son, Ray, he called him "my little guy. He's a perfect little kid. I'm partial, of course."

Asked if he would give them a DNA sample to exclude him as a suspect, Merritt agreed. Because DuGal didn't bring a kit with him, he called the San Bernardino County Sheriff's Department (SBCSD) to send one over with a patrol deputy. DuGal put the swab into evidence, but never did anything with it.

Before heading south, DuGal stopped by the Chick-fil-A where Merritt said he'd met Joseph for lunch, but after thirteen days, the surveillance video had been recorded over.

Chapter 8

Two days later, Detective DuGal executed his first search warrant, which covered the McStays' house, Dodge truck, and Isuzu Trooper.

Although he later insisted he saw no evidence of this, DuGal's warrant affidavit stated, "It is my opinion that the McStay family is the victim of foul play," which established probable cause a crime had been committed. "I believe that some or all of the McStay family has been kidnapped or killed. This belief has been bolstered by the intense media attention that this case has received, including several days of pleas to the public through local and national television, without the family or anyone coming forward who are aware of their whereabouts."

At the time, he based his working theory on the food left out in the kitchen, indicating the family "left the house very quickly"; the lack of communication with family and business associates; the abandoned Trooper; their pets left outside without food; and the inactivity of their cell phones.

Asked later how he entered the locked house, he couldn't remember, only that "we got in legally." But when he and his team walked in at 10:30 a.m., they immediately felt the impact of Susan's cleanup.

"Everyone in our group was disappointed," recalled forensic tech Denys Williams. "But [Susan] was distraught—her kid was missing, maybe she was in a little bit of shock. I don't know. I just know that she did clean up. I wouldn't be surprised if she was just trying to find a way to stay busy. But, it was like, 'oh, no,' because it makes such a difference."

DuGal briefed his team—which included several other detectives, a state Department of Justice (DOJ) agent, two criminalists, two cadaver dogs, and their handlers—on what had changed since he'd been there four days before.

"The popcorn was gone, the eggs were gone," Williams said. "The only food I remember was the apple on the stairs with a little kid's bite out of it. I'd heard that there were maybe some shoes on the floor, stains, maybe, on the carpets—not red stains, just stains—and the house was hard to tell if people were actually living there or not, because it was messy."

However, after six hours of taking photos and searching for clues DuGal might have missed initially, they still couldn't find any blood or signs of a struggle in the house. The only brownish-red stain they found was on a book cover, which tested negative for blood. He didn't send the dogs inside, because they were only trained to "alert" at the smell of human decomposition.

DuGal asked Williams, who took 745 photos, to get one of the window blinds in the office, which were bent where Michael said he'd climbed in, but didn't remember "doing the damage." DuGal deemed that "forced entry, but legitimate."

DuGal didn't ask Williams to take DNA swabs or dust for fingerprints, because he couldn't identify any signs of forced entry or that a crime had been committed.

"It's not how we do business," DuGal testified later. "It's not how we could do business."

Dusting areas with black fingerprint dust leaves behind a sooty material, like the residue from a smoky oven fire, so investigators use it cautiously.

"We were very aware this family might come back," Williams said.

As they searched drawers in the kitchen, office, den, and the recycling bin outside, they collected various documents, including a "notice to vacate" the apartment in San Clemente.

A few other items became of interest later: a black-light device no one could recall leaving behind; the dining table, where investigators sat doing their paperwork; a pale spot on the carpet near the front door, which they thought might be a bleach stain; and three pairs of Summer's favorite tan Uggs, which were left on the front doorstep, in the master bedroom closet, and in the Dodge truck.

The investigators seized four cameras, three computers, an external hard drive, and four old cell phones. Joseph and Summer's current phones, which weren't used after February 4, were never recovered.

It was several years before a computer forensic expert realized Joseph had been using a Dell Inspiron laptop for much of his business accounting work since October, which they never found, either. In the Dodge truck, the investigators found Joseph's soccer gear on the floor in back, a video camera, and kids' toys, but the key was missing.

Next, the investigators picked up the Trooper from the tow yard in Chula Vista and took it to the crime lab, where they processed it the next day. The vehicle was locked, and the keys were nowhere to be found, so a tow-truck driver had to open the door for them.

From the position of the driver's seat, DuGal could tell the previous driver was shorter than his six-feet-one-inch frame. Summer was five feet five inches and Joseph was five feet nine inches. Merritt was six feet two inches.

The children's car seats were attached to the rear seats, which were packed with belongings, leaving little or no room for a fifth person to sit or avoid crushing items on the floor, say, in an abduction situation.

"We took every single thing out of there," Williams recalled. "By then I was getting more and more suspicious."

If the family had to leave the country suddenly, she wondered, why would they leave behind a tub of Joseph's allergy and cold meds, nasal sprays, antibiotics for a respiratory infection, and two inhalers?

"I'd heard that one of the boys was on asthma meds, and was severely asthmatic, and they took that medication everywhere they went," she said.

The cargo area was packed with toys—a Pottery Barn Kids refrigerator and sink for a playhouse—and covered with a sheet. If they were going on a trip or planning to disappear into Mexico, Williams figured they would have removed those from the car.

"So, by this point, I was absolutely willing to believe that they'd been killed or kidnapped," she said.

They also found four DVDs in a Ross bag, a checkbook for Joseph's business account at Union Bank, and four business cards for representatives at the San Clemente branch.

The steering wheel and gearshift lever were covered with a pliable and porous foamy material, which is more difficult to wipe clean, so Williams scrubbed it with two swabs for DNA. She also scrubbed the gearshift, four-wheel-drive lever, radio dials, and the heater-A/C dials with two swabs. If the DNA levels were low in certain areas, she figured a profile might not turn up if she only used a single swab for each area, but it might if she combined areas.

Here's our best chance of getting some evidence of whoever last drove this car, she thought.

That decision was later criticized by defense attorneys, who said each area should have been swabbed separately.

Within a few days, DuGal had identified the numbers for the family's landline and cell phones, which he used to seek search warrants for T-Mobile, Time Warner, and Sprint records.

Although the judge approved and sealed those warrants, he also cautioned DuGal: "I think there's just barely probable cause.

Don't come back to me with another search warrant outside of this family until you have good probable cause for any other investigation."

So, DuGal said, "I was pretty much froze[n] for search warrants at that point unless I could find more evidence" that a crime had been committed. Until then, this had to remain a missing persons case, which came with certain restrictions.

Many observers, and even other investigators, later criticized this passive approach, questioning why DuGal didn't try a different judge, or try again after some period of time when it was clear the family was gone for good.

DuGal agreed through a mutual acquaintance to be interviewed for this book once he retired but changed his mind without explanation. In fact, after facing criticism for the handling of this case, no one with the SDSD, including retired Sheriff Bill Gore, agreed to be interviewed.

Five days after Dan Kavanaugh said he'd returned from Hawaii, he met with Sergeant Roy Frank, who assured him he "wasn't under any criminal investigation."

Like DuGal, Frank didn't seem to question Kavanaugh's access to Joseph's personal email account. He also perpetuated Kavanaugh's narrative about his executive role at EIP, saying, "Plus you're a business partner, so——"

"I'm a business partner," Kavanaugh repeated, offering to give them access to Joseph's "actual email through my phone or whatever, if you need to look at the last few emails he sent, I sent."

"I understand there's three people in EIP," Frank said. "It's you, the webmaster; Joseph, the owner-operator; and Charles, or Chase, you call him."

"It's actually a little different than that," Kavanaugh said, describing himself not just as the "webmaster," but as the only person who could save EIP from going under while Joseph was away, and the one who had the most to lose after investing so much time and money into the company.

"'Cause if I didn't come in and, like, save it, he's [Chase] done. I've spent the last five years of my life investing, down to a thread, just to make sure that site stays up. All this internet marketing time and just profits that we took, we weren't greedy, we invested back into the site to make it" work like it does now. When "you search for water fountain in any variety, we're top five on Google." He also claimed he and Joseph were starting a new water ionization business.

Frank asked about the accounts he'd heard from "family members and friends" concerning the "buyout," where "you're paid fifty grand" to build and optimize the website, and "you were almost about to be paid off as the webmaster, and then it would be Joe's exclusively."

Kavanaugh disputed this scenario, throwing out percentage splits he claimed he could back up with earnings spreadsheets for the past six years. He also contended he worked solely for EIP.

"I've put all my eggs in that basket," he said.

Initially, Frank pushed back, saying his numbers didn't add up or match what Merritt had described. "If [Joseph] only made thirty-six grand a year, how in the hell did he afford his family and a brand-new $330,000 house?" he asked.

Still not satisfied with Kavanaugh's answer, Frank pushed back again. "Again, I'm not challenging you, I want you to help me," he said, but the numbers still didn't make sense. Nonetheless, Frank seemed to accept Kavanaugh's contention that he should operate the business, even over Joseph's family.

"I was going to tell you, the family keeps calling me and saying we want to run the business," Frank said. "I said, 'Well, you need to get a hold of Kavanaugh and Chase, because that's their business, it's not law enforcement business.'"

"Exactly," Kavanaugh said, adding that he had "every intention to set a trust up. You guys aren't even asking, but this is at least what his family said, and what I think's fair. They're gonna have a lawyer draw up, like, a trust account, and then I'm gonna, of course, still run the site."

Kavanaugh went on, "The family, they can run a business, but how could that help us? How could his mom, who just wants something to do, who's probably real emotional," and keeps asking customers if they've seen her son, when they just want to buy a fountain, only to make the "business fail, 'cause she doesn't know the fountains, and this builder guy, Chase, does."

At this point, Kavanaugh had only positive words about Merritt: "He is a good builder of what he does, probably one of the best Joseph found to make that stuff." Kavanaugh also claimed he'd discovered Merritt through a guy at a trade show, and referred him to Joseph.

Kavanaugh said he knew something was wrong when he couldn't reach Joseph, because they'd just talked about a $2,000 payment to cover his rent in Hawaii. "Two days later, I'm, like, Joe, come on dude, you've always sent this with PayPal instantly."

"Why does Joe have to send you money if you both have access to the account?" Frank asked.

Kavanaugh explained Joseph sent him money from his bank account via PayPal, but Joseph and his dad had recently created a second merchant account to run sales through. "So that's definitely something to look at. He could have been capturing some side sales and could have been deleting them in some type of an accounting way."

According to Merritt, that separate account and "side sales"— which secretly cut Kavanaugh out of profits on the custom fountains—is exactly what he and Joseph were in the process of establishing via QuickBooks. However, Patrick was never involved in that.

By now, the detectives had heard some of the resentments and interpersonal conflicts DuGal was waiting for, many of which tracked back to Summer. But Kavanaugh went even further, encompassing the entire McStay clan: Summer was a controlling woman who spent too much money and kept Joseph away from his friends. Michael took too long to report the family missing, and Patrick had ulterior motives for trying to horn in on the business.

Kavanaugh also said he'd seen an email in Joseph's account about a two-million-dollar life insurance policy. At some point, the SDSD learned Joseph had obtained a $500,000 policy for himself in June 2008, naming Summer as the beneficiary, but he'd cancelled it after buying the house.

As the detectives explored theories for the family's disappearance, such as a deal gone bad, Joseph getting into financial trouble, or hiding money and not reporting his true income, Kavanaugh offered them one more scenario: the family had fallen prey to a "professional weirdo on the internet," which rang uncannily familiar later on.

"It would take so little for an internet predator of even novice ability to come and go, oh, look at this," he said. "Actually, I want to rape that little kid, or I want to kill her, or whatever. . . . Looks like they have money. They moved into a brand-new house. Doesn't look like they have big dogs and security. I'm just gonna wait 'til he leaves, stop him on the corner, make him disappear, and then come in when it's just his wife and kids. Tell them to put all their cell phones here. Two little kids can't fight back. Walk that way, or I'm gonna blow your brains out."

Kavanaugh also suggested that the detectives investigate a man whom other family members had also mentioned: "Summer's previous ex, have you looked into him at all?"

He recalled accompanying Joseph to Summer's house in Big Bear early in their relationship, where she said they had to hide if "Jojo," her crazy ex, showed up. "He's, like, a Navy SEAL or something," Kavanaugh said.

Chapter 9

Tracy Russell, Summer's sister, was still unaware of her disappearance two weeks after the McStays had gone missing.

When they'd last talked on the morning of February 4, Summer had committed to bringing the boys to meet Tracy's new son for the first time and stay for a sleepover. The sisters hadn't seen each other in two years, but they'd always talked about having babies around the same time so they could play together.

Summer had come late to motherhood, because she hadn't found the right man to father her children until she met Joseph. He was three years younger than her, though she told everyone she was five years younger than him.

Now that she had Gianni and Joey Jr., she didn't like people interrupting her "family time," and she certainly didn't want to hang out with Joseph's ex-wife Heather and her family. She also didn't let just anyone into her "circle," including Susan Blake, who was still close with Heather.

Tracy's son was born prematurely on Halloween in 2009. Because Summer didn't believe in vaccinations, they all had to wait until the baby had his immunization shots before he could meet his cousins. Despite doctors' warnings, Summer even refused a neonatal screening test for Baby J, citing religious grounds.

"She went by her own teachings," Tracy said, calling Summer "somewhat of a cornflake. She had a whole way of life. She walked with a purpose and a passion."

As Tracy recalled their last conversation, she said, "I was telling her that I couldn't work anymore now that I had a baby. She had a whole new career figured out for me. She was going to do the marketing, and I was just going to do the work. Just big sisterly advice: hurry up, have another baby." Tracy replayed that conversation in her mind in the years to come, mulling the would'ves, could'ves, and should'ves of it all.

When Summer didn't follow up about the sleepover, Tracy left her a message saying she loved her and asked her to call back. But Summer was funny that way, so Tracy didn't think much about it until she got a call on February 17 from a woman she thought was with the SDPD.

The woman said she was trying to locate Summer's brother, Kenneth Aranda, so Tracy assumed the woman was chasing a stolen-identity case, and told her Kenneth lived in Hawaii.

"Oh, you're Summer's sister," the woman replied.

"Yes," Tracy said.

"Let me connect you to homicide."

As she waited on the line, Tracy was terrified, because she knew whatever was coming next couldn't be good.

After being informed that her sister's family was missing, Tracy arranged to meet Detectives DuGal and Fiske at her house in San Bernardino that night. Knowing her mother couldn't handle the news by phone, she and her husband Joe decided to pick up Blanche and drive her to the meeting with no explanation. But Blanche was no fool and wouldn't take silence for an answer.

"What's wrong?" she kept asking Joe in the car.

Summer had called Blanche on February 4 as well, letting the boys talk to their grandmother for about forty-five minutes.

Tracy had been right to worry. After hearing the details from detectives, Blanche started to unravel and never really recovered.

"I pretty much lost my mom in this tragedy, too," Tracy said. "It was horrible, wondering and waiting." But they all knew Summer wouldn't stop calling all of them at once. "If Summer wasn't in contact with me, she was in contact with my mom. If she wasn't in contact with my mom, she was in contact with me and my brother. She never would have just disappeared."

When the detectives asked if Summer feared anyone in her life, the consensus was her ex, Vic Johansen. The former Marine had threatened to cut off Bear's head, which was why Summer insisted on taking the dog when they broke up.

Blanche and Tracy had no clue where the McStays could be. They were also baffled why the Trooper had been left near the border.

"I know [Summer] didn't like Mexico," said Blanche, who was equally puzzled about why her daughter had left her prescription sunglasses behind on the kitchen counter. "She can't see without her glasses."

"She's pretty much blind at night," Tracy added.

As the nation witnessed with media saturation of the Gabby Petito case in 2021, missing-persons cases can draw widespread public and media interest, more so when young children are involved, and even more when an entire family vanishes without a trace.

The coverage about the McStays started locally and quickly spread to major newspapers and TV stations throughout Southern California. By February 18, it had already spread to national media outlets, including *Nancy Grace*, and ultimately went international with outlets like the *Daily Mail*.

Bloggers and amateur sleuths jumped on the case with fervor, dissecting every new development and theory, as they analyzed, and often criticized, actions and remarks by Michael, Patrick, and Susan.

This led to the airing of much speculation and dirty laundry about the McStays, as people debated why the family of four would leave their house so abruptly and in such disarray. Who, exactly, were they, and why would anyone want to harm them and their two adorable little boys?

Chapter 10

Joseph's mother, Susan (Gredick) Blake, got pregnant right out of high school in Akron, Ohio. She married Joseph's father, Robert Ashley, but when they split up shortly after Joseph was born on November 20, 1969, Ashley was no longer part of their lives.

In 1971, Susan met Patrick McStay, who, at twenty-five, had started a transportation management job after serving three years in the U.S. Army. They got married the following year, and their son Michael was born in January 1973. Patrick adopted Joseph that same year, and from then on, considered Joey to be his son, just like Mikey. But that marriage didn't last long, either, ending in divorce in 1975.

Sometime after Patrick got a job in Houston, Susan moved with the boys to Dallas. But because the boys had to take a plane every time they visited their father, Susan eventually moved closer, to Sugar Land, then back to Dallas.

In 1986, Susan met Tom Blake while he was in town on business from Northern California. After a year of dating long-distance, Susan brought Mikey across country to live with Tom in San Rafael. At the time, sixteen-year-old Joey wasn't getting along with Susan, so he stayed with Patrick.

As Patrick chronicled in a self-published book, *McStays, Taken Too Soon: A True Story,* Joey started running with a group of teenagers who got into trouble with the police one night, but the officer told Patrick he hadn't taken Joey to the station because he was a good kid. Patrick had advised Joey not to be so trusting, and to be more careful of the friends he hung out with to avoid "guilt by association." But this continued to be difficult for Joey, who saw the good in people and shrugged off the rest.

A few months after Susan moved to California, she was talking to Joey on the phone, which she then handed over to Tom.

"Someday, I hope to meet you," Tom said.

The next day, Joey called from the San Francisco airport. "Can you pick me up?"

Soon afterward, Tom flew down for business to Orange County, where it was a sunny seventy-six degrees, and he realized why the boys kept begging to move to "SoCal." The boys longed to surf, so Tom bought a home near the beach in Laguna Niguel. He and Susan got married several weeks after moving there.

Tom opened Tutor and Spunky's Deli in Dana Point (Spunky was his nickname for Susan), where Mikey worked while he and Joey attended Dana Hills High School. After Joey graduated with the class of 1988, he took classes at Saddleback College.

When he was about eighteen, Joey used and sold ecstasy he got from a guy in Texas. But once he and his brother became involved in church activities, Joey stopped getting high and went to the other extreme, becoming a health nut.

Mikey tried moving to Houston to develop a closer relationship with Patrick, but they didn't get along. Susan claimed they actually came to blows, so she had to ask Mikey's boss to put him up in a hotel and drive him back to California.

Susan and Tom moved with the boys to Monarch Beach, within walking distance of a gnarly surf spot, but ultimately, that marriage broke up, too. "Blood is thicker than water," Susan told Tom.

After the divorce in 1994, Mikey decided to move to Hawaii.

Joey bought a gun that year, and at some point, changed his name from Joseph Allen Ashley to Joseph Bryan McStay.

Joseph was always an entrepreneur at heart. Although he did odd jobs and worked at Costco, he started his first business at seventeen by weaving bracelets and surfboard leashes out of neoprene scraps, selling them to friends and surf shops. He moved on to building tabletop water fountains in the garage, bartending at night for extra income.

After a brief stint back in Texas with Patrick, Joseph returned to Orange County, where he met a blonde named Heather Martin. As the daughter of Rock Martin, who owned a custom jewelry store in Laguna Beach, Heather supported Joseph's business endeavors. The young couple got married on August 8, 1992, and lived in San Clemente.

With Patrick's help, Joseph bought a boutique called Naturally Dana Point, where he and Heather sold his fountains, scented soaps, and other items.

"Dad, I think I can do really good with this," he said.

In September of 1996, Joseph and Heather had a son, Elijah. They also bought an undeveloped beachfront lot in Belize, about six miles south of the Mexican border, where Joseph wanted to build a house someday.

As his fountain business grew, Joseph asked his brother to come back from Hawaii to be his partner in a new company, Naturally DP Fountains, in 1998. After buying a green Dodge truck, and renting an industrial space in San Clemente, they built fountains together—tabletop water features, with tiers of slate or a nautilus shell, in California gold-panning bowls. Although Joseph's primary focus was accounting and packaging, he added a little ceramic turtle into each fountain as his signature.

However, that venture never had a chance to take off, because a woman with a company in San Francisco saw their features at a trade show and accused them of stealing her "zen" designs. According to Patrick, who was at the show, he told the woman they'd never heard of her company, and that Joseph had designed his fountains and packaging with his own style, incorporating little twigs. But she sued them nonetheless.

The costs of fighting the lawsuit sunk the brothers' business. Michael and his wife lost their house in Lake Forest, and Joseph's marriage to Heather suffered as well.

While Joseph was trying to keep his head above water, Heather had an affair and got pregnant. Joseph said he was willing to raise the child with Heather, regardless of who fathered it. Although Heather told Joseph she'd stop seeing her lover, the relationship didn't end until Joseph told him about the baby.

Joseph was devastated when Heather decided to leave him anyway. They separated on July 17, 1998, although she didn't file for divorce until June 2000, citing irreconcilable differences.

They shared legal and physical custody of Elijah. Joseph was supposed to pay Heather $395 per month in child support, though he apparently missed some payments, because court documents described him as a "debtor" in 2003.

Joseph kept both businesses, which were sole proprietorships. He also took on all related liabilities, including the costs of fighting the lawsuit and an $18,000 promissory note from Patrick.

In an unrelated development, the same week Heather left Joseph, her longtime friend Michael McFadden was arrested for brutally beating a former girlfriend for sleeping with another man.

McFadden's charges, including attempted murder, burglary, assault with a deadly weapon other than a firearm, and infliction of great bodily injury on a child under five, were reduced in a plea bargain. After pleading guilty to two felonies—assault with a deadly weapon and making a criminal threat of death or bodily harm—he was sentenced to two years and eight months in prison in March 2000.

Heather had known McFadden even longer than Joseph, because they'd both worked at her father's store, where McFadden designed and sold jewelry. He also lived in a studio apartment at the Martin family's house.

Heather wrote and visited McFadden during his fifteen months in prison. After he was released on parole in June 2001, her father let him return to the store, and she married McFadden seven months later. They went on to have a daughter, whom Joseph used to watch during Elijah's Little League games. Mc-Fadden coached the games, but by then, the situation was so amicable that the two men surfed together and hung out at birthday parties.

But this took some time. Joseph had sunk into a depression from the domino effect of the lawsuit, separation, and divorce. Struggling to pay his legal costs, he took out two bank loans and racked up debts on eight credit cards, while trying to heal his broken heart.

With Patrick's help, Joseph kept the boutique going while also collaborating on a new venture with his buddy, Guy Joseph, in 2000. To supplement Joseph's retail sales, Guy obtained a business license to run a home-based internet retail business, Earth Inspired Products, in San Clemente, and Joseph designed a simple website for it, earthinspiredproducts.com.

Billed as "bringing nature to you," EIP sold his tabletop water fountains, made of copper, slate, glass, and driftwood. It also sold "Dancing Water Tables," known as furniture fountains; wall-hanging features that sent water cascading down sheets of glass; and items that had been selling at the boutique, including "bamboo chimes, luminaries, wood carvings, aromatherapy soap, sheepskin boots, sandals, and more."

Guy also took out a business license for Integrity Electronics in 2002, a venture he and Joseph ran for several years, refurbishing hard drives in an industrial park and reselling them online.

Nonetheless, Joseph was still having a rough time. He didn't earn enough from these businesses to cover his $117,000 in legal debts, so he filed for Chapter 7 bankruptcy in June 2004.

The following year, Patrick came out from Texas to try to help jump-start Joseph's fountain business. Filing a fictitious business name for Earth Inspired Products in Orange County as a partnership, Patrick opened bank accounts with ATM cards and a merchant account to take credit cards. Joseph had power of attorney and was a signer on the account, but their $50,000 credit line was under Patrick's name.

Joseph hired Dan Kavanaugh, then in his early twenties, to upgrade EIP's simple website and improve its visibility using search engine optimization (SEO) techniques. As the website became more sophisticated, it moved up in Google searches, and company profits began to grow.

Guy had introduced Joseph to Kavanaugh a few years earlier, when he was still a high school kid who built websites. In the interim, Kavanaugh had taken classes at Saddleback, learned internet marketing, and earned the nicknames "Hacker Dan," "Dan the Hacker," and "The Hacker Kid." In exchange for the occasional software, Joseph threw Kavanaugh money when he was short, and let him drive his 1983 Volkswagen Vanagon.

Joseph was rooming with McGyver McCargar at the time, so the three of them sometimes surfed together. If Kavanaugh stayed late, working on Joseph's computer, he'd sleep on the couch.

By 2006, Joseph's credit had improved enough to dissolve the partnership with Patrick and return EIP to a sole proprietorship in his own name. His seller's permit application to the state Board of Equalization listed him as the owner, the partnership with Patrick as the former owner, and Merritt's company, IDesign4U, as one of two major suppliers. Kavanaugh's name never appeared on any official EIP paperwork, government or otherwise, until months after Joseph disappeared.

Chapter 11

Summer was born Lisa Virginia Aranda to her fourteen-year-old mother, Blanche, on December 27, 1966, in the San Gabriel Valley of Los Angeles County. Summer never met her father, who took off before she was born.

When Blanche landed in juvenile hall, her mother, Virginia, assumed custody of Summer, as she did with Tracy when she was born three years later.

By nineteen, Blanche had been married and divorced. After moving to Chicago, she got her daughters back and started seeing a man she didn't know was married, becoming pregnant with Kenneth in the mid- to late 1970s. Blanche married again in the early 1980s, but left her husband due to physical abuse.

Blanche and her children returned to live with their grandmother in California until Blanche met a new man, and they moved into his house in Temple City. In 2010, she went by the name Blanche Almanza.

Summer was still going by her birth name, Lisa, in high school, when she briefly dated Albert "Al" Vergara, who was three years older. They broke up because, even at sixteen, Summer had strong opinions and kept mostly to herself.

Summer went to live with Blanche's boyfriend's mother and

dropped out of high school. After Vergara reached out one day, they started dating again, only this time, they fell in love and moved into a trailer in south El Monte, which he'd bought from his father. When family meddled in their wedding plans, the couple decided to elope at the Hitching Post in San Bernardino. Summer was only nineteen.

She finished high school by taking adult classes while working at Enterprise and L'eggs, then went on to earn two associate's degrees by attending community colleges in Pasadena and Mission Viejo.

A voracious reader, Summer was intelligent, and encouraged Vergara to return to school, too. He didn't realize it at the time, but later said she "wasn't quite as confident as she thought she was," and was actually "very vulnerable."

Vergara said he believed Summer was ashamed of her Latin heritage, seeing it as a stigma due to the stereotype of a "beer-drinking, labor person, and not the most respected race." She was embarrassed that her mother had three children with three different fathers, and she didn't want to live in a mobile home.

Frequent arguments sent them to counseling as they tried to save their marriage, but Vergara finally moved out. They never had children, because they both knew their relationship wasn't going to last.

After seven years, Summer was the one to suggest divorce. Vergara agreed to take on their $20,000 in debts, but said if Summer wanted part of his pension, she had to assume half the debt. She declined, so he gave her their car and the trailer, which she sold to move to Anaheim Hills and Laguna Niguel and to buy a green Isuzu Trooper. Summer started telling people she was nineteen, because she felt like she was rediscovering the youth she'd lost to her marriage.

In 1996, before she and Vergara were officially divorced, she took a trip with Kenneth to Amsterdam and Paris. When her European friends nicknamed her "Summer Girl," she liked it so much she decided to keep it. Adding the last name of Martelli, she became Summer Martelli, which was reflected on her real estate license in 2002.

After marrying Joseph, she was drawn to the idea of a combined last name for the boys, Martelli-McStay, similar to the one she'd previously used, Aranda-Martelli. Detectives attributed her numerous aliases to her eccentric personality, but she told Patrick she used different names because a woman in Houston had stolen her identity.

Although she claimed to have Italian heritage, it's unknown why she chose the name Martelli, which traces back to a Giovanni di Guglielmo Martelli, a lawyer in Florence, Italy, in the 1300s. Giovanni is a longer form of Gianni, or John. Giovanni "Gianni" Versace was a fashion designer, who was murdered, ironically, by serial killer Andrew Cunanan in 1997. It appears her nickname for Joseph, Giuseppe, morphed into the name of their firstborn son, Gianni Giuseppe Martelli-McStay.

In the summer of 2004, Joseph was a single part-time dad, looking for love.

After going six years without finding someone he cared for as much as Heather, Joseph was immediately taken with Summer, calling her "my sweet Colombian princess," and she with him. They couldn't keep their hands off each other. McCargar advised them to "pace yourself," but they didn't listen.

A few months into the relationship, Summer called her brother in Hawaii and told him she was dreaming that she was pregnant.

"I'm going to go to the doctor," she said.

It turned out she was right. She'd been pregnant since November.

Before then, Summer and Joseph had been having secret rendezvous and communicating by email, because she was still sharing a four-bedroom house, two and a half hours away in Big

Bear Lake, with her boyfriend, Vic "Jojo" Johansen. He'd bought the place in 2002, her first sale as a real estate agent.

She and Johansen had also been running a business together called Adrenaline Pushers, where Johansen taught kids and adults how to surf. He'd recently expanded into ski lessons, traveling back and forth from Mammoth Lakes to see Summer—until she rebuffed his kisses.

Summer wanted to extricate herself from Johansen, but needed to be careful, because he had a volatile personality. The police had been called to their house several times during arguments when he'd punched walls in anger, though he never hit Summer. He was, however, arrested and charged for threatening a neighbor and her twelve-year-old daughter.

"I was a Marine, and I know how to kill," Johansen told the neighbor, who called the police and obtained a restraining order against him in April 2004.

After six days in jail, Johansen pleaded no contest to making criminal threats, a misdemeanor. He got three years' probation, which was revoked twice when he was deemed a fugitive for failing to attend his required anger-management program, but he eventually completed the sessions.

Johansen had, in fact, served in the U.S. Marines as a field radio operator and forward observer from 1995 to 1999. After that, he moved to San Clemente and attended Saddleback, where he met Summer.

Shouldering a tax lien and a bankruptcy, Johansen let his house go into default several times, but Summer wanted to prevent it from foreclosure, so he put it in her name in January 2005.

Patrick McStay loaned her money via a rental agreement so she could remodel the house, which she eventually sold to her tenants for $415,000. After repaying Patrick, she still was able to put $40,000 into savings.

Once Summer had moved into Joseph's duplex in San Clemente

in 2005, Johansen emailed her to say he was happy for her and her new family.

"You can still call me if you ever need help with anything," he wrote. "Don't forget about me. I am still out here."

He was still in touch with her in late December 2009, when he wished her a happy birthday, signing off with, "I love you . . . forever and ever, Vic."

By then, the McStays had moved to Fallbrook and Johansen had moved within two miles of the McStays' former apartment in San Clemente. He was arrested in the early morning of January 10, 2010, after refusing to leave the OC Tavern, which Joseph used to frequent because it was next door to his office. Johansen spent several days in jail, pleading guilty to interfering with a business.

Joseph had taken over the apartment in San Clemente, which was two blocks from the beach, from his mother when she moved to Ventura County. After Summer moved in, she insisted on giving birth to their boys in a plastic pool in their living room with the help of a midwife.

Joseph's family wasn't invited, but Summer asked her sister to be there for Gianni's birth in July 2005, which Tracy remembered as "one of the most beautiful experiences of my life." Likewise, in 2007, Summer flew Kenneth in for his annual visit from Hawaii to coincide with the birth of Joey Jr.

Summer was very pregnant when she, Gianni, and Kenneth ran into her ex-husband at a restaurant in Sierra Madre in 2007. As Vergara told detectives later, he "felt that day was a gift," because she looked so happy.

After Baby J was born, Summer and her family posed for photos in the front yard with a giant stork placard, announcing the baby's birth weight and size. Susan called the baby chubby, which hurt Summer's feelings, but somehow the nickname Chubba stuck.

"He was just so chubba chubba, and that little red mark [on

his forehead], it was so cute," Kenneth said. "Summer was a very good mother. Never left their side, tended to their needs, very protective and very picky about those things."

Summer was "elated" to be a mother, Tracy said. "It was what she wanted to do, be a mom, a wife. They were living a beautiful life together." Although Summer was a stark contrast to Joseph, who was "fun, free-spirited, always joking, always laughing," they were inseparable, "touchy-feely, [and] in love."

Summer and Joseph waited to get married until after both boys were born.

"Joey wanted a big wedding," Susan said. "Usually it's the girls who want a big wedding."

Summer's four closest friends were her bridesmaids, including real estate agent Diane Cirignani and photographer Jesi Silveria. Michael was Joseph's best man, with Elijah, McCargar, and another longtime friend, Nick Pomponio, as his groomsmen.

Summer was adamant about who she wanted there, and who she didn't. When she learned Joseph was searching for her birth father to invite him, she dashed off an angry email. Taken aback by her tone, Joseph, who hadn't met his birth father either, immediately backed off. She'd sent him a similar email while pregnant with Joey Jr., threatening to leave if he didn't heed her frustrations with his ex-wife.

Summer initially invited her sister and mother to the wedding, only to disinvite them over pet peeves only she could understand.

"That's Summer," Tracy explained.

Summer still expected her brother to come, however, and when he didn't, she told him that she and Joseph were hurt he didn't show up to walk her down the aisle.

Joseph and Summer said their vows and took communion on the lawn of a woodsy private venue near Mission Viejo on November 10, 2007.

"I can get my green card now," Summer joked afterward, which left Michael scratching his head.

The attendees danced into the night under a covered patio.

"It was all a blast," Susan recalled, who beamed from the front row during the nuptials, then joyfully watched her grand-children frolicking together, as Joseph danced with Cathy and Taylor Jarvis—Chase Merritt's partner and their daughter—and Summer danced with Merritt.

Every morning in San Clemente, Summer and Joseph had oatmeal and coffee at a nearby eatery, then took the kids to the park or the beach before Joseph headed to the office. Joseph often surfed by the pier a few blocks away.

The couple didn't want to give up this mellow beach life, but they couldn't afford a house by the coast, so they reluctantly set their sights on foreclosure properties inland.

In August 2009, they found a five-bedroom ranch-style home in Temecula that sounded so good the family drove out to see it. Joseph posted video of the excursion on his YouTube channel.

"This is our dream house we found up in the hills of Temecula," Joseph says in his surfer voice, with a hint of southern twang. "We're literally on the top of the mountains. That's the road comin' in. It's dirt, just like Texas. And here's our circular driveway, four-car garage, ranch-style. Look at that! We're in the mountains of Temecula. It's ah-maaaaazing."

When this house didn't work out, they bid on the home on Avocado Lane. They'd planned to move once escrow closed, but their landlord went to court to evict them after their neigh-bor complained about the toys that Summer kept buying until they filled half the driveway.

The McStays were so busy house-hunting, taking care of the kids, and running EIP while Joseph was sick, that neither of them responded to the eviction notice. When they realized they had only three days to pack and go, it was too late to ask the court for more time, so they had to stuff all their belongings into three PODS storage units.

Because Susan Blake was in Ventura County five days a week for her job, they took their terracotta-potted plants to her house in Corona and stayed there for three weeks until escrow closed. During that period, Summer planned a birthday party for Joseph at a Mexican restaurant in Laguna Beach and rented a limousine to take them there.

Her friend Diane had promised to watch the boys, but called last minute to say that her husband John would babysit instead. Summer refused to allow a man to watch her kids, so she called the whole night off. Susan suggested Summer and Joseph take the kids for a joyride in the limo anyway, which is how the now nationally recognized photo of the four of them in the limousine came to be.

Such rash decisions and volatile behaviors weren't uncommon for Summer, who sometimes calmed down after expressing her quick temper and acerbic tongue, but also mulled over events or held grudges at other times. Although these outbursts caused rifts within Joseph's family as well as her own, Summer seemed content with her close-knit family of four, which explains why most of their family photos feature only one parent at a time.

Summer seemed closest to Patrick, who had similar characteristics, and also had a soft spot for his daughter-in-law. "She could probably go down on Bowery Street and cuss with the best of the sailors," he said, describing her as "very passionate" and "pretty feisty."

Although Tracy characterized her sister as "very strict," "bossy," and "anti-everything," Summer held a special place in her heart, because she never purposely harmed anyone.

Summer was often depicted in contrasting extremes, such as headstrong but sometimes withdrawn. "She was difficult, absolutely true. But she was also great," her ex-husband, Vergara, recalled. "When you were with her alone, she was wonderful.

When others were involved, she felt the need to put up her wall. But I don't believe she was mean-spirited. She had an incredible need to keep certain people at arm's length."

As these stories were relayed to detectives, they seemed to fit a pattern of victimization and paranoia. Two people close to her said they thought Summer might be bipolar. Although no one mentioned any formal mental-health diagnosis, Johansen said she smoked pot and took Paxil for depression when they were together.

Summer apparently knew her behavior could be erratic, because she was looking for a homeopathic supplement called "Anger" to treat it on February 4. The pharmacist she spoke with remembered their call later, because Summer argued and hung up on the pharmacist after she said the product didn't exist.

When Susan testified at trial, her tone seemed to have a tinge of disapproval, or perhaps frustration, as she described Summer as "a very protective mother" over her two boys.

"She was always worried about something," she said. "She had them with her at all times."

Susan never publicly revealed the source of these feelings, but she listed Summer's odd behaviors privately to detectives: She didn't get up until 10 a.m., so Joseph had to make breakfast for the boys. She wouldn't drive at night or over bridges. When Blanche was over when Joseph came home from work, Summer made her go to another room, and Blanche only complied because Summer threatened not to let her to see the grandchildren otherwise.

Although Summer's family seemed to accept these behaviors, Susan said she felt she had to speak up.

"I even told her she needed drugs," she said.

Chapter 12

Five days after the family was reported missing, Detective DuGal asked the National Center for Missing & Exploited Children (NCMEC) for help distributing fliers featuring photos of the family. San Diego County Crime Stoppers offered a reward of up to $1,000 for information leading to an arrest.

The fliers described the McStays as "endangered missing," and listed birthdates and identifiers like Joey Jr.'s strawberry birthmark and Joseph's tattoos. When Susan saw the fliers, she was surprised to see Summer's birthday was in December, and shocked that she was forty-three—ten years older than she'd claimed at her last party in July. Susan said she wouldn't have cared, but she wondered why Summer would lie about that.

Summer's brother and Joseph's father suggested, independently, to DuGal that the McStays might be in Cabo San Lucas with Joseph's high school friend Jimmy, who ran a surf camp there. This theory grew stronger after Guy Joseph was "freaked out" by a call from an unknown Hispanic man, asking if he knew Jimmy.

Although Jimmy told DuGal he hadn't seen the McStays, the disturbing call fueled Guy's theory that "Mexican drug lords had committed a home invasion and took the family across the border because Joseph was going to sue a Mexican restaurant in

Los Angeles" after they'd "stiffed" him for tens of thousands of dollars.

That restaurant was Provecho on Wilshire Boulevard, which is now closed. The dispute apparently stemmed from a differing interpretation of "architectural plans" that were to be approved before a waterfall installation.

"Chase was asked time after time to produce shop drawings," a Provecho rep wrote in an email to Joseph in July 2008, but all he gave her was a "pencil scribbled, vague, incomplete sketch."

"How could it be ready for installation? I have not approved it," she wrote, telling Joseph he could "choose to believe" Merritt had made himself available, but he hadn't returned their calls.

Joseph replied that they'd installed the first portion of the waterfall to fit the restaurant's design and dimensions after Merritt finalized them with the architect. Once they were paid the outstanding balance, Merritt would finish the job.

After negotiations fell apart, Provecho cancelled the order and reversed its deposit payment. Joseph tried to dispute the chargeback, saying he had "every intention" to complete the "one-of-a-kind custom" job, "despite the client ignoring the executed contract."

However, Provecho's credit card company sided with its client, which left Joseph with a hefty loss, $19,000 of which had already been paid to Merritt for labor and materials. He and Joseph discussed filing a contractor's lien against the restaurant, but ultimately agreed to split the loss.

Detectives soon learned Joseph was the only family member with a valid passport. Summer's was expired, and investigators found only one of the boys' birth certificates in the house. That meant they couldn't have gained lawful entry to any foreign countries, but DuGal asked Interpol to post the family's photos on its missing persons site nonetheless.

Within two weeks, the U.S. Border Patrol told DuGal that neither of the McStays' vehicles had crossed into Mexico in the past six months, so he requested surveillance footage of the pedestrian walkway into Tijuana for the evening of February 8, when the Trooper was towed from San Ysidro.

A group of volunteers watched many hours of video until one identified a grainy ninety-second clip of two adults, each apparently holding a child's hand, as they walked casually across the border around 7 p.m. But the camera angle was from behind, so their faces weren't visible.

DuGal showed the clip to Joseph's and Summer's relatives and McGyver McCargar, but none of them could identify the group with any surety, only that the woman was wearing boots resembling Summer's favorite Uggs.

Susan Blake thought the family might have crossed the border to fly to a resort in Belize, but she said Summer was thinner than the woman in the video, and the man didn't walk like Joseph, with his duck-like gait.

"It doesn't look like my son," she said.

Nonetheless, DuGal posted the clip on YouTube on March 5, writing in a report that "Susan believed it was probably her missing family, but wished she could see their faces to be sure."

Michael McStay didn't believe Joseph would've taken his family to Mexico, especially without telling him.

"The bottom line is, if that's them crossing the border, with all the media coverage all over this thing," he told *The Orange County Register* in late March, "my brother would have picked up the phone and said, 'Mikey, I'm all right . . . Tell Mom and Dad I'm OK.' We are a tight-knit family."

Several days later, an RCFL analyst, who had been searching the family's computers, found evidence to support DuGal's theory that they'd gone, voluntarily, to Mexico: on January 27, someone had queried About.com for travel and passport requirements for children going to Mexico. The same session included visits to websites for Chuck E. Cheese and other family-oriented activities, as Summer was apparently planning a late birthday party for Joey Jr.

Summer had also emailed a seller on Craigslist about buying Rosetta Stone Spanish-language software and having it delivered at Joseph's soccer game on January 29, where his friends saw him shake hands with two men in the parking lot after the game.

In the meantime, DuGal obtained a slightly enhanced version of the border video, which revealed that the man and both kids were wearing knit beanies, as Joseph and the boys habitually did.

As DuGal became more convinced the McStays were in Mexico, he alerted the families to the new findings, which sparked a push to distribute fliers throughout Baja California. Although the FBI had already been briefed on the case, DuGal asked again for help south of the border in April and submitted the border-crossing video to the *America's Most Wanted* TV crew during a shoot at the house in May.

Also during the shoot, Susan and Blanche retrieved the boys' placentas from the freezer so DuGal could have the DNA extracted from the umbilical cords. This information went into central databases, along with Joseph's and Summer's dental records, to assist with identification if any bodies or remains were found.

Chapter 13

Early in the investigation, DuGal retraced Joseph and Summer's steps via cell phone records and voicemails. By all appearances, February 4, the last day they were seen, was an ordinary day. In between calls to her sister and mother that morning, Summer contacted Smith & Noble, inquiring about window coverings.

Now that the boys were getting older, she spoke with her bridesmaid, Diane Cirignani, about getting back to work as a real estate agent and listing the Fallbrook house as a satellite office for the Cirignanis' agency. She said she'd already printed up new stationery and had purchased Rosetta software to help her communicate with Spanish-speaking clients. She'd also ordered an Italian CD, because the languages were so similar.

Summer made a credit card purchase at a holistic pharmacy in Vista at 2:11 p.m., then headed over to Ross for the second day in a row to buy baby clothes and beach bags.

Meanwhile, Joseph called Merritt several times as he headed north to meet him for lunch. His phone pinged cell towers in Rancho Cucamonga at 12:52 and 1:01 p.m., then accessed the internet seven times until 2:39 p.m.

He called Merritt twice as he was driving south, at 3:03 p.m. from Ontario and half an hour later from Norco. By the time they spoke for another three minutes at 4:18 p.m., the call pinged off Joseph's "home" tower in Fallbrook.

Someone made a call to Joseph's cell phone at 4:25 p.m. from the McStays' landline, but it didn't go through, because the caller hung up after only ten seconds. Susan Blake was the last caller to their home phone at 5:39 p.m.

Summer texted Joseph at 5:05 p.m., but he didn't receive the message until 5:47, which indicated he either lost power or turned off his phone after checking his voicemail at 4:30, then turned it back on to check messages and call Merritt for another three-minute conversation.

The final call made from Joseph's cell phone was to Merritt at 8:28 p.m., lasting one minute or less.

McCargar also helped to reconstruct details of his last days with the family, which dovetailed with Merritt's account.

Because he'd introduced Joseph and Summer, McCargar often acted as a mediator between them. Before they disappeared, he told Detective Hillen, Summer called to complain about Chase Merritt, who was over at the house. She knew he had a criminal record, and she didn't like him being around so much. But the bottom line was, she just didn't like him. Period.

Summer said Merritt had just undermined her in front of her children. They'd ordered pizza for dinner, so she set up the kid's table with plates, knives, and forks, then served herself and Joseph at the adult table. Merritt, who was standing at the island in the kitchen, grabbed a slice out of the box and started eating it with his hands, which upset Summer.

"You're eating like a pig," she said. "I'd prefer it if you just leave."

As Joseph tried to smooth things between them, Merritt got a plate, knife, and fork and ate his pizza the way she wanted.

She and Merritt had also argued over the use of corporal punishment. When Merritt said he'd spanked his son Ray for refusing to say "sorry" to one of his sisters, Summer disapproved, saying, "You broke his spirit." She didn't hit her kids. She simply told them to stop doing whatever they were doing until they got bored and moved on to something else.

Seeing how stressed Summer was about the remodel, McCargar told her to stop worrying about Merritt and Joseph's work matters.

"Just relax and let Joey handle it," he said.

He'd seen how Joseph operated before—his goal was to keep his workers motivated, as he had with his young webmaster, Dan Kavanaugh. Even though it was Joseph's company, he'd tried to help Kavanaugh feel he had an emotional investment to keep him engaged.

"C'mon, let's go," he would say. "You are my partner, let's make this happen."

But that was before Kavanaugh threatened to shut down the website or link it to porno sites. The last time McCargar was at the house, painting, on February 3, Joseph said he'd about finished buying out Kavanaugh, and had moved him over to a water manufacturing website to keep him occupied so he wouldn't interfere with EIP.

McCargar recalled that the day he'd started painting on January 31, a guy stopped by to talk business with Joseph. He figured it was Merritt, because he sensed the awkwardness between the man and Summer.

The boys were constantly underfoot that day. Joseph got upset when one of them took a wet brush outside and painted the Dodge truck's bumper, so he and Summer took them to the park to let McCargar make some progress.

After the family returned, they all chatted around the banister as Summer recalled undergoing hypnosis during her pregnancy and identifying Bear as her "guardian angel." Joseph proposed going to a microbrewery nearby for some pizza, but McCargar said it was getting late, and suggested a beer later in the week.

He'd planned to come back February 2, but had to call and cancel because of his girlfriend's ultrasound appointment. When Summer scolded him, he hung up on her. Then came her angry string of texts.

Respect for us is where on your list? she wrote. You gave us your word of honor.

She was like a sister to him, but he thought her reaction seemed like "a little overkill." He was upset that she was upset, though, so he showed up the next morning at eight thirty to do a half day. Visibly surprised and maybe a bit embarrassed, Summer left to run some errands as he was masking the kitchen with blue tape.

After removing the cabinet doors and drawers, he painted the island. He was still there when Merritt stopped by to chat and try out some LED lights in the living room with Joseph.

The next day, McCargar and Joseph were talking in his office while Summer was at Home Depot, buying a different color paint, because she said they'd used the wrong one the day before. As they commiserated about dealing with their difficult partners, McCargar said his pregnant girlfriend was acting hormonal, and Joseph said he felt like "splitting" sometimes, but hung in to keep the family together.

Very early in the investigation, the SDSD learned that Summer became alarmed when she saw her boys exhibit inappropriate behavior in early September 2009. Also wondering why Gianni had tried to "French kiss" her several times, she questioned him with the video camera running.

Summer had already earned her "protective" label by accusing a daycare worker at a local gym of inappropriate behavior with her boys. She fought for a membership refund and won.

Before long, she became convinced that Elijah's stepfather, Michael McFadden, must be involved in a chain of events that resulted in her boys' behavior. When Joseph called Heather to inform her, he said "God told Summer" about it.

After filing an official complaint with Child Protective Services (CPS), citing her age as eight years younger than she was, Summer confided in her mother and a couple of close friends. She also took Gianni to a counselor, who filed subsequent reports with new information.

Not surprisingly, Heather didn't want Elijah to be around Summer, and enrolled her whole family—including Joseph—in therapy. Summer refused to join the sessions, and also wouldn't let her boys spend time with their half-brother.

The McFadden family and Susan Blake denied that any such behavior had occurred, but the ensuing investigation—in which Summer's claims were ultimately found to be unsubstantiated—clearly generated great tension, anxiety, and estrangement between all involved.

Caught in the middle, Joseph decided to find a separate counselor to help heal his family and his marriage, so he asked Susan if she knew of a good one. If Summer refused to attend the sessions, he'd go alone.

"I want to get my family back on track," he said, noting he and Summer hadn't had sex in a year.

By the end of January, Susan had found one relatively close to his house for $140 an hour, but Joseph never had a chance to go.

In the meantime, Summer confronted McFadden, who responded with a voicemail, telling Joseph to "muzzle" his wife, or he would do it for him.

These accounts fit with others that Summer had been responsible for isolating Joseph and the boys from friends and family. But the very nature of these allegations—and the involvement of several agencies in neighboring counties—fueled speculation that this stressful situation could have contributed to Joseph's protracted illness, and more importantly, could have spurred the family to leave town.

Given McFadden's violent criminal record and his angry reaction to Summer's accusations, the SDSD identified him as a person of interest within three days of the missing persons report.

But in an interview with Detective Hillen on February 19, McFadden said he had nothing to do with the family's disappearance. He denied threatening Joseph, and claimed he'd been at work in Laguna and at home in Oceanside the day the family was last seen.

McFadden said he didn't remember any particular call or communication with CPS on February 4, and he had no idea what had happened to the McStays. But he didn't think it was good.

"People just don't go missing," he said.

Although it appears the SDSD cleared McFadden pretty quickly, DuGal still suspected the CPS investigation could have contributed to the family going missing. DuGal stated in an email that "CPS informed Summer her complaint was unsubstantiated on February 4," which "possibly had a major effect on whatever happened" at the house that day.

DuGal may have based this theory on speculation by family members, however, because a CPS case worker tried but couldn't reach Summer to update her on February 5. Summer had left a message for Gianni's therapist the day before, saying she wanted to schedule another appointment because the boy was "having anger issues." Heather wasn't officially notified the allegations had been found to be unsubstantiated and that the case was now closed until February 23.

DuGal was worried Patrick would go public with details of the CPS investigation. But other than a brief mention in a TV news story in late 2013, the only hint came when a stack of search warrant affidavits was unsealed in 2015, noting that among the items seized from the McStays' garage was an educational pamphlet, titled *Helping Children With Sexual Behavioral Problems.*

*   *   *

As a result of this family drama, Joseph had to split his time over the holidays in 2009. Susan joined Joseph's family at Thanksgiving for dinner at a casino near the house, but when he brought Elijah to Susan's in Corona a couple of days before Christmas to celebrate with Michael's family, Summer and the boys stayed home. That's when Joseph told Susan about the allegations reported to CPS, but didn't go into detail and asked her not to tell anyone.

On Christmas Eve, Susan brought over gifts for "the little guys" and spent the evening with the family. She was shocked to find her gifts unopened in a cabinet above the refrigerator several months later.

Chapter 14

As Joseph's business grew, so did his desire to increase profits by producing more and bigger custom fountains and by
selling fewer made by outside manufacturers. He'd always handled all the sales and accounting, but he thought he could also
handle his own IT work now that the website was established.

He'd already paid Kavanaugh more than $80,000 to build the
site and update the SEO since 2005, but even before the threats,
he'd been relying on him less and less. Joseph hired Authority
Domains Inc. (ADI) in 2007 to take on some of those functions,
and by 2009, ADI was his primary contractor. As a result, Kavanaugh's income from EIP had declined dramatically, from
$40,000 a year to only a couple hundred dollars a month.

Joseph also wasn't giving Kavanaugh any portion of the sales
from the custom waterfalls he and Merritt were manufacturing.
In fact, he'd been hiding those sales from him.

Kavanaugh told detectives in 2014 that he only learned about
these hidden sales because he happened to see a custom-fountain
query come in to the website. He didn't mention the threatening
messages he sent to Joseph afterward, only the discovery that
triggered them.

Joseph notified ADI of the threats by email, forwarding his
message string with Kavanaugh as a proactive heads-up in case
something happened in the future.

"The success of eip is much more critical to me than to him. I can't couch hop as he could, I have mouths to feed," Joseph wrote ADI, noting that no matter how much he paid Kavanaugh, the young man spent it immediately, "part[ying] like a rock star."

In contrast, Joseph wrote, he'd learned to save his money to provide for his wife and three kids, which required the website to stay up and running.

"I can't have EIP disappear off the face of the earth and end up back in a cubicle working for someone else," he wrote. "I will not be malicious as [Kavanaugh] is being, and perhaps we can work through this or part ways amicably, I don't know."

Joseph started sending "buyout" payments to Kavanaugh via PayPal and checks, which he listed on an Excel spreadsheet named "Dan pay off," on February 19, 2009. It showed a couple of smaller amounts toward the year's end, but his bookkeeping wasn't consistent, because by the time he disappeared, he'd told McCargar, Merritt, and Patrick McStay that he'd already made, or was about to make, the final payment, and had kicked in a 1994 BMW as part of the deal.

Accounts varied on the total amount. Merritt estimated it was more than $20,000, with maybe $2,000 left to pay. But, he said, "Dan was no longer part of the business."

Patrick said Joseph had finished paying off Kavanaugh—after three installments of $10,000—by late 2009. "Dan Kavanaugh was more or less bought out or paid off to shut him up and get him away from the whole thing," Patrick said on the Websleuths Radio Podcast. However, because Joseph was a softie, he tried to placate the volatile young man by agreeing to team up with him on a water-ionization start-up.

"Joey was nonconfrontational. He didn't like arguing," Patrick said. "[His] business was going tremendously well," so he still sent Kavanaugh small payments if he "ran a little short," on top of the monthly website maintenance fee, just to keep the peace.

Despite the messages documenting that Kavanaugh was the one who originally proposed the buyout, he still insisted to investigators that he was a "general partner" and had a fifty-fifty ownership in the business.

Although Michael and Susan accepted Kavanaugh's involvement in the business and access to EIP's finances, Patrick told DuGal as early as March 2010 that Kavanaugh had no legal authority to do any of that.

"[Kavanaugh] tried to claim he was a manager and a silent partner, and he was never a manager of squat," Patrick said on the Websleuths podcast. "He was like a subcontractor. Dan was never a partner in anything."

This was confirmed to DuGal in February 2011 by Joseph's tax accountant, Paul Dutton, who forwarded an email from Joseph stating that he'd mistakenly checked "general partner" on a tax form.

"I have no partner, therefore should not legally file a partnership tax return," Joseph wrote in November 2009. "Please change this EIN to a sole-proprietor entity."

Patrick believed he was the only person to whom Joseph and Summer had given their email passwords. He told DuGal that he believed Kavanaugh had hacked into Joseph's PayPal account and attempted to start paying himself as early as February 6. Patrick warned DuGal that this would all come out if the FBI got involved, but his tips about Kavanaugh seemed to fall on deaf ears.

Patrick also expressed concern about his own son, Michael, having access to Joseph's accounts, saying Michael owed Joseph at least $10,000 in loans. Susan voiced similar concerns about Patrick having access to Joseph's finances.

Joseph's business activities provided the major thrust of DuGal's investigation, but the detective was never able to connect the dots to anyone with a motive for murder.

Joseph's friends said that, in addition to hiding the custom jobs from Kavanaugh, he also tried to hide his true income from Summer, as Merritt claimed. Several of them described her as a "shopaholic" or "pack rat," constantly buying things she didn't need on Craigslist or Amazon, which sometimes forced Joseph to tell her there was no money in the account.

Susan Blake waited until August 24, 2010—after the house had gone into foreclosure—to tell DuGal her son had also been hiding money from the government. Susan said he'd "stored a large quantity of cash in his safe-deposit box which was actually unreported income," DuGal's report stated. "She believed Joseph would have had access to this safe-deposit box's money for living expenses."

DuGal tried to find this safe-deposit box, but the fraud investigator at Union Bank said there wasn't one in Joseph's, Summer's, or his business's name at any institution subscribed to CrimeDex. The only possible exception was the local Mission Oaks National Bank in Fallbrook, which refused to disclose information without a subpoena, so DuGal stopped searching.

In retrospect, this missing cash raises questions about the motivation behind the numerous visits Susan and Michael made to "clean" the house. It also provides another possible incentive for someone wanting to rob or kill the missing family.

DuGal noted that Joseph's tax filings also seemed inconsistent. His EIP return for 2008 showed gross receipts of $491,701, with a gross profit of $202,096. Yet the McStays' personal return showed business income of only $67,128, which his accountant said didn't reflect the "very profitable" business that his family had claimed it was. Dutton said Joseph had given him "sketchy" income and expense information, with numbers crossed out and penciled into a spreadsheet, and no backup documentation.

When Dutton finalized the return, Joseph owed $12,671, but he said Joseph was informed later that he owed additional interest and penalties, because he hadn't paid enough in estimated quarterly taxes.

Chapter 15

By all accounts, Joseph had developed a close relationship with Chase Merritt during their four years of working together.

After seeing or hearing about Merritt's work at a trade show in 2006, Joseph called to ask Merritt if he was interested in a job that required water to flow uphill, which his other contractors couldn't do. Merritt said yes, and the feature ended up at a library on the East Coast.

Merritt soon became Joseph's go-to guy for welding and metal work for his bigger custom features. Along the way, Joseph started creating design drawings on his computer as they discussed where to put the wiring, plumbing, and pumps.

By 2009, "they were starting to do a lot more volume, and not just volume, but [building] more expensive waterfalls," Cathy Jarvis recalled.

That fall, Joseph decided to capitalize on that trend by consolidating his operations into a warehouse, where he could boost custom fountain sales even more by increasing EIP's "manufacturability." To this end, Merritt said, they agreed to contract out the stainless-steel work he'd been doing, because it was difficult for him "to keep up" as a one-man manufacturing operation, especially with his coronary heart disease.

Merritt found MSM in October and arranged for them to bid on projects, then provide the steel and welders to put the framework together.

"I can bring in the work," Merritt told MSM. "You don't have to go out and find the work. And we'll pay you directly."

That allowed Merritt to close his factory showroom in Pomona, where he had about fifteen finished waterfalls on display and clients could watch new ones being built. He sold his equipment to MSM and put the displays into storage.

He and Joseph had been splitting the sale price with 65 percent to Merritt and 35 percent to Joseph, because Merritt often bought materials out of his portion, which left him with about 15 percent profit. Under their new arrangement, Joseph bought the materials and supplies himself, paying MSM directly for steel and labor.

From then on, Merritt oversaw the metal work, finished the edging and stonework himself, then either packed the components for shipping or delivered and installed them locally. This actually increased his profits, he said, because he no longer had to pay the overhead on his factory showroom.

As a sales rep for Bluworld of Water, which manufactured water features, Gina Watson had worked with Joseph since 2006. But by late December 2009, she'd noticed Joseph's orders had markedly slowed.

"Why haven't you given us more bids?" she asked, in what turned out to be their last conversation.

Joseph told her about his expansion plans, that Merritt was building bigger waterfalls at a metal shop, and they were going to buy new equipment to scale up even more. Watson understood his desire to raise his profit margins, because he only made 25 percent when he resold a Bluworld fountain he didn't have the expertise or resources to assemble himself.

Explaining he had a quote from a Paul Mitchell salon and one from an ice cream shop, he asked her for prices on some parts he needed. In turn, she passed on some scuttlebutt she'd heard about Merritt's work.

"He's screwed over some customers," she said, recounting a story about one waterfall "so flimsy and thin that it was actually springing multiple pinholes at once."

Another customer, she said, claimed that Merritt had taken a $50,000 deposit for features, "but never came forward with the final product." Instead, he changed his address, his phone number, and tried to start over.

But Joseph wasn't deterred. "I know," he said. He was aware of Merritt's past problems and that he didn't manage his money well, but they were going to build this business together, with Joseph in charge of the money and sales.

"I can handle him," he said. "He'll do it right for me. I've helped him and his family, so he's loyal to me."

In the next month or two, Watson heard more stories about screwups affecting Joseph's customers, one of whom "had a copper feature that was all banged up because [Merritt] hadn't shipped it right."

"It's kind of weird, my last conversation with Joey was about Chase," she said. But "everything I was saying started coming true."

Chapter 16

Michael McStay and Susan Blake made a brief effort to keep EIP going so it would still be there when Joseph returned.

Because the deposit on the Paul Mitchell job had been paid in January, Merritt traveled to the New York salon in late February to do the installation, where he was paid the balance. He said he passed Joseph's portion to Kavanaugh and Susan.

Meanwhile, Michael renewed EIP's website domain name, registered earthinspiredproducts.com as a new DBA, and opened a new account at Chase Bank on March 16 so funds from incoming orders didn't get "comingled" with Joseph's existing accounts. He didn't have much of a choice, though, because he had no access to Joseph's accounts or passwords.

A week later, he added his mother as a signer to write checks on the account, then went back to running his own fire sprinkler business.

"I had a lot going on," Michael said. "Looking for my family. I was juggling a lot. I just set up the business entity so they could continue."

Things started falling apart soon after Susan and Merritt met to discuss next steps with Kavanaugh at his high-rise apartment in downtown San Diego. As he installed a new version of Windows on Susan's computer, Susan said Merritt kept asking for more money to complete pending orders, and Kavanaugh refused, until the two of them were yelling at each other.

Merritt had a different take. Because Susan had taken a leave from her job, he suggested she handle the sales calls and orders, like Joseph used to do. Merritt would come up with bids, and she could close the sales.

Kavanaugh had promised to handle the phones, but he was "sleeping until noon and not returning phone calls," Merritt said.

Merritt claimed they'd already talked about the new arrangement before the meeting, but Kavanaugh balked once they got there.

"Nobody's taking over shit. I'm running this," Merritt quoted Kavanaugh as saying. "You are a dime a dozen. There's only one of me."

Kavanaugh said the argument escalated until Merritt threatened to throw him over the balcony. But according to Merritt, "What I said was, 'You're fortunate I'm not someone else, because someone else would have thrown you off that f'ing balcony.' I was livid with him."

Either way, Susan was so scared by the cussing, screaming, and threats that she left the apartment.

"There was no second meeting," Merritt recalled, chuckling.

Trying to press the issue with her afterward didn't help matters. In his view, Susan had the power to wield over Kavanaugh to keep the business going, but "she was meek and mild and she wouldn't do it. That pissed me off. I let her know that, and it escalated from there."

This wasn't only about protecting Joseph's business, he told her; his own business "was going to die," too, without the income from EIP. "You're going to let Joseph's business completely fail. You're ruining a lot of peoples' lives here."

Susan had another perspective. She told investigators that tensions grew because Merritt was taking money but wasn't producing fountains as promised. She'd expected that once he got paid, he would reimburse her for the money she'd paid out of her personal bank account, but he never did.

Records show she paid him $5,410 in checks from that account between late March and mid-May, and $19,700 in April and May from the Chase account. She also paid $2,800 to Kavanaugh.

Merritt maintained he was only paid for jobs he completed, and was still owed money after writing himself checks for the Paul Mitchell and Saudi Arabia jobs using Joseph's Quick-Books account. He said EIP sales and manufacturing basically came to a halt until March 31, when Susan was paid for a new waterfall, and called to ask if he wanted to build it. This was the first of several projects he did for her through mid-May.

"That's why Ms. Blake was making payments to me," he said.

But in May, after "four, six, or seven weeks" of working on Joseph's business, Susan said, she, too, stepped away.

"My mother and I focused on finding our family and forget the business," Michael testified later.

That, in turn, left a void for Kavanaugh to take over the business and push out Merritt for good.

Chapter 17

Without the ability to serve search warrants, DuGal had to seek records on a voluntary basis. He sent out a CrimeDex alert, informing major banks that he was investigating a missing family, but had no warrant.

The few bank records he obtained reflected no activity on Joseph's and Summer's credit cards after February 4, and no transactions "directly related" to them other than those DuGal attributed to "keeping the business going."

In March, DuGal wrote to PayPal asking for Joseph's billing and payment records, which he received on a CD that he reviewed for "evidentiary information." Seeing none, he gave it to a financial crimes detective "to see if there were other persons we should look at in this case."

It's not clear how detailed these records were, but there was activity in Joseph's PayPal account. Kavanaugh's PayPal records, which were obtained years later, showed that after he'd requested and received $25 from Joseph's account on February 3, his next requests were cancelled or didn't go through.

That changed on February 10, six days after anyone had last seen or spoken with the family, when Joseph's password was reset and Kavanaugh received $900. The next day, he received $200 more. After a second password change on February 12, he received three payments totaling $4,800 that day, and $3,000 more the next. Not counting the $1,000 for Elijah's child support, Kavanaugh collected $7,900 from Joseph's account after he disappeared and before he was reported missing on the 15th.

To broaden its search, the SDSD set up a tip hotline and sought leads from coverage on national TV shows, including *Nancy Grace*, because every time a story aired, it generated more tips.

Armchair detectives, bloggers, psychics, and forensic science students across the nation were trying to solve this mystery, posting findings from public record searches and identifying possible suspects on social media, the Websleuths website, and other online message boards.

They also forwarded their theories, questions, and suggestions to DuGal: Did he know Joseph had posted a video on YouTube showing his new house? Did the McStays have their house re-keyed after buying it in foreclosure? Had DuGal interviewed the neighbors Summer invited to her home—not a suggested practice—to talk to them about selling theirs in short sales?

As these reports flooded in from all over the United States, Mexico, Canada, and even Australia, DuGal spent much of his time chasing down well-intentioned leads that went nowhere.

After Susan decided she didn't want to coordinate search efforts with her ex-husband Patrick, he and Michael set up separate websites and Facebook pages, while Susan hired her own private investigator. Michael invited Patrick to come out and get more involved, but only if he didn't spend most of the trip in casinos, gambling.

Unable to focus on work, Susan took a leave from her home-building job for nearly a year, praying Joseph would knock on her door one day and say he was sorry.

"I never gave up hope," she said. "Never."

Encouraged by leads from her investigator about "sightings" of the family south of the border at a Walmart in Merida and a restaurant in El Rosario, Susan hit the road to post fliers in grocery stores and gas stations as far south as Cabo San Lucas.

She also emailed Joseph and posted the messages online, hoping he would answer or someone would put them in touch: "Where are you? Why can't you call your mom? There's something bad happening, I'm here to help you."

But when her son and his family didn't turn up, Susan slipped into a depression. A friend had to come and stay with her, "because I was losing it," Susan told detectives.

Patrick teamed up with Gina Watson, the Bluworld account rep, to cull through thousands of Joseph's and Summer's emails. He shared select findings with DuGal and certain reporters, and posted others on his sites. After an initial interview, however, Patrick declined to cooperate with this book.

One item he flagged for DuGal was Joseph's email to ADI, which included Kavanaugh's threats and stated that Kavanaugh "was no longer going to be in control of EIP's website." Patrick also forwarded DuGal an email to Joseph, warning that someone had tried to access his QuickBooks account on February 8. Patrick was sure that person was Kavanaugh, because the credit card information wasn't familiar.

After working with Joseph for several years, Watson believed she understood his business, and echoed Merritt's concerns that Susan and Kavanaugh didn't know how to run it. When Kavanaugh tried to order a Bluworld fountain from Watson, using Joseph's credit card number, she said no, he had to use his own.

"Dan was a contracted employee rather than a partner," she said, so he shouldn't have been sending invoices to customers in early February, before Joseph even disappeared, or taking money from Joseph's PayPal accounts before he was reported missing.

"Never in the history of that account had Dan helped himself to PayPal funds or to Joey's funds, that wasn't the way their relationship worked," Watson said. "You can look at the pattern of transactions and see that never happened before."

But when DuGal asked Kavanaugh about the transactions, he contended he had permission from Susan and Michael to pay himself, to keep the business and website running, and to pay child support to Elijah.

"When I clarified with them and I got a unilateral answer that, yep, that was okay, I had no reason to question what they were doing at that point in the investigation. None," DuGal testified later.

In fact, DuGal described Kavanaugh in his reports as "very cooperative" in providing information about EIP finances, stating, "Daniel intended to attempt to continue running the business in Joseph's absence."

After DuGal got access to Joseph's QuickBooks account from Kavanaugh on May 27, he asked the financial crimes detective to review it, as well. But the detective found nothing of note other than Joseph made about $100,000 in annual profit from his business.

DuGal was more focused on Merritt, especially after receiving a complaint from a paying client who hadn't gotten her two fountains.

"I'm getting calls from dissatisfied customers," DuGal told Merritt on June 8, 2010.

DuGal's call was prompted by a woman at Geis Construction who wanted to know her legal options. She said she'd sent Kavanaugh $6,250 as a deposit on a $12,500 order, but still had no fountains. So DuGal called Kavanaugh, who said he'd sent Merritt $5,000 from his personal bank account for materials to build them.

"In theory he sent you five grand to get 'em going," DuGal told Merritt.

"But he did not," Merritt said. "Dan never paid me."

DuGal didn't ask to see Merritt's bank statement, but it showed he did receive that money from Kavanaugh.

Merritt told DuGal that EIP hadn't paid him, either, and he was still owed $14,000. "I'm doing the waterfalls to get 'em done for Geis, but I have not been paid."

"Then you had them send your wife money for crating or shipping or something? Why did you involve your wife?" DuGal asked, referring to the $2,000 Geis had sent to Cathy Jarvis at Merritt's request.

"I involved my wife because I do not have a checking account," he said.

"It sounds like you're robbing Peter to pay Paul, and I understand it," DuGal said.

"Honestly, that's exactly what I've been doing. I've been trying to just survive, keep things rolling, and get the waterfalls out," Merritt said, although this was tricky, because he and Susan weren't really talking, and he'd had a falling-out with Kavanaugh.

"Excuse my language, but he's a little prick," he said. "He thinks he knows everything."

Apparently, Kavanaugh had told their Saudi client that Merritt no longer represented EIP and if he did the work, EIP couldn't guarantee it, so Kavanaugh was going to try to find another builder. Kavanaugh had also been telling clients—and DuGal—that "Chase was both manufacturing the fountains and ripping people off," selling fountains meant for one customer to another. Kavanaugh told DuGal that anyone could find complaints about Merritt by Googling his company, "IDesign4U."

But Kavanaugh never found someone else to do the Saudi job, Merritt said, and now his visa was about to expire. He said he'd been hospitalized because he got dizzy when he stood up, and by the time the client asked him to come and install the fountain, he had to get his visa extended, *and* serve the out-

standing twenty-three days in jail. So things had gotten complicated.

Merritt contended Kavanaugh had taken in something like
$35,000 after Joseph disappeared, but he wasn't using it to com-
plete fountains or to pay Merritt. He'd tried to warn Susan that
Kavanaugh was "lying to you, he has his money, he's duping
you," but she was afraid Kavanaugh would shut the website
down.

"She kept telling me, 'I'm gonna take over the phones,' but
she never did, and he [Kavanaugh] just kept using her, taking in
checks. Earth Inspired Products is pretty much a dead company.
This whole thing has completely devastated my whole life."

Switching topics to news reports of the family being sighted
in Mexico, Merritt asked DuGal, "How is it going with the investigation with Joseph?"

"I have no idea where he is. None," the detective replied, saying those leads never panned out. "I believe they probably went
south at the beginning of February. I don't know if he's further
south or came back north."

DuGal told Merritt to resolve the situation with Geis, and not
to ask anyone else to send money to Jarvis, because he didn't
want any more calls.

Geis subsequently overnighted $1,950 to Walker Sheet
Metal, which had the fountains on site, then issued a check to
Merritt for $4,000 to finish the job after he sent them photos of
the fountains as "90 percent complete."

After Kavanaugh told DuGal he was going to file a police report, "because he thinks he is also a victim," the detective
dropped the issue.

Nine years later, when detectives from another agency followed up, they learned a Geis superintendent had to fly to California to load the fountains onto a truck and drive them back.

"We couldn't get anybody on that end of the world to make
good on the delivery," the Geis rep said.

What DuGal and other investigators didn't know or over-looked, was that six days after Kavanaugh's personal bank account was overdrawn by $40 in January 2010, he sent that first invoice to Geis, asking for the $6,250 deposit to be paid by credit card to his personal account.

Why was Kavanaugh collecting money for waterfalls on February 2, when Joseph was still very much alive, and still handling all the sales, deposits, and accounting?

On June 7, the day before DuGal's call to Merritt about Geis, Kavanaugh took the first formal step to lay claim to Joseph's business as his own. He set up a new Bank of America account with a $3,600 deposit, proclaiming himself sole proprietor of EIP.

In mid-June, Merritt flew to Saudi Arabia to install fountains for that client, who had already paid $61,400 for them.

Too big to be shipped by air, the parts had been sent by ship on March 5. Once they arrived, Susan Blake paid for Merritt's visa, but he said no more money came in to EIP from that project, because the client bought his airline ticket and paid him a per diem directly for his four days of supervising the installation.

"Pretty much I just pointed," he said, because he didn't have an official work visa.

Merritt emailed Susan from there on June 17, saying he was "trying to take care of these people" and would handle "all other loose ends" when he returned. But in the meantime, he asked her not to make any other commitments for him.

"You and Dan have successfully screwed up this business beyond repair, despite my pleas, and then tried to turn the blame on me, so as far as I'm concerned, I have no commitment to you," he wrote.

Nine days later, Merritt sent her another angry email after hearing she'd told people he was wanted by the FBI for fraudulently taking money for waterfalls, and not supplying them.

"You and I know that that is not true," he wrote. "I was in Saudi Arabia and not able to get in touch with my client for a while, but telling them that I was wanted is slander."

He said he'd installed all but the last few components for the Saudi waterfalls, which he wanted to discuss with her. But he threatened to "take legal action" if she defamed him again.

Chapter 18

Early on, Susan Blake invited Summer's mother to her house in Corona to learn more about Blanche's family. She also asked Blanche to help her clean and do laundry at the McStays' house in Fallbrook.

Because Blanche didn't have a car, she drove to Fallbrook with her cousin, Kathy Sanchez, who helped wash the boys' clothing. Sanchez said someone had washed the futon cover, so it had shrunk and was unraveling, and she couldn't get it back on.

As the months passed, Susan knew the house would soon go into foreclosure and be sold at auction, so she focused on selling and distributing the family's belongings.

"If there's anything you want of your dad's, take it," she told Elijah as they walked through the house. But all he took were his dad's surfboards, bikes, some music, and one of his shirts.

When she testified later about their walk-through, she said, "Grandma is supposed to be stronger, so I did my best."

Blanche was alarmed to hear from the McStays' gardener, whom she'd previously befriended, that Susan and Michael were removing property from the house. So, Blanche and Tracy showed up to find Michael loading the refrigerator, microwave, washer, and dryer into the Dodge truck, which Michael had been driving since Susan had a new key made.

Michael said the police told him they could do what they wanted with the house and its contents. So, Susan sold the appliances, gave the boxes of unused flooring to Joseph's ex-wife, and put the balance of Joseph's bank account toward college for Elijah.

"We made this very clear to Blanche and them," Susan told detectives. "Anything that goes out of this house that can be sold, that money is going back to [Elijah]. Period."

Although Susan invited Blanche to take any sentimental items she wanted, Blanche was upset to see Susan throwing away things that Summer might have wanted to keep. Why do that if she thought they were coming back?

Blanche asked for family photos, so Susan gave her some pictures and videotapes, unaware that one tape contained Summer's conversation with the boys, which led to the CPS investigation. At some point, Susan told detectives, she gave Blanche the Trooper.

When Union Bank froze Joseph's accounts, the automatic payments for his home mortgage and storage PODS stopped, sending the house into foreclosure in August. The PODS' contents were auctioned off even after Susan allegedly paid the $3,000 outstanding balance.

"They said because we didn't have a power of attorney or something, they held onto them and sold it anyway," Michael testified.

However, a PODS company official told DuGal that family members had "elected to not pay the bill." Summer's family made the same decision about the storage unit containing her belongings from Big Bear.

Chapter 19

As the one-year anniversary of the McStays' disappearance approached, Detective DuGal believed he'd exhausted leads from people he'd already interviewed, so he sent a group email to Joseph's Facebook friends in January 2011, looking for new tips.

But DuGal continued to keep details of his investigation close to the vest, refusing to answer most questions from tipsters, including Patrick McStay, who demanded updates about his family's case.

As Patrick grew increasingly frustrated with DuGal, his emails became more aggressive on February 8 and 11, when he confronted DuGal about his lack of response to the information he'd been forwarding, such as Kavanaugh's threatening string of messages to Joseph.

"You say you can't bring him in for questioning because 'NO CRIME HAS BEEN COMMITTED' try again, I always thought FRAUD, MISS USE OF FUNDS, CONSPIRACY, INTERNET HACKING, and other acts where [sic] all crimes to be investigated, OH MY MISTAKE you told me that's not your department, those are handled by another department!"

DuGal complained to his sergeant, who told him to stop communicating with Patrick, and informed Patrick that he would be his future point of contact.

This only escalated Patrick's venting on TV crime shows and in online forums, which thrive in the vacuum of investigative secrecy. He also shared findings from his personal investigation, which unnerved DuGal and other family members.

For example, Patrick had alerted the SDSD about the "love you forever" and other emails to Summer from her ex, Vic Johansen, as well as his move to San Clemente, and his arrest there six days after the family went missing. When nothing came of his tip that Johansen may have been stalking the McStays, Patrick complained to KFMB-TV in San Diego that the sheriff's department apparently "never bothered to look into any of this."

DuGal didn't tell Patrick he'd already talked with Johansen in March 2010, when Johansen called to ask for custody of Bear, saying he'd originally been his dog. But Michael had already given Bear to Summer's mother, Blanche.

After questioning Johansen about his relationship with Summer, DuGal essentially cleared him before amateur sleuths posted his criminal history and discussed him as a possible suspect online.

Patrick was also unaware that Michael McFadden was one of the first people of interest the SDSD had interviewed, so he complained online that authorities never acted on the lead he'd given them about the unnamed violent felon who had threatened Joseph if he didn't "muzzle" Summer.

McFadden, whose arrest and prison record were released online by multiple amateur sleuths, was as upset as Johansen at being labeled as a possible suspect.

"I am not a criminal nor did I murder the McStay family," he wrote, calling Joseph his friend. "My family is trying to get through this horrible tragedy as privately as possible, but I am growing tired of all the name calling and mudslinging toward me."

He explained that his "rap sheet" stemmed from one night, which was the last occasion that he'd drunk alcohol, and that he'd been "a solid productive member of society" ever since. He wrote a similar letter to a judge in Orange County years later, requesting that his felonies be reduced to misdemeanors, because he was considering a run for public office someday. His request was granted.

Meanwhile, Michael McStay's description of Summer as Colombian was still fueling speculation on his popular website and elsewhere that a drug cartel, the Mafia, a religious cult, or even Summer herself, was to blame for the family's disappearance.

Michael dismissed these theories as ridiculous. "These are just normal, everyday Americans," he told the *San Diego Union-Tribune*. "This is a loving family."

These speculative theories prompted Summer's friends to defend her character. Although they conceded privately to detectives that her personality may have been to blame if the family had met with foul play, they said Summer never would have harmed anyone, especially her own family.

"Summer was flakey, headstrong, gullible, and somewhat paranoid," one friend wrote to DuGal in February 2011. "What she was not was a murderer."

Summer's family was upset by this negative scuttlebutt, too. Despite her moods and erratic behavior, they knew her as a kind, loving person.

Michael's behavior was subjected to criticism as well, putting him on the defensive for "raiding" or "plundering" the house, first the computer, then the appliances. When he drove past one of Joseph's neighbors in the Dodge truck, saying, "Worst-case scenario, I'm gonna be your new neighbor," the woman told detectives she found it strange that he was driving his brother's truck and talking so soon about moving into his house.

But mostly, people kept coming back to his remark to *The Orange County Register* in March 2010: "My fear is that I'm looking for two adult shallow graves and . . . my two nephews' crosses," which proved to be a curiously prescient statement once their remains were discovered.

Similarly, Patrick drew fire for his attacks on the SDSD and his confrontational tone with Websleuths members, whom he felt were judging him and his family and coming up with outlandish theories.

"I got mad," Patrick said, rejecting the notion that the McStays had gone voluntarily to Mexico, which he no longer believed. Or that Summer killed Joseph and ran off with the kids, or vice versa; Michael killed his own brother; Elijah was somehow mixed up in this; or Joseph was involved with drugs or the cartel.

Joseph hadn't surfed in Mexico since the 1990s, and hadn't bought slate or iron rods in Tijuana for fountains since the early 2000s, he said. Joseph wouldn't have taken Summer and the boys down there, because he thought it was too violent, and Summer wouldn't have gone unless Joseph deemed it safe.

However, Patrick still thought that they might be in Costa Rica, where Joseph had talked about retiring, so he asked the English-language newspaper, *A.M. Costa Rica*, to run a story in January 2011.

"There is a possibility that they may have left the States on their own under a cloud of misunderstanding (no violence, no crime, no problem with police), or may have been mislead [sic] in order to get them to leave," Patrick said in the article.

Merritt also disputed the drug theory. "Any suggestion that [Joseph] was involved with the cartels is nonsense," he told the *Daily Mail*. "Joseph was the most honest person I had ever met. He wouldn't even drop litter, let alone get involved in anything more serious. Even the thought of being involved in drugs would have sent him into a fit of paranoia. There's no way he would have been caught up in crime. He was just not that kind of person."

Chapter 20

Although the SDSD never confirmed this publicly, the agency considered Merritt to be "a person of interest." But DuGal couldn't find him in 2011, because he'd repeatedly moved and changed his cell phone numbers.

Tipped that Merritt was working at Aragon Construction in Pomona, DuGal located him on June 9. Merritt said he and Cathy Jarvis had separated a few months earlier, so she and the kids were staying at a motel until she could move to her parents' in Arizona, and he was living in a mobile home. Jarvis later said that she and Merritt had already been sleeping in different rooms as early as ten months before the McStays disappeared.

DuGal and Merritt set up a polygraph exam for June 16, but Merritt left a message to cancel that morning, saying he had to go to Arrowhead Regional Medical Center. DuGal tried having Merritt paged there, but he hadn't checked in, so DuGal called Jarvis, who confirmed they'd broken up and she was now in Arizona.

Later that morning, Merritt's sister Juanita called DuGal, concerned that the stress of the investigation was exacerbating Chase's heart condition, because he'd suffered a minor heart attack and was being admitted to the hospital.

Four days later, DuGal got a call from Merritt's attorney, who said he'd advised his client against taking the polygraph. DuGal replied that Merritt wasn't a suspect, and the lawyer couldn't stop police from interviewing a witness in a missing persons case.

DuGal finally got hold of Merritt again on June 21, when they discussed Merritt's concerns about the exam, including his attorney's prediction that he would be harassed "if anything at all shows up."

"If I had evidence that you were a suspect in their disappearance, then I would be coming after you to arrest you," DuGal said. "That is not what I'm doing."

During their ninety-minute call, Merritt said he'd been trying to keep a low profile because the media had been hounding him. It gave him a bad case of déjà vu, because his brother had been wrongly arrested as a suspect in the Hillside Strangler case in 1977.

"They plastered his face and name on every major newspaper and every major news station across the nation," causing trouble for Merritt at work and his siblings to be "tormented at school. [The media] were sitting outside our house for weeks."

As a result, he said, Juanita lost her business, and their mother was hospitalized. "That's the biggest reason that I, right from the very beginning, told you when we interviewed, I want to stay as far away from this thing as I possibly can."

"Yeah," DuGal said, "and I don't blame you at all."

DuGal outlined Merritt's previous statements that he wanted to cover during the polygraph and said he also wanted to talk about a new lead: someone had been messing with Joseph's QuickBooks account around the time he went missing.

Apparently, it didn't register with DuGal, but Dan Kavanaugh and Patrick McStay had both given him the same tip at least a year earlier. Patrick said he believed it was Kavanaugh, and Kavanaugh didn't give DuGal enough information to understand the tip's significance, omitting that both he and Merritt had independently been making changes to Joseph's account. DuGal only pursued the issue after getting more specific information from another tipster, who had obtained access to Joseph's emails.

"This is one of the questions I have that I didn't know when I [first] interviewed you," DuGal told Merritt. "I know Joseph had QuickBooks online. Somebody ordered QuickBooks Pro, and it was right at the time that they were missing or were about to go missing."

DuGal didn't reveal that this "somebody" had called the customer service desk on February 8, 2010, claimed to be Joseph and used his Mastercard number, but gave them Merritt's cell phone number. Or that the person asked for instructions on how to export and back up the online account files, then delete the account.

But Merritt filled in the gaps without skipping a beat: "[Joseph] was having a problem with Dan and the PayPal account, because Dan was able to access his QuickBooks, his checking account, everything, and he wanted to get him out of it."

"Get Dan out of it?" DuGal asked, recalling Merritt's original story that Joseph was hiding this information from Summer.

"Right, right. So, he asked me about it, and I said, 'yeah, I think that's a good idea,' because I had access to his Quick-Books," Merritt said. "I mean, he had access to my books, I had access to his. Hell, I could even write checks."

Merritt said he didn't remember asking for the QuickBooks Pro CD to be mailed to Joseph's former business address in San Clemente, where DuGal told him it was sent—twice, and was eventually returned—because he thought the software could be downloaded without a CD, which is true.

"I don't think Dan would have been doing it, so it would have been me," Merritt said. In fact, he added, if DuGal went through Joseph's voicemails, he should find one from Merritt, explaining all of his QuickBooks activities, which checks he'd written and when, since their meeting on February 4.

"I'm almost positive that I called him and left a message saying exactly what transpired."

At this point, neither of them knew Kavanaugh had also been in Joseph's QuickBooks account, changed the password, and kept the account active by setting up a new credit card payment from someone named John Pugsley in September 2010. Or that a second order for the QuickBooks Pro recovery CD was submitted on March 4, 2010, a day after Kavanaugh changed the password and locked Merritt out of the account.

DuGal had already tried to track down John Pugsley. He'd reached someone by that name in Los Angeles in May, but the man said it wasn't his credit card. With QuickBooks' help, DuGal determined that the actual cardholder, author John Allen Pugsley, had died on April 8, 2011, and the account was suspended after the last charge to the card was denied.

"It was possible that this was a fraudulent credit card account," DuGal concluded in May 2011, never realizing that Pugsley was actually Kavanaugh's grandfather.

DuGal decided Merritt was the only person involved, failing to connect the dots back to Kavanaugh, who needed access to Joseph's QuickBooks records so he could sell EIP as his own later.

Merritt expressed frustration to DuGal once again that Susan Blake had let "that little twit that ran the website" tank EIP. "If I was ever gonna commit murder, it would be with him," Merritt said, because he'd been forced "to just walk away," which cost him his business, his apartment, and his family. "I lost everything."

DuGal asked if he'd heard Kavanaugh talk "about intentionally screwing Joseph over" for not wanting to keep paying him to maintain a website that was already up and running. "Is that correct? Am I right so far?"

"No, not completely," Merritt said, "Joseph had paid Dan a considerable amount of money [to buy out] Dan's interest in the website. He only had a few hundred dollars left to pay, [and yet]

Dan just said, 'The website's mine, yeah, he never paid me for it, or he didn't finish paying me for it.'"

DuGal said people assisting his investigation "freak out" that Merritt had ordered QuickBooks software for Joseph's account and that Kavanaugh had access to Joseph's emails and accounts, "because they go, well, that's wrong."

But DuGal disagreed. "It's not criminal, and it's not wrong as long as Joey had authorized it, and there is absolutely, in my mind, not only an assumption, but pretty much proved that you guys had been existing that way. That's how the business was running."

Merritt pointed out, however, that it wasn't right for Kavanaugh to be taking money via PayPal "left and right, as far as I know."

"You're saying, after the fourth, or even after they were reported missing?" DuGal asked.

"Even after they were reported missing. I mean, he just kept—"

"I agree, there's a potential that there was money flowing right into his pocket," DuGal said.

Merritt said he could have done that, too, because he had "two or three of [Joseph's] credit card numbers. I had everything just the same as Dan did, but I didn't use 'em after Joseph was reported missing. I told Joseph's mom, 'You need to lock these accounts up. Get Dan away from this. What does he need the money for?'"

"Well, Dan says he was still in business with them and that he was receiving money and he had the right to go in there and do pretty much what he did."

"Yeah, of course."

That's why DuGal said he wanted Merritt to take a polygraph, to rule him out. "I really truly do believe what you're telling me, and once that's done, that's done," DuGal said. "I'm not bugging you because I think you're lying, I just want to say, 'Everything he's told me is truthful, guys.'"

Merritt said he was surprised it had taken DuGal so long to find out about his QuickBooks order. But more importantly, with a whole family of four going missing, "I don't understand why it wouldn't be a criminal investigation."

"Because I have no reason to believe somebody did something criminally," DuGal said. "Not one person has said, 'I think Joey was ripped off,' or 'I think Joey was taken against his will.' That's where you and the public are misguided. A judge needs very specific parameters for me to violate civil rights and go into anybody's accounts and extract information. I can't just go, 'They're missing, so therefore give me.' I have to say, number one, they're missing, number two, we believe it's because of this element."

After talking it over with his family, Merritt decided to take the polygraph, so the detectives could "forget about me and focus on something that might actually help find [Joseph]."

This time, Merritt showed up as scheduled on July 5, 2011. Among the questions to which Merritt answered "No" were:

Did you have any prior knowledge that the McStay family was going to disappear? Have you had any contact with the missing McStay family since they were reported missing? Have you intentionally withheld any information that would help locate the missing McStay family?

During an interview afterward, Merritt told DuGal that one of Joseph's primary concerns before going missing was Summer's complaint to CPS, which seemed close to being resolved, but Joseph was still worried he would be prevented from seeing his oldest son. Merritt said Joseph seemed "settled" in the marriage regardless, because he wouldn't want to leave his kids.

After reviewing Merritt's polygraph chart, one investigator noted some "inconsistencies," but Merritt figured he'd passed when he didn't hear anything more.

Although polygraphs aren't usable in court, the examiner, Paul Redden, determined Merritt's chart showed he was "attempting deception," but said, "It is possible that Merritt has such strong suspicions that could have affected his reactions." However, Redden didn't believe Merritt "had any specific involvement in the disappearance of the McStay family," DuGal wrote.

Redden is the same examiner who said Adam Shacknai's polygraph results were inconclusive in the Rebecca Zahau death case in Coronado, but he believed Shacknai was telling the truth. The SDSD ruled Zahau's death a suicide in 2011, but her family believes Shacknai strangled her, then called 911 to report he'd found her hanging naked, bound, and gagged at the Spreckels Mansion, where she lived with her boyfriend Jonah, Adam's brother. Subsequent outside examiners thought Shacknai's chart showed deception, and a civil jury found him responsible for Zahau's death in 2018. Shacknai contends he is innocent.

Chapter 21

DuGal had been tipped by multiple sources, including Patrick McStay, that EIP had been advertised for sale for $163,800 on the website BizBuySell since May 2010.

As Patrick emailed DuGal, "No one, not Susan, Michael, Dan or Chase have any Legal Authority to sell, operate, manage, or use any of the money that belongs to EIP or Joey or Summer! . . . I believe you or others have a right to turn this matter over to a fraud or other proper authorities to investigate these violations of the law."

However, DuGal didn't call Kavanaugh until July 8, 2011—three days after Merritt's polygraph—to ask if he was still operating the business.

Kavanaugh "claimed he was looking for investors who will cover the debt the company has incurred since Joseph went missing. He believed if he could pay off the debt, he could possibly make the company a continuing success," DuGal's report stated.

But that was a misleading claim. Kavanaugh had already negotiated terms of sale with two buyers—twentysomethings Matthew G. Schneider and Quinatzin Joaquin Quintero—and signed the contract the very next day. The buyers' corporate address in Crown Point was the same as the La Playa Collective, advertised as "a medical marijuana dispensary and art gallery."

"They had, like, a weed store," Kavanaugh told detectives in 2014. "They're these two surfer kids that just had a very small—I didn't know about any of their operation, or anything," he said, claiming they told him, "We want to buy your business and get out of that."

Kavanaugh most likely knew about the "weed store" because he and his friends hung out at Rocky's, the popular dive bar/hamburger joint that was literally next door. He also lived six blocks away. A longtime bartender at Rocky's recalled the "weed shop" as a popular destination that seemed to be operating on the "down-low."

The dispensary's history goes back to July 2009, when Quintero registered a nonprofit "mutual benefit corporation," Tonatuah and The Sacred 4 Inc., with the Secretary of State's Office as a "collective," which could legally sell medical cannabis under the California Compassionate Use Act of 1996. Recreational use wasn't legalized until 2016.

Leo Battista did taxes for various businesses Quintero and Schneider operated together and independently, including their band, Rattlife. Battista told authorities investigating a drug case in San Diego that Schneider "provided cash and inventory" for the collective as a start-up, and "was providing resources while Joaquin was operating [it]," but Battista didn't know where the cash "infusion" originated. Battista also did taxes for Kyle Gillen, whom he said supplied La Playa with marijuana grown at his residence in Pacific Beach.

Schneider and Quintero were working together on the collective in early 2010, but Quintero didn't register his "collective" corporation with the state until late April or obtain a city business tax certificate until June 1, 2010. That annual certificate expired a month before he and Schneider hired attorney Michael J. Leonard for a rush contract job so they could buy EIP from Kavanaugh in July 2011.

"I was paid to write the contract over the Fourth of July

weekend," Leonard testified at trial in 2019. "The buyer was in a bit of a hurry to take this business over."

Nearly two years after the sale, Schneider and Gillen were arrested after a yearlong investigation by the U.S. Postal Service and the Anti-Money Laundering Task Force. They and several co-defendants were accused of mailing ten to twenty pounds of marijuana a week to eight states ranging from Texas to West Virginia, and as far north as New York, which generated $20,000 to $30,000 weekly in cash or wire transfers.

Battista was questioned by investigators after the arrests:

"What type of due diligence did you do to establish that the companies were something more than a place to deposit illegally obtained income from illegal marijuana sales?"

Battista said he "sat with Matt [Schneider] and went over his bank deposits. I took his accounting of the businesses verbally." He conceded that the receipts he saw could be consistent with both selling water features and growing marijuana.

"Couldn't those just be shell companies to route money from the collectives through?"

Yes, Battista said, "since he never saw any supporting documentation for business income and very little in the way of support for expenses."

Based on reports from the pot-by-mail investigation, attorney Raj Maline said he believes EIP was purchased as a front for this operation.

"They needed a front to mail out these drugs," Maline said, referring to the boxes of marijuana and cash packed in bath towels and other scented products to mask the smell and to hide the illicit nature of the interstate sales. "It made perfect sense to buy this. Shipping things out and having things shipped to them."

"It really kind of raised a big question mark for us," Maline said. "When we first learned of it, we were ecstatic. Then, of course, the judge shut us down," so none of it could be presented at trial.

Schneider, Kyle Gillen, his brother Chris, and two other men were arrested in this nationwide marijuana sales operation in May 2013, which resulted in nineteen charges. Quintero was mentioned in the investigative reports, but wasn't prosecuted.

However, Quintero did have a criminal record. He pleaded guilty to committing battery with serious bodily injury in September 2009—two months after setting up Tonatuah—against a man who was found bleeding, unconscious, and his jaw broken, on the sidewalk near the bar where Quintero worked as a bouncer in Pacific Beach. He got off with probation and a fine.

It's unclear how long the pot-by-mail scheme had been operating, but Kyle Gillen had been selling drugs since 2007, "overseeing and financing another dealer's distribution of everything from cocaine and ecstasy to mushrooms and acid. Gillen and the dealer then set up a marijuana growing operation in a Miramar warehouse, hoping to use their medical marijuana permits to grow the plants and then sell them to dispensaries," according to the *San Diego Union-Tribune.*

Schneider and his co-defendants, who lived in neighboring residences on La Jolla Boulevard in Pacific Beach, were arrested there in May 2013.

The authorities also raided a grow house nearby, where they found more than 250 plants, as well as marijuana in various stages of drying, some packed in plastic for mailing. Quintero rented a portion of the warehouse, where his expired tax certificate for the collective was displayed.

When police came to arrest Schneider, he was armed with a shotgun. They found a La Playa Collective sign hanging above the toilet in his bathroom, and records showing that the twenty-five-year-old had $800,000 in the bank and had acquired 3.65 million shares of CannaBank, a publicly traded company. They seized thirty-one pounds of pot, an assault rifle, a loaded .22-caliber semi-automatic pistol, and more than fifty-two boxes of ammunition, as well as cocaine, hydrocodone, Vicodin, and

Xanax. At the Gillens' residence next door, police found a .45-caliber pistol, a bulletproof vest, and a money counter.

Schneider spent eleven days in jail before being released on $150,000 bail. He received a three-year suspended sentence and three years' probation after pleading guilty to a nine-count "sheet" of felonies, including possession of more than $100,000 obtained by illegal drug sales, having a firearm while also possessing cocaine, cultivating and possessing marijuana for sale, and money laundering.

While on probation, Schneider requested permission to go to Mexico on business, which was granted. With the court's permission and his attorney's help, he and Quintero formed Baja Winery Tours, Inc. in 2015.

Schneider and Quintero's contract to buy Earth Inspired Products contained a seller's warranty that it was subject to refund if terms or claims were questioned in the future.

"You wouldn't want him to buy something that somebody else owns," attorney James McGee said facetiously to Leonard at trial in 2019.

"Hopefully not," Leonard replied.

The buyers agreed to assume all liabilities and to pay Kavanaugh $20,000 and 20 percent of net profits for the next year, none of which went to the McStay family, who weren't informed about the deal in advance. Susan Blake told McGyver McCargar later that she had "nothing to do with the sale."

Kavanaugh claimed that EIP was saddled with $92,865 in debt and at least two legal threats, including a lawsuit filed by Fairmont Designs in October 2010, demanding more than $25,000 in damages. Fairmont claimed that EIP had accepted a $10,000 deposit for a fountain in July—after Kavanaugh had taken control—but failed to produce it.

Leonard acknowledged he did no due diligence to verify Kavanaugh was the sole proprietor of EIP or to fact-check Kavanaugh's handwritten notes about the debts, liabilities, or past income, which Kavanaugh documented by submitting Joseph's previous bank statements. How he obtained those statements is unknown.

Kavanaugh told Patrick McStay he'd met Quintero and Schneider at a nightclub in San Diego, but not until after the McStays were missing. Kavanaugh told detectives in 2014 he met the buyers through his then-girlfriend, Lauren.

"I know somebody that might be interested in, like, buying your company, these dudes, Matthew and Joaquin," he quoted her as saying.

Kavanaugh hung out with a group of friends at the beach or in bars in Pacific Beach. Tess Tallman, who was part of the group, said they also partied at nightclubs like Voyeur and Fluxx in the Gaslamp Quarter downtown, where they drank champagne and posed for photos together.

Tallman said Kavanaugh often referred to himself in the third person as "Danimal" in person and on social media, and habitually wore a hoodie to perpetuate his hacker image. Once the McStays' bodies were discovered, she said, she and several of their friends suspected that he had been involved in the family's murder.

Kavanaugh met Tod Davidson in a bar and hired him to work as a sales rep for EIP in March 2011. Davidson told a friend about Kavanaugh's "shady business practice" of collecting money for orders but not delivering products until the business was "upside down." The friend called to report these activities to DuGal in 2012.

DuGal followed up by calling Davidson, who said he believed EIP "had more debt than income," but he hadn't heard about the missing McStays until several customers told him about Joseph. When Davidson confronted Kavanaugh, he said he believed Joseph had gone to Mexico after a business deal went bad.

Davidson told DuGal that Kavanaugh had sold EIP for approximately $25,000 and that he'd also been arrested for domestic violence. DuGal independently confirmed Kavanaugh's arrest from August 2011, but he didn't see that as evidence tying Kavanaugh into the McStay family's disappearance, or as worthy of further investigation.

Patrick Maloy, who also worked for Kavanaugh at EIP, offered to stay on after the sale to handle calls and emails.

Schneider and Quintero had set up a corporation called Earth Inspired, Inc. on July 5, 2011, and bought EIP four days later. That October, they launched Water Feature Supply, Inc., another new "online retail" corporation. But Schneider and Quintero soon lost control of their new business in an ironically parallel scenario of how they'd acquired it.

In anticipation of the sale, Maloy purchased several dozen domain names, including "waterfeaturesupply.com," which he then parked, meaning they weren't in active use. After buying EIP, Schneider and Quintero paid Maloy for the domain name matching their new business and hired him as their national sales manager.

According to the lawsuit they filed against Maloy in February 2012, demanding more than ten million dollars in damages, Maloy watched Quintero set up bank and email accounts with his social security number and passwords while he was living on Quintero's couch.

In December 2011, the suit states, Maloy demanded a third of the company, then hijacked the business by taking over its domain name, email, and business accounts while the owners were away on vacation.

Schneider and Quintero also filed a complaint with the National Arbitration Forum, claiming Maloy was taking orders and money for fountains, but not shipping them to customers. They asked for Maloy to be forced to return both domain names to them.

Maloy denied stealing the business, contending his promised compensation never materialized, so he simply reclaimed his own domain name. Kavanaugh took credit for this, saying he showed Maloy how to redirect the site by changing the main servers and the IP address to another domain name.

"I taught this kid how to be smart online, and he took the company," Kavanaugh bragged to detectives. "Like, straight took it. Walked off. And there was nothing they could do about it."

In March 2012, Maloy's attorney emailed Michael McStay for help proving that the domain name and rights to the website still belonged to Joseph, and that Kavanaugh never had any right to them or to sell EIP. That way, Maloy could keep the website and business running as Water Feature Supply. Michael forwarded the email to DuGal.

In a meeting with Maloy at the OC Tavern, Michael signed a declaration for submission to the arbitration panel, which later denied Quintero and Schneider's complaint, allowing Maloy to retain the company and its website.

Quintero and Schneider had the lawsuit dismissed without prejudice about two weeks later, and dissolved Water Feature Supply, Inc.

After winning the legal battle, Maloy emailed Michael in December 2012: "Since I first learned what Dan had done with your brother's company, I was appalled and to this day I still cannot believe someone had the balls to do such a cowardly thing," he wrote, saying he was happy to return the EIP domain "to its proper and true owners."

He said he was struggling to keep the website in the top Google ranking. If Michael would be willing to add some backlinks from the original EIP site, he said he would send him the drive Kavanaugh gave the buyers when he "illegally sold EIP," which contained McStay family home videos and files from the old site "about Dan and money. It might be useful."

Kavanaugh claimed Maloy's site wasn't successful because it lost its high Google ranking. "All they had was the domain name and no site, really," he told detectives. So, "they just gave the site, the domain name, back to the McStays."

Chapter 22

Detective DuGal got a new lead in the case when the DA's office in New Orleans called him in early December 2011, trying to locate Patrick McStay.

Patrick had been eluding felony arrest warrants for three years after passing "worthless" checks at casinos in 2008—$13,000 at Harrah's Casino in New Orleans and $25,000 at Horseshoe Casino in Bossier City. As he'd told DuGal, Bank of America had also filed a lawsuit against him in late December 2009, citing an old DBA for Earth Inspired Products.

Finally locating him in late December 2011, the U.S. Marshals took Patrick by force at his house in Spring, Texas, breaking his sliding glass door after he refused to open the front door. Complaining of chest pains, he was seen by a doctor, then booked into the Harris County Jail, where he posted $15,000 bail a few days later.

Because his complaint to SDSD's internal affairs about the missing persons investigation went nowhere, Patrick used this time to submit a twelve-point complaint to the Citizens Law Enforcement Review Board (CLERB). His allegations, aimed primarily at DuGal, ranged from misconduct to harassment, mishandling the investigation, withholding information, not cooperating or communicating with him, and "prematurely" dismissing suspects without "proper investigation."

Patrick was arrested again in late March and was extradited to New Orleans, where he served five more months in jail. DuGal forwarded a list of questions to the DA's office there so investigators could ask Patrick if his debts involved Joseph or if they had contributed to the family's disappearance. But Patrick refused to answer any of DuGal's questions, citing his complaint to CLERB.

At its May 2012 meeting, the CLERB panel found most of Patrick's allegations were "not sustained" due to insufficient evidence, or that the SDSD's actions were "justified."

Patrick ultimately wasn't prosecuted for the bad checks because he'd "paid restitution in full" by July 2016.

In June 2012, DuGal met with Summer's mother and sister, who were upset that people were talking about their family on social media and questioning them about the investigation.

"Where are we with this?" Blanche asked, relating that someone said the SDSD had characterized the family as "voluntary missing." DuGal assured them there was no such designation, and that the investigation was ongoing.

Like DuGal, they were disturbed by Patrick's repeated release of speculative details that could harm the investigation. They were also upset to learn Dan Kavanaugh had sold EIP.

DuGal told them he only knew what he'd read on social media about the sale, but his "limited information . . . indicated Daniel may have been a partial owner of the business with Joseph. If Daniel fraudulently sold the business, the new owner would become a victim and would need to report the crime or civilly sue Daniel for his actions."

After Kavanaugh's employee told DuGal about the sale of EIP in March 2012, DuGal never called Kavanaugh to ask him about it. He simply checked to see if any federal consumer-related agencies had opened criminal cases related to Kavanaugh or EIP. Finding none, he noted that in his report.

At that point, DuGal wrote, "I had not discovered enough evidence to show a specific motive of any type," but he would continue to investigate the financial aspect of the case, because money "could possibly have been a motive" in the family's disappearance.

DuGal didn't write up the Tod Davidson interview, or a number of others, for nearly two years, until another agency took over the investigation, because he'd long been convinced the family was in Mexico and wasn't coming back.

"The physical evidence indicates it is probable the family left the residence voluntarily and traveled into Mexico" for unknown reasons, DuGal told the *San Diego Union-Tribune* in February 2011. "I am confident the McStays have not traveled out of Mexico unless they are using an assumed name."

That theory was bolstered later in the year when a tipster sent DuGal a photo of Joseph with one of his sons, who was wearing an animal backpack with a leash attached to it. Reviewing the border video, DuGal noticed the adult female wasn't holding the child's hand as he'd first thought, but, rather, had the child on a leash. The fact that a similar leashed animal backpack was found in the family's Trooper didn't alter his theory.

But such tips had slowed to a trickle by late 2012, when Michael McStay got one last call from DuGal a week after the Thanksgiving holiday. He'd been informed that a hunter had found the decomposed remains of an adult man with a broken tibia and a healed broken collarbone, partially buried in a field southeast of Temecula.

"Did your brother ever have any broken bones?" DuGal asked.

Michael said no, but he still hoped it could be Joseph. It wasn't.

Four months later, on March 12, 2013, DuGal threw up his hands and turned the case over to the FBI.

When DuGal's handoff went public, Patrick McStay was not happy, posting twenty-eight reasons why he believed his son's family had met with foul play on the Missing Persons of America (MPOA) website. He also made it clear that, unlike a male family member, presumably Michael, he didn't think Chase Merritt was involved, after talking to him several times.

"I want everyone to know that the online interview with Chase [in the *Daily Mail*] reported incorrect information and appears that someone may have said I suspect Chase," Patrick told MPOA. "I can tell you personally my son Joey always spoke highly of Chase. Joey liked Chase and Chase always spoke highly of my son."

Although Patrick didn't name names, he listed identifying characteristics and actions of three other "felons or ex-cons" he did suspect, which matched Michael McFadden, Dan Kavanaugh, and Vic Johansen.

Chapter 23

The entire trajectory of the investigation into the McStays' disappearance changed when the motorcyclist found the partial skull near Victorville on November 11, 2013.

About twenty sheriff's investigators, including a five-man homicide team, showed up the next morning for a "grid search" near the two sunken areas, which were designated Grave A and Grave B. Lining up ten to fifteen feet apart, one group walked the surrounding sixty-four acres, marking bones and possible evidence with pin flags, while others focused on the graves. They worked until 5 p.m., then returned at 6:30 the next morning.

As Grave A was excavated, Detective Edward Bachman documented its contents: the skeletal remains of an adult man were wrapped in a blanket or "gunny sack type of material," secured around the neck and body with two knotted white electrical cords, two red tie-down straps, and a hook. His body was lying on his right side, partially facedown.

The fabric was brittle and fell apart in bits as it was pulled away, revealing that the man's skull had a circular hole in the back on the left side. His bones were encased in a T-shirt, Hanes briefs, and brown shorts. One pocket held a loose key; another contained several others on a ring, one of which was embossed with Chateau, a brand of padlock. Some blue masking tape was found in a swatch of white paper towel.

At the other end of the grave were a few child-sized bones, along with a black nose, eyes and whisker, which were eventually matched to a kid's cat-face bathrobe. Inside a child-sized backpack were a paintbrush and a pick from a miniature set of garden tools.

Detective Jose Armando "Mando" Avila documented the contents of Grave B: the bones of an adult woman, including a mandible fractured in two places and a shattered skull, which were covered, but not wrapped, in what appeared to be a white terry cloth robe. A pair of black sweatpants, size small, with a pair of Old Navy panties inside them, were lying above the skull, separate from the other remains. A woman's black sweater and a left bra cup with a frayed edge, as if the bra had been cut down the middle, lay nearby.

This grave also contained the remains of a small child, a pair of correspondingly small blue pants containing a pull-on diaper, a child's backpack, a cell phone cover, and a three-pound, slightly rusty Stanley sledgehammer.

Outside the grave, investigators found the right bra cup, caught on a greasewood, as well as one more red strap, several pieces of a white bath towel, an electrical cord socket, and three empty beer containers. No shoes were found in or around the graves.

If someone were heading north on Interstate 15 from Fallbrook, the gravesite could be accessed by taking the Stoddard Wells Road exit, and heading under the freeway toward the dump. While a local from the High Desert, known more formally as the Mojave Desert, might be familiar with this particular area, the killer also might have chosen this burial site out of convenience. It's the first undeveloped area after Victorville and only a quarter mile from the freeway.

On the morning of November 13, investigators checked the DOJ's missing persons database for a family and were able to identify the most likely victims as the McStays, who had gone missing about one hundred miles south.

A database match with the teeth, still attached to the adults' jawbones, was made fairly quickly to Joseph and Summer.

At 4:35 p.m., the SBCSD issued a vague release to the media, disclosing only that investigators had completed their "scene examination" in Victor Valley, where they had recovered the remains of four persons from two graves.

"Every available resource will be utilized in this investigation to identify the suspects involved in this heinous crime and bring them to justice," Sheriff John McMahon said.

That evening at six o'clock, five detectives from the SBCSD met with two from the SDSD at the Victorville station, where Detective Troy DuGal briefed them by cell phone.

Detective Bachman scribbled down these highlights: "DuGal felt Joseph's tax records did not match his lifestyle and felt Joseph was possibly putting money away outside of bank accounts. Joseph paid Merritt and Kavanaugh under the table."

Although Joseph's family denied he was "involved in any type of illegal activity or drug use during the initial stages of the investigation," Bachman wrote, DuGal later learned "through family members Joseph used and sold ecstasy while in high school . . . [and] stored ecstasy in his freezer. . . . DuGal believed, based on the evidence he was able to obtain, the McStay family entered Mexico and had no record of them returning to the United States."

It took two days for Dr. Chanikarn Changsri, the chief forensic pathologist, and Alexis Gray, a forensic anthropologist, to complete all four autopsies, which began the next morning.

With only a partial skullcap, four skull fragments, and three ribs, they finished examining the smaller child, assumed to be Joey Jr., in an hour and sixteen minutes. The fracture to his skull was deemed to have occurred after he was already dead.

The autopsy on the older child, assumed to be Gianni, took a bit longer, because they had more bones with which to work.

Changsri said the skull fractures showed he'd been hit with a blunt instrument at least six times, just like his mother, whose skull was shattered into forty pieces.

Because Summer's jaw was broken in two places, her bra had been cut in half, and her sweatpants and panties weren't on her body, it appeared she might have been raped before being killed, but it was impossible to say definitively with no vaginal tissue to examine.

Joseph's skull also had deep fractures, reflecting at least four blows with "a lot of force," two from behind, to create the sizable hole in back. Changsri later testified this type of wound would have produced enough blood to start "to pool" around the head.

The pathologist found perimortem fractures in all the victims—meaning they were inflicted at or near the time of death. Joseph's right tibia and one left rib were broken, indicating he was likely beaten right before he died. Antemortem bone injuries, occurring more definitively before death, show signs they have started to heal before the victim's heart stops, while postmortem injuries look dry and cracked.

Because most of the smaller child's bones were missing, it was impossible to determine the cause of his death, but it was ruled a homicide, like the rest of his family, because his partial skull showed a similar semi-circular hole and fractures around the temple area. The cause of death for his brother and parents was deemed multiple blunt-force trauma to the head.

Although Bachman testified at the preliminary hearing two years later that the sledgehammer was "consistent with" the injuries, and prosecutors said at trial it was the assumed murder weapon, the coroner's investigative reports were less definitive, stating it "could not be ruled out as the murder weapon." Changsri, who testified it was a "possible object that was used to cause these injuries," could only estimate that the bodies had been in the ground for at least two years.

Chapter 24

As the original reporting party, Michael McStay was the detectives' first call on November 14, 2013.

The night before, a TV reporter in San Diego had asked him to comment on the bodies found in the desert, but he declined, because he hadn't heard confirmation from law enforcement that they belonged to his family.

When he got the call from Detectives Bachman and Stan Wijnhamer, they were parked in front of his house. Because he was out on a fire sprinkler job in Orange, they agreed to meet him at a Starbucks.

He thought they were just going to sit down and chat, but after leading him to a table outside, the detectives informed him they'd found and identified Joseph and Summer via dental records. Michael began to weep as they told him they were awaiting DNA results for the children's remains, but he knew in his gut they were his nephews.

The official results arrived from the state DOJ on November 22: the white bone that had caught the motorcyclist's attention was confirmed to be part of Joey Jr.'s skull.

Knowing his mother would be devastated, Michael waited to make sure Susan wasn't in a meeting or driving when he delivered the news. It was her day off, but she'd come into the office to catch up on some work.

"Are you alone?" he asked.

Once he determined his mother was in a safe place to talk, he said, "They found them."

"Where are they?"

"No, Mom. Joey and Summer are dead."

Susan felt as if a boulder had hit her in the chest. "No, no," she said. "What about the babies?"

"Yeah, Mom. They found 'em. They found 'em all."

After nearly four years of waiting, hoping, and praying for a miracle, Susan collapsed to the floor in her office.

"I didn't want to believe it," she said.

She was such an emotional wreck that one of her construction crew had to take her home. Her best friend, who had seen the story on the news, drove over right away to take Susan back to her house so Susan didn't have to grieve alone on the worst day of her life.

Someone had to get word to Elijah, who thought his father had abandoned him, so Michael called Heather and told her, too. Then he went home to tell his three daughters their Uncle Joseph had gone to Heaven.

Summer's sister, Tracy, was getting her hair done that day. Even though Tracy's husband Joe kept calling, which he never did while she was at the salon, she didn't catch on that something was wrong.

It wasn't until she pulled up to Joe's parents' house, where he was visiting with their son, that she knew. As he walked out to meet her, he was clearly distraught. Leaving their son behind, they got straight into the car and drove to their house to meet with detectives.

After hearing the news, Tracy looked at Sergeant John Gaffney to see if he was sure. He was.

It only got worse from there because she had to notify her brother and mother. "My brother was all the way in Hawaii, and it was the last phone call I'd ever want to make to him," she said. "It was devastating." But worse still, "I had to drive up the mountain [to Big Bear] and tell my mother that her four babies were gone forever."

That evening, news outlets all over Southern California began making the possible link to the missing Fallbrook family.

The next morning, Joseph's and Summer's families drove separately to the SBCSD station to meet with detectives before the agency held a news conference.

Sheriff McMahon told reporters about finding the graves and the bones scattered around the area, but he withheld specifics, such as the suspected murder weapon and cause of death. He said it was too early to know whether it was "cartel-related," but emphasized that no one was being ruled out as a suspect.

Susan sat there, feeling numb, as Michael stepped up to the microphone.

"It's not really the outcome we were looking for," he said tearfully, "but it gives us courage to know that they're together and they're in a better place."

Patrick McStay wasn't in town, but he was quoted throwing barbs at the SDSD once again. "I could probably have hired some Boy Scouts that would have done a better job," he said.

Now that they knew the details, he told CBS News, "Either there was a hired killer who killed them, or the children could have recognized them, this person. To kill a child is something totally different. You have to be a cold-blooded killer."

Rather than admit any mistakes, the SDSD stood firmly by its previous findings. Spokeswoman Jan Caldwell characterized her agency's work as "incredibly thorough," claiming the case went cold because "it's almost impossible to work a case without information flowing in."

Despite the fact that the family's remains were found one hundred and sixty miles north of the border, Caldwell still wouldn't let go of the idea the McStays had voluntarily gone to Mexico. "We still think there's a strong possibility that they did," she told CNN.

The McStays' neighbors told reporters they were shocked to hear that the family had been murdered so soon after moving into their new house.

"We have a pretty good Neighborhood Watch, but this is very odd," one of them said. "I was praying that it would be a witness-protection program case, or something. It's very sad."

It was some time before Susan Blake learned the gritty details, "that Joey was tied up with a rope or wire around his neck and his legs, and they were beaten with, not a hammer, a sledge-hammer, and your mind is, like, why? Who?" she said later.

Like the sheriff, San Bernardino County District Attorney Michael Ramos didn't publicly disclose the murder weapon, only that "it's an object that could have come from the home or somewhere else."

A couple of weeks later, Susan stopped at the store on her way to work and saw her family on the cover of *People* magazine, with the headline "Mystery in the Desert." As she leaned over to pick it up, she started having trouble breathing. She wanted to grab the entire stack, but she only took one.

"Oh, this poor family, they just went *poof*. What could have happened to them?" the cashier asked obliviously as she rang up the magazine.

Susan couldn't hold a funeral right away, because investigators were still examining and documenting the remains, so she and her son Michael organized the memorial and paddle-out ceremony they thought Joseph would have wanted.

"Joey walked the walk," she said. "He was a strong Christian."

When Chase Merritt called Michael to ask if he could attend the service, Susan, who was in the room at the time, said no.

"I'm sorry, you cheated me out of money and you cheated my son out of money, so absolutely not," she said.

The Saturday service was at noon on January 4, 2014 at the Vineyard Community Church in Laguna Niguel, which Joseph and Michael had both attended. Among the several hundred people who packed the pews were Joseph's soccer teammates, high school classmates, and close friends of twenty-five years from surfing and Bible study.

Touched by the outpouring of love, Susan listened intently to all the stories about Joseph's generosity, and the funny anecdotes she'd never heard. Like the time he went to Italy with his surfboards and left them with the local kids. Or when people called him the Train Man, saying, "Would you let the guy with the long hair who looks like Jesus off at the next stop?"

"There was maybe one prayer because so many people wanted to talk," she said. "It was just beautiful. Beautiful."

That afternoon, about twenty surfers, including several local kids who wanted to join in, paddled out to form a big ring next to the San Clemente Pier, where Joseph used to surf.

"Even in his death, people like Joe," Michael said.

Susan handed out orchids to mourners on the pier, so they could say a prayer and throw petals into the water, while the surfers wore her leis like halos. The water was cold as Summer's brother, Kenneth, and his children released the leis and said a prayer, joining the other surfers in cheering and splashing to celebrate the family's life and next journey.

"That was kind of just a goodbye," Kenneth said, but it "really spoke for Giuseppe and Summer. They loved the ocean, they loved the surf. The boys would be surfing right now."

Afterward, everyone was invited to a buffet at the Dana Point Marriott to tell more stories.

It was six months before Susan could bring herself to drive out to Victor Valley, where well-wishers had created a memorial at the gravesite, planting flowers and four white wooden crosses in piles of white gravel, adorned with teddy bears labeled with the boys' names.

She and a girlfriend got lost on the way, driving around the wash until they found the spot, where they put hats on the crosses, planted more flowers, and pushed solar lights into the ground.

"I didn't want the babies to be in the dark," she said.

But once was enough. Susan never went back, choosing to visit her family at El Toro Memorial Park in Lake Forest, where she laid them to rest properly, with the grandest headstone on the grassy slope.

The front of the headstone lists all four names and birthdates, with this inscription: Riding the waves in Heaven. The back side reads, McStay Family: Although you have departed from this earth, you will never truly leave us, for you remain in our hearts and will be forever loved.

"The hurt will never go away," Susan said. "You miss their sounds and their laughter, and now I go to a gravesite and talk to them. I'll never, ever be the same. Never."

Patrick McStay didn't visit the desert gravesite memorial until CNN reporter Randi Kaye took him there with a film crew. He said he couldn't help but imagine what his loved ones had been thinking as they were being driven down that dusty road.

"They had to know it wasn't good, and that's the part that I don't want to think about."

Chapter 25

The SBCSD investigation, which would last nearly a year, involved more than two hundred interviews and dozens of search warrants. A motion by a group of Southern California media outlets to unseal those warrants was denied on January 7, 2015, but their request to unseal SDSD's four warrants was granted.

The group's second petition, approved after the preliminary hearing six months later, resulted in the release of a select thirty-three warrants, unveiling three hundred pages of insights into the investigation's early days.

Although Detective DuGal had publicly stated he was handing his investigation over to the FBI, the Trooper was the only item to actually reach that agency. The files of documents, recorded interviews, and other physical evidence never left SDSD custody, which the San Bernardino County team only learned at a meeting with the FBI for the "handoff."

Because many SDSD interviews and handwritten notes had never been compiled into investigative reports, the SBCSD had to wait for DuGal and others to hastily dictate and submit those narratives, now with 20/20 hindsight. Thousands of pages of investigative reports, correspondence, tips, and other physical evidence were then forwarded to the SBCSD.

* * *

As the new team of detectives reviewed these materials with fresh eyes, they analyzed what their predecessors had and had not done.

In 2022, SBCSD Lieutenant Ryan Smith, who started working this case as a detective, seemed reluctant to criticize the other agency's efforts, saying he understood the "constraints" of San Diego County, where a search warrant affidavit goes to a prosecutor before a judge, whereas in San Bernardino County, a detective can go directly to the on-call judge. But even so, he said, he would have tried to obtain additional warrants as it became more obvious the McStays weren't coming back.

"I absolutely think there was more out there and certainly, as no one could find the family, there's even more reason to write a search warrant," said Smith, who eventually became the case agent and assisted the prosecution team at trial. "They go in to process the house and [say they] didn't find anything. I would argue they did."

For example, Joseph's and Summer's families said, "It was very unlike them to be out of touch," and, "coupled with Mitchley's surveillance [video], you have a car, which isn't the McStays', leaving the McStay residence. I certainly would have pressed for getting a search warrant for more video." In addition, "their phones, bank accounts, are not connecting, there are no large withdrawals, no evidence that the family packed up to go."

Smith said he also would have applied for a warrant looking for phone pings for the handful of people of interest in the case. So, now that they had probable cause, this was one of the team's first tasks, starting with McGyver McCargar, Dan Kavanaugh, and Vic Johansen. They also began to flesh out a more comprehensive timeline for who was where and when during the first half of February 2010.

Bachman reviewed Kavanaugh's cell phone records, but saw

nothing suspicious, stating in his case summary that Kavanaugh
had already handed them over to the SDSD.

Developing a master list of people to interview, the SBCSD
approached those who had already been questioned, knowing
they could ask more pointed queries this time, such as who
might have wanted to kill Joseph and Summer.

San Diego investigators "kind of missed the mark a bit,"
Smith said, because "their interviews were really geared toward
why would [the McStays] go missing."

Michael McStay named Chase Merritt and Dan Kavanaugh
right off the bat, but Susan Blake said she didn't know of any
enemies. Patrick McStay repeated his previous concerns about
Michael McFadden and Kavanaugh, noting Kavanaugh had
sold EIP to two men who ran a marijuana dispensary.

Patrick told Detective Avila that he and his son Michael
talked in August 2011 about going after Kavanaugh "for selling
Joseph's business. Michael gave Patrick the number to call
Quintero. Quintero told Patrick he did not handle the finances
and referred him to Maloy." Patrick said Maloy told him that
Kavanaugh owed $100,000, and that the sale not only relieved
this debt, but also paid Kavanaugh $20,000.

"Before Patrick learned about Kavanaugh and his dealings
with Quintero, Maloy, and Schneider, Patrick believed McFadden was responsible for Joseph's family disappearance," Avila
wrote in his report. "From the money perspective, Patrick believed
Kavanaugh was involved in Joseph's family's disappearance. From
the violence perspective, Patrick suspected McFadden."

Then, on January 16, 2014, the case took another turn.

Avila was notified by Ann Bate, a supervising probation officer in San Diego County, that Kavanaugh had been arrested on a
probation violation for a felony domestic violence arrest and
made some curious incriminating statements about the McStay
investigation to officers on the ride to jail.

Before they could seize his laptop in the lobby, Kavanaugh tried, unsuccessfully, to give it to another probationer, whom he'd previously met in jail. Probationers' property and computers are subject to search at any time without a warrant.

Avila drove out the next morning to collect the laptop and hear more about Kavanaugh's statements: Kavanaugh told the officers that he'd met Joseph McStay when Joseph "lived in his mother's garage and he (Kavanaugh) had made Joseph rich," Avila's report states. Kavanaugh said Joseph's "business partner, who lived in Victorville, owed Joseph $30,000, and they met 'that' day because Joseph was going to fire him" due to the debt and because "the man was nothing but problems." After Joseph disappeared, the Victorville partner "strong-arm(ed)" Kavanaugh into helping him with the business and hired "Hispanic immigrants" to transport and assemble the fountains. The Victorville man "would do anything for money," Kavanaugh said.

The officers couldn't recall if Kavanaugh identified the Victorville man by name, but believed he "mentioned Merritt."

To evaluate the context—and timing—of Kavanaugh's statements to the probation officers, it's important to consider media reports from around that time.

A week after the family's remains were discovered in the desert, the British *Daily Mail* ran an exclusive interview with Merritt, detailing his last meeting with Joseph and their excitement about the big jobs coming in.

Merritt said he figured the SBCSD detectives would be "back in touch with me. I'm surprised they haven't been already."

But he dismissed his past crimes as a nonissue, because they happened decades ago. "I have never done anything violent; I am the least violent man on the planet," he said.

A couple of weeks later, KFMB-TV ran its own "McStay Murder Mystery" series, exploring the backgrounds of Merritt, Kavanaugh, McFadden, and Johansen.

The first story focused on Merritt, noting he'd been convicted for receiving stolen property and burglary in the 1970s and 1980s. Kavanaugh's profile ran five days later, stating he'd pleaded guilty in two domestic violence cases involving physical fights with girlfriends that occurred after the McStays' disappearance.

Nonetheless, Kavanaugh told KFMB, "As far as you asking me if I'm a violent person, the answer is a resounding no. Definitely not."

Merritt had already made it clear to DuGal what he thought of Kavanaugh, and vice versa, but Kavanaugh seemed even more determined now, possibly as a way to deflect this new, unwanted attention on his criminal background toward Merritt.

Kavanaugh's Google search records, which became part of the court record, indicate he'd been following news and online discussions about the McStay case closely. On the evening of November 14, when discovery of the remains was first reported in the media, Kavanaugh searched for "four bodies found in the desert news" at 6:11 p.m. and for "victorville" at 6:18 p.m.

In the next several days, he checked whether his name was linked to the murders or other possible suspects, including Merritt, McFadden, and Johansen, searching for "dan kavanaugh mcstay," "mccstay chase merritt," "dan kavanaugh," "mcstay suspect," and "summer mcstay ill turn on you."

In late December, seven months after Schneider's drug arrest hit the news, Kavanaugh also searched for "Matthew Schneider, Joaquin Quintero" and "Tweety Quintero," as well as "facebook delete everything from your timeline."

After a KFMB reporter showed up at his door, Kavanaugh called his probation officer to warn that he might be on the news. Until then, the officer hadn't been aware Kavanaugh was connected to the McStay case, but his call "caused probation officers to watch him closely," Avila's report states.

Asked by the reporter if he knew where the large sums of money withdrawn from Joseph's business accounts had gone,

Kavanaugh acknowledged he had transferred those funds to his accounts, but said he had the permission of Susan Blake and Michael McStay.

"I actually transferred it to myself with Mike's knowledge," he said. "None of that money went to me. That money went to vendors, welders, and manufacturers. Mike and I and his mom tried to salvage and run the business that we had built for a long time. I created all of the traffic to the site. Joe did very little. He just answered the phone. I built the entire business."

Chapter 26

The SBCSD dug a little deeper into Dan Kavanaugh than the SDSD, but still seemed to largely accept his alibi, his partnership claims, and his word about his activities in Joseph's PayPal account. In fact, they didn't even interview him until September 2014, six weeks before arresting their primary suspect in the case.

While DuGal accepted Kavanaugh's statement that he'd left for Hawaii on January 7 and returned on February 17, 2010, Avila actually tried to confirm those dates.

Avila contacted Homeland Security and the Transportation Security Administration (TSA), but was told they didn't keep flight records for passengers unless they were on a "no-fly" list. So Avila contacted Hawaiian Airlines, where a web support specialist checked passenger lists and confirmed that Kavanaugh flew to Hawaii on January 7, but he said Kavanaugh's return flight was actually three days earlier, on February 14.

Curiously, Bachman signed a warrant affidavit on December 27, 2013, stating that Hawaiian Airlines said Kavanaugh didn't fly to Hawaii until February 6, two days after the McStays disappeared, which eventually caught the attention of defense attorneys.

The February 6 date, which would blow up Kavanaugh's alibi,

wasn't mentioned in Avila's final investigative report, which also wasn't written until mid-August 2014—eight months after he'd called the airline, and months after detectives had focused their investigation on another suspect.

When the defense tried to raise this discrepancy at trial, the judge called it "triple hearsay," and wouldn't allow the jury to hear it.

The SBCSD also went further than the SDSD by asking the state for paperwork concerning the ownership of EIP. In a call to the state Board of Equalization, Bachman learned Joseph had filed a permit application on November 28, 2006, listing himself as EIP's sole owner. In fact, Bachman's case timeline refers to Kavanaugh's sale of EIP as "illegal." Nonetheless, the warrant affidavits repeatedly state Kavanaugh "partnered together in Joseph's business," while Merritt "was hired as a designer/builder."

Detectives seemed to accept Kavanaugh's contention that he had the family's permission to transfer money from Joseph's PayPal account to keep the business going, even though records show he'd started doing that days before Joseph was reported missing.

"They (the family) said, okay, do what you got to do," Kavanaugh said.

Detective Joseph Steers, who interviewed Susan Blake on August 28, 2014, stated in his report that she "knew Kavanaugh had access to the business' PayPal account . . . Blake never expressly gave Kavanaugh permission to utilize the [PayPal] accounts, but she also never seemed to deny it."

More specifically, Steers stated, "Blake authorized Kavanaugh to take two payments from the business account of $2,000 each to provide child support for [Elijah] McStay while the family was missing." However, she acknowledged at trial that she wasn't monitoring Kavanaugh's business transactions.

Patrick McStay continued to insist that Kavanaugh had no claim to Joseph's company. He sent detectives paperwork from Joseph's Better Business Bureau (BBB) account to prove that Joseph listed himself as EIP's owner when he registered in 2006, and that Kavanaugh added himself as "manager" after Joseph disappeared, despite telling detectives he was a partner. Kavanaugh subsequently removed Joseph's name as CEO and replaced it with his own.

Patrick also forwarded several BBB complaints from May 2010 through February 2011, which stated EIP had collected payments for fountains but never shipped them. One customer said he'd placed an order, then received a call from Kavanaugh requesting a check for $4,296 as down payment. The check was cashed, but no waterfall was sent, and Kavanaugh ignored the customer's follow-up calls and demands for a refund. Such unresolved complaints finally resulted in an "F" rating for earth inspiredproducts.com and the revocation of EIP's accreditation on May 25, 2011.

Detective Ryan Smith, who joined the team later in the investigation, reviewed Joseph's PayPal account and debit card transactions, noting log-in attempts and password changes on February 10 and 12, 2010 were "consistent with Dan Kavanaugh's statement of accessing PayPal." However, Smith didn't note in his report that Kavanaugh's IP address was *in San Diego*, not in Hawaii, when he made those transactions.

Asked about Kavanaugh's activities in 2022, Smith told the author that even if detectives were confident that Kavanaugh stole from the business and then sold it, they couldn't prosecute him for the alleged theft for several reasons, primarily because "you don't have a victim." Smith said the detectives also saw no direct connection to him murdering the family.

"It sounds kind of brash," Smith acknowledged, but even if Kavanaugh stole from Joseph, Joseph was no longer alive and thus unable to make that claim, which is necessary for a prosecution to occur. "So, how can you prove or disprove to the pros-ecution's level? He's saying he's 'an equal partner, fifty-fifty, Joseph wasn't done buying me out.' But the only person who can truly disprove that is Joseph. The fact of the matter is, it's all hearsay without the owner of the business. There's no way you'd ever be able to prosecute that."

But if detectives believed or even suspected Kavanaugh's sale of EIP was illegal, why didn't they look into the sale or the two buyers? And why did prosecutors block the jury from hear-ing details about that?

In prosecutor Britt Imes's view, the "complete nature" of Kavanaugh's business relationship with Joseph and EIP was "very unclear and gets more unclear due to their disappear-ance."

There was "no clear answer to who had access to what, be-cause nothing is in writing," he said in 2021. "There's no con-tracts, a lot of it is very verbal-handshake type of agreements." Nor did Joseph write Kavanaugh "regular payroll checks."

As a result, they couldn't tell if Kavanaugh was authorized to use Joseph's PayPal account to "make purchases all over the North Shore" of Hawaii in January and February 2010.

Despite Joseph's agreement to buy Kavanaugh out of the business, Imes noted that Kavanaugh still had access to the website and PayPal accounts, so "how far along they'd gotten in finalizing those terms is not real clear."

Kavanaugh still had access on behalf of the business "to sales, website stuff, or his own income for his services. This was up until they were missing, and continued afterward, because Mike, Susan, Dan, and even Merritt, were trying to keep the business running. So that's where it became really clouded."

Asked if he knew anything about the EIP buyers and their his-tory, Imes played it cool. "I honestly don't recall. But I believe someone—I don't know if it was actual or purported buyers—did get in trouble at some point. Remember the sale is a long time after the disappearance. I don't have that information at my fingertips of recall. It vaguely rings a bell, but it was not allowed to come into trial."

So, if the prosecutors knew any further details, it appears they chose to overlook them, because they didn't see what Imes called "a natural link."

Asked if he was aware Kavanaugh had a criminal record consisting of two domestic violence convictions, Imes replied, "Vaguely."

Chapter 27

Because DuGal had only checked the McStays' Isuzu Trooper for blood, the SBCSD detectives sent the DNA swabs DuGal had collected to their crime lab.

On February 18, 2014, the DNA analysis by the Riverside/San Bernardino Cal-DNA laboratory arrived. In what Bachman clearly saw as a break in the case, he stated, "Criminalists matched DNA collected from the Trooper to Merritt," after Merritt said he'd never driven the car. Bachman cited this as probable cause in subsequent search warrant affidavits.

But the reality was not that definitive. The two swabs of the steering wheel actually reflected a mixture of DNA from at least three people: "Assuming the presence of three contributors with Joseph McStay Sr. present as the major contributor and Summer McStay present as a trace contributor, Charles Merritt is included as a possible minor contributor," the report stated.

The two swabs of the gearshift, four-wheel-drive lever, radio controls, and heater-A/C control panel proved even less definitive, also showing a mixture of at least three people. Assuming Joseph was the "major contributor," the report stated, Summer was a "trace contributor," and Merritt was even more iffy as "a possible trace contributor."

Merritt's DNA also didn't turn up on the driver's interior door handle, which any driver must touch to exit the vehicle. That handle, power windows, and door lock controls reflected the presence of at least three individuals, with Joseph as the major contributor and Summer as a trace contributor. "Due to the complexity of the genetic information," no further conclusions were made about the second trace contributor.

The lab also analyzed two swabs taken from the sledgehammer, but detected no blood. DNA testing on the sledgehammer was a bust as well: because "a low level of human DNA was detected," and only "one weak allele, the presence of an 'X' at amelogenin," the sex-determining gene, no further testing was done. (A female has XX chromosomes, and a male has XY chromosomes.) A hair fragment was found, but because it lacked a follicle, there was no DNA to test.

Nonetheless, it's evident from the interviews the detectives conducted from this early point on that their focus had narrowed to Merritt as a promising suspect, based on this DNA "match," and his ties to the High Desert, where he grew up and his family still lived.

But if the McStays were, in fact, killed with the sledgehammer, wouldn't at least a small amount of their blood or DNA be detected on it, especially given the gaping holes in their skulls? The fact is, investigators never found blood anywhere they searched, including several residences and vehicles.

Investigators also couldn't make any connection between paint at the McStays' house and items in the grave, though it wasn't for lack of trying. A warrant obtained in August 2014 to return to the McStays' house states that detectives believed the murders occurred there, and that a "large amount of blood spatter" could have been painted over to no longer be "visible to the naked eye." They collected two sets of paint chips on separate trips, which were sent to the FBI for analysis. Forensic analyst Diana Wright said paint from the kitchen and living room was excluded from the "smear" of paint on the sledgehammer and the "drop" on Summer's bra in the first set. The second came back as "inconclusive" due to "subtle [chemical] differences."

Chapter 28

By mid-March 2014, it became clear this case was too massive and complicated for the homicide team to conduct interviews, write warrants, and process evidence effectively while still in the "on call" rotation, with new cases constantly coming in.

District Attorney Michael Ramos said publicly that investigators had narrowed their focus to Merritt as their prime suspect within six months of finding the family's remains, but it appears to have been even sooner than that.

Internal investigative documents show the investigation was stalled, with little, if any, substantive work done between mid-March and July 2014, after the agency formed a task force of detectives who were taken out of the regular rotation.

Avila, the case agent, was promoted out of homicide, and all the other original detectives were reassigned except Bachman, who took over as case agent on the new team, joining Detectives Ryan Smith, Dan Hanke, and Joseph Steers and Sergeant Chris Fisher.

Sean Daugherty, a "major felony" prosecutor with extensive homicide experience in the Victorville office, was assigned to handle the case.

The SBCSD only forms task forces to handle cases that are "extremely manpower intensive," and this one "did the bulk of the investigating," Smith said. "I do recall our captain saying this is one of the biggest [murder] cases our county ever had, so we all knew it was a very big, complex case. We've had a lot of crazy critical incidents, but not with a suspect who is unknown and a whole family is murdered."

Earlier in the year, Bachman had written a warrant for Merritt's cell phone records from AT&T, which were under his partner's name, Catherine Jarvis.

Once they came in, Smith saw nine calls to Joseph between February 5 and 9, ranging from fifty-three seconds to two minutes and three seconds, which suggests that Merritt did leave voicemails, as he'd claimed. Kavanaugh's records show twelve calls to Joseph after he went missing, for a minute or less.

In DuGal's report about Joseph's and Summer's voicemails, he said none of the twenty-five messages that filled Joseph's mailbox had come in before February 15. However, the thirty-one messages that filled Summer's mailbox went back to February 4, including those from Susan, Patrick, and Kavanaugh, referring to messages they'd left for Joseph or tried to leave after his box was full.

DuGal never asked anyone if they, or T-Mobile, had deleted those early voicemails to Joseph, several of which showed up on the callers' phone records. Smith deduced that an "unknown party" had deleted them from Joseph's phone or with a remote device, using his password, which allowed his mailbox to fill up again.

Smith speculated that, during Merritt's longest call to Joseph on February 9 at 8:56 a.m., he could have been listening to and then deleting those messages. But Merritt didn't call Joseph again, so that doesn't explain what happened to messages left over the next five days.

Merritt's phone records were also given to Kevin Boles, a special agent from the FBI office in Riverside, to triangulate Merritt's location between corresponding cell towers during those crucial ten days before Joseph's family was reported missing. His findings helped to flesh out the timeline and support the narrative that Merritt killed the family after turning off his phone, or putting it into airplane mode, to avoid tracking during the murder and while he was cleaning up the crime scene.

On the night of February 4, Boles noted a period of three hours and thirty minutes during which Merritt missed six calls that went to voicemail, all from Cathy Jarvis. The period started after a 5:48 p.m. call from Joseph and ended at 9:32 p.m., when Merritt called Jarvis back.

Joseph's records reflected a call from his phone to Merritt's at 8:28 p.m., which didn't show up on Merritt's because his phone didn't connect with any cell towers during that three-and-a-half-hour period.

Although Merritt and Jarvis claimed he was home watching a movie that night, his 9:32 p.m. call to her pinged off a tower in the Mira Loma area, about twelve miles south of his usual "home tower."

Merritt's phone also showed a nine-and-a-half-hour gap in activity after that call until he checked his voicemail from Upland at seven o'clock the next morning, February 5, during which time investigators believed he was looking for a place to dump the bodies. Merritt headed west on Interstate 210 to the 14 freeway near Angeles National Forest and then to Santa Clarita, where his phone pinged at 10:45 a.m. Several minutes later, it pinged a tower to the south near San Fernando.

He was back in Rancho Cucamonga for four calls between 12:49 and 3:54 p.m., after which his phone didn't connect to any tower for six hours. When he called Jarvis at 9:17 p.m., he was near Riverside, heading north on the 15, the same route he used to return home from the McStay house. After that, his phone was inactive overnight for thirteen-and-a-half hours, which, detectives said, gave him plenty of time to clean up and paint over blood at the crime scene.

But after six hours off the grid, why would he be heading north only to turn around and return to the McStay house for another thirteen hours?

The next time he used his phone, at 10:46 a.m. on February 6, it pinged in the Victorville area at a tower near Interstate 15. Investigators believed that's when he was burying the bodies, because the call put him "in a position to access" what is known as the Quartzite cell tower, on a hill northeast of the gravesite.

His next calls, at 11:30 and 11:52 a.m., pinged a tower in Oro Grande, north of Victorville, then connected with a tower a little south at 11:53 a.m. After that, his call at 12:49 p.m. pinged a tower in Hesperia, followed by one at 1:30 p.m. in Oro Grande "from a direction pointing south." Four of those calls were to Cathy Jarvis.

Using the same logic, however, why would he leave his phone on while burying the bodies in broad daylight, in the middle of a rainstorm, and so close to the freeway?

On February 7, Merritt called Joseph twice around 3:47 p.m. His last call that day was ninety minutes later, the start of a fourteen-hour window of inactivity until 7:26 a.m. on February 8, when his first call hit his "home tower."

Merritt got only one incoming call that morning, but it went straight to voicemail and didn't ping a tower, so they couldn't tell where he was. But detectives believed the six-hour window after that first 7:26 a.m. call gave him enough time to drive to the McStays' house, pick up the Trooper, drop it in San Ysidro, and somehow get back home. Merritt was heading north when his phone pinged a tower in Corona at 1:30 p.m., and he was back in Rancho Cucamonga for a call twenty-three minutes later.

Detectives later learned there was activity on Joseph's Quick-Books online account that day at 2:20 p.m., when checks were written to Merritt, then deleted. Joseph's online subscription was cancelled at 2:44 p.m., followed by Merritt's call to the customer service line at 3:11 p.m., pretending to be Joseph and asking to upgrade to QuickBooks Pro.

Merritt made his last call to Joseph at 1:07 p.m. on February 9, which pinged a tower in the Temescal Valley near Susan Blake's house, where he stopped before heading to Joseph's, rather than the converse, as he told detectives.

His phone pinged in Fallbrook twice that afternoon, when he called Susan. He then headed to the Pechanga Resort Casino in Temecula, where his phone hit the same tower for nearly eight hours.

One of the task force's first actions was to serve a warrant for Cathy Jarvis's phone records on July 8. Six weeks later, they were cross-checked with Merritt's.

Her records showed six calls to Merritt while she was home the evening of February 4, but most were "zero seconds" in duration. Merritt's records showed those calls went to voicemail within five seconds or less, which fit with his phone being off.

If he was at home with her or in the apartment complex, like he'd said, why was she calling his cell phone? The detectives concluded he wasn't actually there, so she couldn't have seen or heard his phone ring on the kitchen counter as she claimed.

Hoping to bolster their theory that the murders occurred in the McStays' house, detectives went through the McStays' family photos and those taken by the SDSD, trying to identify items from the gravesite, such as the bath towel material, child's backpack, electrical cords, and material wrapped around Joseph's body.

As McGyver McCargar had said, the cream-colored futon cover, featured in a photo of the boys sitting in their PJs, was missing from Deputy Tingley's photo. Although they thought it resembled the fabric that encased Joseph's remains, the defense challenged this premise at trial by comparing enlarged photos of the cover with the material from Joseph's grave, which appeared to have different weaves. The defense also showed witnesses a photo of a pillow and futon cover, which McCargar said seemed consistent with the cover that was apparently on top of the dryer the day the SDSD searched the house.

Detective Smith interviewed Kathy Sanchez about her claim that she found the cover in the laundry room and tried to get it back on the futon. However, he said he didn't put this detail in his report, because Sanchez kept referring to a top and a bottom cover, which didn't exist.

The defense later framed that omission as further evidence of confirmation bias—where any evidence to the contrary, pointing at another suspect, or away from a particular suspect or theory, is ignored or dismissed—saying, "They only reported facts consistent with their theory."

However, no one argued with the premise that the terry cloth robe hanging on one of two hooks in the master bathroom, where it appeared that a matching robe was missing, looked similar to the material covering Summer's remains.

Although the first team of SBCSD detectives had already conducted interviews with friends and family, the task force went back for more information from key witnesses like Susan Blake.

When Detectives Steers and Hanke interviewed her in August 2014, it had been four and a half years since Joseph and his family had been killed, so her memory was fuzzy in some areas. She also remembered certain events differently each time she talked about them, which can happen when seminal events occur during a traumatic time.

This being the third set of detectives since her son's family had disappeared, she expressed frustration with the SDSD investigation, saying she never truly believed her family had gone to Mexico.

As she answered their questions, Susan reiterated what Joseph told her in November 2009 about wanting Kavanaugh out of the business and his plan to expand and consolidate his IT and manufacturing work under one roof.

"Joey was wanting to get his own IT guy and mentioned to me that, 'I'm buying him out, mom.' So I just thought Dan the Man was going to be gone, and then he'd still have Chase and the welders and everybody in one spot. That was his goal."

But regardless of what she said, the detectives kept repeating back to her that Joseph had wanted both Kavanaugh *and* Merritt out of the business, which she inadvertently confirmed twice.

"So you talked about buying Dan—that Joey was going to buy Dan and Chase out," Hanke said.

"Uh-huh," Susan said.

The third time, they asked her more directly: "Did he ever tell you that he was planning on getting a new—you say IT guy—but did he ever say that he wanted a new builder or welder?"

"No, he didn't say as much about Chase, wanting to get Chase out. He wanted to get more Dan out. Because [Dan] acted as if he could just flip the switch and shut his whole business down. And Joey couldn't get it back and up."

Nonetheless, the narrative that Joseph had wanted to "sideline" or fire Merritt from the business—as Kavanaugh had claimed—was set in the detectives' minds, despite statements by Susan, Patrick McStay, McGyver McCargar, and Merritt that Joseph wanted Kavanaugh out after he'd threatened to destroy EIP.

Susan said Joseph mentioned that Merritt had "some gambling problems" and also that "Joey gave money to pay some debts and stuff," but it was the detectives who conflated those two statements.

"Joey had mentioned that Chase had a gambling problem, and Joey helped him out with some debt as far as that goes," Steers said.

"Correct," she said.

When the detectives asked who she thought might have killed

her son's family, she said she had a bad feeling about Merritt, but she seemed more focused on Summer's ex, Vic Johansen.

"Have you seen him yet?" Susan asked.

"I can't tell you that."

Her surviving grandson, she said, lived in fear that the killer was going to come for him next.

"That's why we kept [Elijah] out of the public eye, as you see, as much as we could to protect him."

When she asked if they had looked at Merritt, they replied, "We're investigating everybody—including you."

She finally gave up, saying she didn't mind that they couldn't or wouldn't answer her questions. "I just want the job done this time," she said.

"Well, if you want it done right—" Steers said.

"That's right."

"—then that's what we're doing."

As the detectives looked for direct physical evidence linking Merritt to the murders, they tracked down the man who assumed ownership of Merritt's white C3500 Chevy truck in August 2011, hoping to find the victims' DNA or blood in it.

When Merritt could no longer make the payments, Cathy Jarvis called the dealership, from which he'd purchased four other vehicles, and said the truck had transmission problems. She asked the owner if he would repossess the truck and call it even. He agreed and sold it at auction.

The same dealership sold a 1997 BMW to Merritt, who agreed to pay $500 down, and repair a water feature for the $1,200 balance. Merritt did neither, but the lot owner couldn't locate him to repossess the car.

When the Chevy truck's new owner consented to a search in August 2014, detectives saw that the cargo bed had been painted white, but not the interior, which the crime lab searched for blood, hair, skin, fibers, or DNA. As the warrant stated, the "presence of blood and DNA can be located years after [an] incident and after the suspect cleans the vehicle."

They measured the wheel-base diameter at seventy-three inches, which matched one set of tire tracks at the gravesite, but otherwise, investigators came up empty.

Smith said he believes blood was in the truck at one time, because under his scenario, Merritt backed it up to the McStays' garage and loaded the bodies into it. However, "[four] years later, we just didn't have any luck. It had been auctioned, it had changed owners. There just wasn't anything there."

The detectives also took photos of the truck in "very low ambient light" with the lights on and compared them to the white truck in the Mitchley surveillance video, concluding the images were "consistent."

After realizing the vehicle in the video "was not the Trooper, which was the common narrative from San Diego," Smith said they came to believe the killer left the Trooper at the border as a ruse.

Delving deeper into the QuickBooks activities that DuGal had only touched on, detectives served a warrant for Joseph's records from Intuit, the parent corporation. Cross-checking them with Joseph's and Merritt's phone and banking records, they pieced together what looked like a check-forgery scheme that Merritt tried to cover up.

Joseph had two QuickBooks accounts, one called Contact, dating back to 2004, and one called Custom, created in 2008. Both had to be tied to a bank or PayPal account to pay or receive money directly, but Joseph had historically used them as an online ledger.

Those activities changed on February 1, 2010, however, when someone logged in to the Custom account as Joseph and added "charles merritt" as a vendor in all lowercase letters. Merritt was already listed in the Contact account, but the first letter of each name was capitalized, as was Joseph's general habit before February 1. Similarly, someone added "metro sheet metal" as a vendor to the Custom account on February 5, also in lowercase letters.

Smith found four checks written to Merritt that were deposited or cashed between February 2 and February 9. The records showed the account was accessed on February 2, 4, 5, and 8, when several of those checks were backdated to February 4, printed, then deleted from the ledger. Furthermore, the signature didn't look like Joseph's, which DuGal had noticed, as well.

Detectives knew Merritt was swimming in debts, and based on his bank records, he was struggling to pay bills due to money mismanagement and gambling at casinos. Then came Joseph's email on February 1, saying Merritt owed him $42,845.

Within a day or two of sending that email, detectives believed Joseph discovered Merritt had gone into his QuickBooks account, and was stealing from him by forging and cashing checks. Already frustrated by problems with the quality of Merritt's work, Joseph called his bank from the car to check details, then confronted and fired Merritt at their lunch meeting on February 4.

This conclusion was partly based on two calls Joseph made to Union Bank that day—one brief call at 11:51 a.m., then a seven-minute call at 12:15 p.m.—as well as the four business cards from the San Clemente branch found in his car.

Smith acknowledged they were unable to identify anyone at that branch to confirm this theory. "No one recalled talking to him specifically and they didn't have any phone-recorded messages around, but we followed up on that," he said.

They also ignored another possible reason for those bank calls: Patrick's advice that Joseph change the name on his account due to Patrick's "bad debt" and lawsuit. Michael suggested to detectives that his father's caution to Joseph more likely stemmed from "loan sharks" coming after Patrick, and possibly after Joseph and EIP as well, because Joseph sounded

Summer and the McStays' older son, four-year-old Gianni, play in the sand in San Clemente.
Photo courtesy of San Bernardino County Superior Court (SBCSC).

(Left) Joseph with their younger son, three-year-old Joey Jr., also known as Baby J or Chubba, who always wore a hat to hide his strawberry birthmark. (Below) Gianni and Joey Jr. often hung out on the fold-out futon couch in the family room.
Photos courtesy of SBCSC.

The McStays had been renovating their new home on this quiet cul-de-sac
on Avocado Lane in Fallbrook since closing escrow in mid-November 2009.
Photo by Caitlin Rother.

Due to the remodeling, the five-bedroom house had very little furniture,
so the family was sleeping on air mattresses in the master bedroom.
Photo by San Diego County Sheriff's Department (SDSD).

The lamp was still on in the home office, where Joseph's brother, Michael, climbed through this rear window to get inside and open the locked front door.
Photo by SDSD.

The interior of the house was in disarray, with painting tape and supplies in the kitchen, and clothing piled high on the master-bedroom closet floor.
Photo by SDSD.

The family's Dodge truck was parked in the driveway,
where a newspaper dated February 5, 2010 was tucked under one wheel.
Photo by SDSD.

The family's other vehicle, a white Isuzu Trooper, was found on February 8, 2010,
parked in a strip mall in San Ysidro, within walking distance of the border into Mexico.
Photo by SDSD.

Detectives didn't secure the McStays' house the night they were reported missing, February 15, 2010, so Joseph's mother returned to clean and straighten up the next day.
Photo by SDSD.

When investigators returned on February 19 with a search warrant, they were surprised and upset to see that the condition of the house had been altered.
Photo by SDSD.

Several investigators sat at the dining room table with paperwork, but no one saw any blood or signs of a struggle anywhere in the house.
Photo by SDSD.

Investigators found food sitting ou[t] including this apple on the carpeted stair[s] with a small bite taken out of i[t].
Photo by SDSD[.]

The kids and the family's two dogs loved their new backyard, where they could run around together. The office window, where Michael McStay climbed in, is on the right.
Photo by SDSD.

Before Fallbrook, the family lived in this duplex apartment
a couple of blocks from the beach in San Clemente.
Photo by Caitlin Rother.

Joseph loved to surf and often rode the waves by the San Clemente pier.
Photo by Caitlin Rother.

The San Bernardino County Sheriff's Department (SBCSD) launched a homicide investigation after a motorcyclist found this sun-bleached piece of bone in the High Desert off Interstate 15 near Victorville on November 11, 2013. *Photo by SBCSD.*

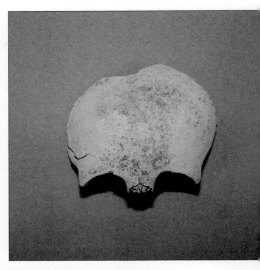

Investigators identified two shallow graves, marked as A and B (the latter shown here), each containing the remains of one adult and one child. The remains were identified by dental records, and later confirmed by DNA, to be those of the McStay family. *Photo by SBCSD.*

Each grave had a separate pair of tire tracks leading to it, one with a wheel diameter of 73 inches, the other with a 76-inch diameter. *Photo by SBCSD.*

A three-pound Stanley sledgehammer, presumed to be the murder weapon, was found in one of the graves, along with a toddler's spoon, mini pick, and paintbrush, which were inside a child's backpack.
Photos by SBCSD.

Summer's sweatpants and panties were found above her head in the grave; her bra was cut in half, with one cup in the grave and one outside, leading to the theory that she may have been sexually assaulted.
Photos by SBCSD.

Joseph's business associate,
Charles "Chase" Merritt,
had a nonviolent criminal record of theft,
burglary, and receiving stolen property,
dating back to the late 1970s.
Shown here in a 1988 prison photo.
*Photo by California Department
of Corrections and Rehabilitation (CDCR).*

The SBCSD arrested
Merritt on the street in
Chatsworth on November 15,
2014 on suspicion of
murdering the family.
*Photo grab of SBCSD
video by Jimmy Dorantes.*

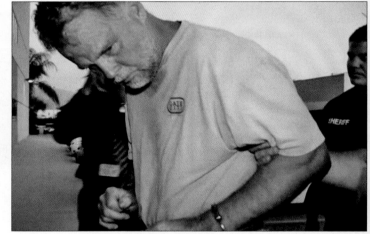

Merritt has a son
and two daughters,
featured here during
a family trip to the
Grand Canyon in 2006,
with former longtime
girlfriend Cathy Jarvis.
Photo by Cathy Jarvis.

Prosecutors claimed a neighbor's surveillance video showed Merritt's truck leaving the McStays' driveway at 7:47 p.m. on February 4, 2010. However, no blood was found in the truck. *Photo by SBCSD.*

February 6, 2010
Photographs of Cell Tower from Crime Scene

Prosecutors said Merritt's phone pinged off this AT&T cell tower near the gravesites on February 6, 2010. The defense claimed that the tower was faulty, that its data was wrong, and that if Merritt was in the desert, he was visiting family.
Photo by SBCSD.

Merritt fired several sets of attorneys, representing himself in between.
He fired James Terrell (right) and Jimmy Mettias (standing) after the preliminary hearing in 2015.
Pool photo by Kurt Miller/The Press-Enterprise (P-E)/Southern California News Group (SCNG).

Judge Michael A. Smith presided over the case through sentencing.
Pool photo by Kurt Miller/P-E/SCNG.

Michael McStay and Susan Blake spoke to reporters at the day's end of the prelim, after the judge determined there was enough evidence to send the case to trial. *Photo by Caitlin Rother.*

Merritt's trial began at the San Bernardino Justice Center on January 7, 2019. *Photo by Caitlin Rother.*

The prosecution team (left to right): Lieutenant Ryan Smith of the SBCSD and prosecutors Britt Imes, Melissa Rodriguez, and Sean Daugherty. *Photo courtesy of San Bernardino County District Attorney's Office (SBCDAO).*

During the trial, the prosecution took the jury to visit the desert memorial to the family, which had been created by local sympathizers. It was taken down after the trial ended. *Photo courtesy of SDCDAO.*

Merritt stood with his defense attorneys, James McGee (left) and Raj Maline (right), for the verdict on June 10, 2019.
Pool photo by Jennifer Cappuccio Maher/Imperial Valley Daily Bulletin/SCNG.

Summer's sister, Tracy Russell, gave her victim witness statement at the sentencing hearing on January 21, 2020.
Pool photo by Watchahara Phomacinda/P-E/SCNG.

Merritt cried at the hearing, where he was
sentenced to death, and told the McStay family
that he did not kill Joseph, Summer,
and their two little boys.
Pool photo by Watchahara Phomacinda/P-E/SCNG.

Sent to death row at San Quentin State Prison,
Merritt claimed he was wrongly convicted.
Photo by CDCR.

CDC# BL4162 Date: 01/30/2020

Susan Blake moved the family's remains
to a private cemetery in Lake Forest,
where she visits them.
Photo by Caitlin Rother.

like he was "scurrying" when they'd talked two days before he disappeared, and Joseph had cut the call short.

The most recent QuickBooks transactions didn't show up during the forensic examination of the McStays' computers, only on the activity log provided by Intuit, which meant they had been done from a different computer. Cathy Jarvis told detectives Merritt used an AT&T cellular "air card" to access the internet, since he couldn't connect using the landline in their apartment, but they couldn't link these transactions to any of his computers. Joseph's Dell laptop also was never recovered.

Still, Smith thought Merritt's story about meeting with Joseph to get blank checks didn't hold water, which led prosecutors to suggest there was no substantive meeting at all, even though Joseph's phone activity showed he was in Rancho Cucamonga for ninety minutes before he headed south.

"He says, 'I was there to pick up these checks,' but he also claims he had access to write checks, so why would Joseph give him a check?" Smith said. "There's a handwritten hundred-dollar check, and on the same day, there's a computer [generated] check."

While searching the house, the SDSD found a number of blank checks for Joseph's checking account, but a block of seventy-six was missing. The checks that looked forged were also out of numerical order with those used for valid purchases, so investigators believed Merritt had taken a box of them when he loaded the family's belongings into the PODS. However, there was no evidence he tried to cash the missing checks.

Merritt told DuGal in July 2011 that he'd signed Joseph's name on the blank checks because he needed to buy materials to complete the pending jobs and to pay himself. He also admitted calling QuickBooks on February 8, contending they were switching to the desktop program to keep the account out of Kavanaugh's hands.

Although DuGal apparently bought that story, San Bernardino detectives saw it as part of the cover-up, partly because Merritt posed as Joseph when he called the QuickBooks customer-service line at 3:11 p.m. on February 8, when he spoke to Sean Augustine for 107 minutes.

When Merritt called back the next morning, he got a different representative, Ryan Baker. Identifying himself as Joseph again, Merritt raised Baker's suspicions by saying he *needed* to delete the online account and expunge the data from the server, including the administrator log-on and password.

Baker testified later that he remembered this "very unusual" call because of Merritt's vehement tone, but conceded he didn't have access to notes from Merritt's previous call to Augustine about downloading the new program and transferring account data to the desktop Pro version, which Baker conceded was "a pretty normal thing."

Baker said he'd only received a few requests to delete an entire account in his five years on the job, and each had involved fraudulent activity, such as avoiding the IRS or a dispute between business partners. Most businesses wanted a copy of the account information, prior to cancelling.

"People want to protect it, not get rid of it," Baker testified.

Only the master administrator could delete an account's information, so he emailed Joseph a link to request it. The "reinstall" CD was to be used if or when the account holder no longer had access to the link.

Because Merritt didn't have access to Joseph's email, he couldn't click on the link. When Baker didn't hear back from Joseph, he closed the case on February 13.

The prosecution called Baker to testify later, and the defense called Baker's supervisor, Annette Dron, to contradict him.

"It's one of our most frequent questions, [how] to export data from QuickBooks online to QuickBooks Pro," Dron said, the latter of which carries no subscription fee. She said it also wasn't unusual for users to delete their online information, "because they didn't feel comfortable with their data online at that time."

As the SBCSD searched for other incriminating evidence tying Merritt to the murders, they uncovered more stories that he was a con man. One former business partner said Merritt spent work income on personal expenses, which eventually forced the partner to dissolve their business at a $15,000 to $20,000 loss.

They also found a longtime associate, bail bondsman Jimmy Flores, who thought Merritt was not only "worthless," but also could be dangerous.

Flores told Detectives Smith and Hanke that he'd met Merritt at a swap meet twenty years earlier. "I know that bastard inside out," he said. "He is the killer of the McStay family. Where they found the bodies, Chase's sister lives over there."

Flores recalled bailing Merritt out of jail after a commercial burglary arrest in Alhambra. On the way to court, Merritt stole a wheelchair from a convalescent home and rode it into the courtroom, carrying a bag of medication, as a ploy to evoke the judge's sympathy. After the hearing, Merritt dumped the chair at a 7-Eleven.

Although Merritt wasn't violent in the past, Flores said he still believed Merritt was "involved in some way" with the murders. Maybe Joseph had discovered Merritt was conning or stealing from him, so Merritt killed him before he could report it to authorities.

These claims were ultimately ruled irrelevant by the judge, which prevented the prosecution from presenting them at trial, but they fit a pattern of behavior that contributed to their overall narrative.

Public records, and now witnesses, showed Merritt had left a trail of debts, tax liens, small-claims judgments, and bad feelings across Southern California, forcing frequent moves for the whole family. But did that really make him a child killer?

Chapter 29

Search warrant affidavits and investigative reports show SBCSD detectives identified Dan Kavanaugh, Vic Johansen, and Michael McFadden as "possible suspects," though they were never named publicly even as "people of interest." Detectives interviewed all three men in August and September 2014 to "close every door we can," as Smith put it.

McFadden, who was interviewed on August 22, refused to take a polygraph and was wary to talk without an attorney because a self-published author had dedicated an entire chapter to him as a possible suspect.

To check McFadden's alibi that he was at home or work the day the McStays went missing, detectives wrote a warrant for his cell phone records after already checking his wife Heather's back in February.

Heather, who was also interviewed that day, said she still believed the murders had to do something with Summer, because she "could make a lot of people angry" and whoever had killed the family must have been angry at her, because Joseph was always "very easygoing."

The last time Heather saw him was at a family counseling session, prompted by Summer's CPS complaint. She said Elijah and her husband Michael had both denied the allegations, but Michael was angry enough to call Joseph and tell him "to control his wife and to keep her from making accusations that had no facts or basis to [them]."

At that time, Michael was driving two white vehicles, a Ford Explorer and a Toyota 4Runner SUV, but he said he'd only driven through the 1-15 corridor near Victorville on his way to Vegas.

Ultimately, both McFaddens were cleared.

Vic Johansen's phone records showed he was in Orange County when the family disappeared, and outside of California right afterward.

When Detective Bachman contacted him, Johansen also expressed concern about talking without an attorney, claiming he'd been identified as a suspect in the media.

"Johansen wanted to cooperate with the investigation but was fearful he would be implicated in the homicide even though he did not have any involvement," Bachman wrote in a report.

After speaking to his worship group, Johansen agreed to be interviewed in South Lake Tahoe on September 4, when he downplayed the "love" emails he'd written to Summer, saying he was lonely and depressed. When he ran into her in San Clemente in 2007, she was happy to be pregnant as she pushed Gianni around in a stroller.

He'd subsequently heard from a former roommate on Facebook that the McStays had gone missing, but he had no idea who might want to harm them. At that time, he said, he was driving two white vehicles, a Toyota Land Cruiser and a Chevy truck.

He agreed to give Bachman a DNA sample, and he, too, was cleared.

Detectives also checked McGyver McCargar's cell phone records to see if he was anywhere near Fallbrook, San Ysidro, or Victorville the night the family went missing. They showed he was in Lake Forest, in Orange County, where he was on a call with someone between eight and nine o'clock.

When he was on the phone at night or in the early morning

hours over the next few days, he was primarily in the Laguna Beach area, where he worked as a bartender, or in Fullerton.

"The block of time where McCargar does not receive any calls is consistent with him sleeping after work," Smith wrote, so his alibi checked out, as well.

Investigators conducted two more interviews, separately, on September 20, with Michael McStay and Dan Kavanaugh, both of whom agreed to take a polygraph.

Michael told them he thought Kavanaugh was a "douche-bag," and he was going to "beat his ass" if he ever saw him again, but he believed even more firmly that Merritt was responsible for the murders. Michael's polygraph on September 25 showed his answers were truthful.

The SBCSD held on to Kavanaugh's laptop for nine months until his four-hour interview, his first with that agency since it had taken over the case.

In a preliminary call before the meeting, Kavanaugh told Detective Hanke he had "nothing to with that [the murders], as you know," and wished detectives had called sooner, because "maybe I could help you solve the case."

Kavanaugh repeated the false claim that it was he, not Joseph, who had launched the waterfall business, bragging that he was also the savvy one who made it successful using SEO techniques.

"That's basically how I started Earth Inspired Products, how I got the company profitable, how I met Joe," he said. "So, he was kind of working for me, and I was just kind of doing everything. I was never paid to build the website. I own half the business with Joseph. He never paid me a cent, so people's misconceptions could not be more inaccurate."

He also claimed he found Authority Domains, Inc. and decided to hire them to do SEI. "Joe had no part of my relationship with them. They didn't want to deal with Joe at all."

Painting himself as a victim, he contended Joseph tried to steal the business by working covertly with Merritt. Joseph "established a relationship with Chase, kind of like behind my back, and he's, like, 'Yo, let's maybe do something on the side here, and I'll pass you some custom work. And you don't really need to talk to Dan.' Now, I'm, like, my name would later come up as just a web designer that never got paid for my site. No, I built that. I did everything."

"I see," Hanke said.

"So, he kind of tried to do some side shady shit with Chase," he said.

Kavanaugh didn't meet Merritt until after Joseph disappeared, when "he hit me up and was, like, hey, what's up? I got your number from Joseph's dad or Mikey."

In their first conversation, Kavanaugh said, Merritt claimed Joseph had instructed him to change the QuickBooks password and delete the online account "so that his wife wouldn't find it or wouldn't see it. I'm, like, what online QuickBooks account? We have an Earth Inspired Products, but he had created a second one, EIP Fountains, on my QuickBooks account that I didn't even know about." Merritt told Kavanaugh this was the account where "the majority of the money, large deals, was being recorded."

In fact, these were both Joseph's QuickBooks accounts, and this is essentially what Merritt had told DuGal, although he didn't admit that he and Joseph were trying to hide the custom jobs from Kavanaugh until his interview in July 2011.

Asked who created the second account, Kavanaugh said, "Joseph and Chase. Joseph created it, and then that was their little side hustle" for custom fountains, "just specific ones, like the expensive shit."

"He's like, 'Joseph didn't want [Summer] to find out about this hundred-grand in sales that we just did.' Because Joseph was telling his wife, apparently, according to Chase, and I think that from the best of my judgment now, this is the case. He wasn't really making that much cash. Because he had it in his mind, like, he'll have a little side thing, where half the money is going—more than half."

Kavanaugh said he was angry when he saw a lead for a restaurant fountain project come through the website about a year before Joseph disappeared and realized he was getting cut out of profits on custom jobs like that one.

"Joseph was surprised when I called him out on it," he said. "Obviously I see incoming leads on the website. How dumb are people, right?"

But the restaurant deal eventually went south. "I was, like, completely left in the dark from the get-go," he said. Then, a week before Joseph disappeared, he mentioned the restaurant debacle to Kavanaugh, and said he'd filed paperwork to sue the company. "Didn't tell me that Chase built it."

"That's going to be something we're going to look into," Hanke said. "Had you ever been to that house in Fallbrook?"

"Never been to the house. Still never been to that house."

Kavanaugh said he knew where it was, because Joseph had sent him the address on Google Maps, and it was on company documents. He also claimed that Joseph had uploaded a video driving to the house to YouTube.

"With his kids and shit," Kavanaugh said. "That's not smart to put that kind of stuff on the internet."

Shortly after the family went missing, he said, he saw the email from QuickBooks, alerting Joseph that his email and passwords had been changed and the account was "deactivated."

When Merritt "started to be irritating to me," Kavanaugh said, he went into the original account through Joseph's log-in and reset the password, reactivated that account, then reset the password for the new account, using one of Joseph's other email accounts to lock Merritt out.

"Chase had updated both of the passwords and attempted to delete both accounts, I believe," he said. "I just reset the password, I changed the email address. I'm not giving him access to anything."

"I know that Joe probably would not have given him access to those accounts," he said. "Because why would you give just the welder access to the company bank, like the QuickBooks account? Maybe the QuickBooks online account that he was just dealing with Chase on was so that they could reconcile the costs."

He said he also didn't think Joseph would have used that account to print checks, because he'd sent Kavanaugh handwritten checks and wired him money, but primarily paid him via PayPal. Detectives discovered, however, that Joseph had recently issued both printed and handwritten checks to vendors such as MSM.

Later, Kavanaugh said, "I created my own QuickBooks account that I started from scratch, recording new transactions," but kept Joseph's original ledger so an accountant could enter some transactions "so we could sell the company. They needed the transactions. They needed the profit and loss."

Kavanaugh urged Hanke to confront Merritt about the QuickBooks activities, "because he's going to buckle. And when those questions get brought up to him and he gets put on the spot, he's not going to say the same thing that he told me. I'll go on the stand and tell people what he told me. You know what I mean?"

"Yeah, absolutely."

"I'll testify or whatever, dude. I'm not afraid of that guy at all."

Two days later, Kavanaugh took the polygraph, answering "No" to this question: Did you plan or participate in any way in causing the deaths of the McStay family?

The examiner said Kavanaugh's chart showed "insufficient responses," so the test was deemed "inconclusive." Per protocol, the examiner repeated the test two more times, but got the same result.

After all these interviews, a warrant dated September 26,

2014 indicated the detectives still didn't have enough evidence
to arrest anyone: "There is no direct evidence which establishes
the identity of all the persons responsible for the McStay family's murders."

When Kavanaugh asked Hanke not to involve his ex-girlfriend,
Lauren Forest-Knowles, in backing up his Hawaii alibi, the detective replied, "It's something that, you know, we might have
to follow up on," but Hanke said he wouldn't ask about their relationship issues.

Kavanaugh described her as "kind of a party animal," and a
"loose cannon." She "didn't have the most positive things to say
about me," which he said Hanke could find posted online. He
said he didn't talk to her anymore, omitting mention of her restraining order against him in 2011.

In an interview with Hanke two weeks later, Forest-Knowles
confirmed Kavanaugh had been with her in Hawaii in January
2010. She said the trip was only supposed to last a few weeks,
but they stayed until Valentine's Day. She showed Hanke a receipt for her plane ticket home, for which her mother had paid.
She later said she came home early because she "did not like it
in Hawaii."

As proof of their time there, she sent Hanke a couple screenshots of posts, dated February 4, from her Facebook page,
where she went by "LoLo Mi KnoKno." But as the defense
pointed out, Kavanaugh couldn't be definitively identified in either shot, and the February 4 date reflects the day the photos
were posted, not taken.

Although a hooded figure was labelled as "Dan" in one of
them, the face was so blurry that two women who know him
personally said they couldn't tell if that was him, one of his
brothers, or a mutual friend who lives in Hawaii. In fact, they
both suggested the awkwardly positioned hooded figure could've
been photoshopped in. The other photo featured a man sitting on
the beach with his face obscured by a video camera.

Forest-Knowles characterized Kavanaugh as a controlling liar and a "bullshitter" who was arrested for domestic violence against her, but she didn't think he had anything to do with the family's disappearance. She, too, said Joseph had bought him out, but Kavanaugh still "took money out of Joseph's accounts to pay business expenses and also for personal use," because he believed he was owed more money.

In January 2012, a tipster had sent DuGal a revealing message about Kavanaugh, posted on cheaterville.com in December 2011, and suggested DuGal contact the author, "LoLoKnoKno." This post, to which Kavanaugh was apparently referring when he spoke to Hanke, was part of SDSD's investigative file, but there is no indication DuGal knew Kavanaugh's alibi witness had written it.

LoLoKnoKno's post paints Kavanaugh in an extremely negative light as she recounts the low points of her three-year relationship with him. She claims she only learned about his behavior from friends who "ratted him out" after he slept with multiple other women during a single year: "He is a master manipulator," she wrote in part. "He's such a great liar, he can convince ANYONE of ANYTHING. LADIES!!! DO NOT trust this sorry excuse for a man."

Chapter 30

In a last round of checks, the detectives followed up on a few remaining leads and theories.

Joseph's longtime friend Guy Joseph had suggested the murders could have stemmed from the Provecho waterfall debacle, because Mexican mafia and drug cartels are known to invest in restaurants. But after Detective Hanke contacted Provecho and gathered more information about the dispute, they concluded that it only confirmed Merritt did shoddy work.

"During the course of this investigation, no nexus to a Mexican Drug Lord or Cartel has been identified and there is no evidence showing the McStays were involved in any type of drug trade," Smith wrote.

However, they were still exploring one other possible drug and underworld connection.

A gun-registration check in September turned up a 9-millimeter FEG Union semi-automatic pistol that Joseph had purchased in Monarch Beach in 1994, which hadn't turned up during SDSD's search of the house.

Susan Blake recalled Joseph had acquired a gun "for protection," but she mistakenly thought it was while he was living with Summer in San Clemente.

In a separate check for any other law enforcement agencies

that had run the serial number, they found two: one by the Little Rock Police Department in 1993 and one recently by the Nevada Highway Patrol (NHP).

In a call to the NHP, they learned Joseph's gun had been recovered from a silver 1997 Mercedes sedan, which was abandoned with two flat tires on the rocky easement of the northbound on-ramp of Interstate 15 near the Las Vegas Strip around 5 a.m. on May 30, 2014.

About ninety minutes later, NHP troopers picked up two men who were walking on the freeway about a mile from the car. Drunk and belligerent, they claimed a cab driver had thrown them out after an argument, which would have been against state law. The men, who were from Mountain View, California and Las Vegas, respectively, claimed they were heading to Caesar's Palace, even though they were walking in the opposite direction.

The troopers suspected the men had abandoned the Mercedes to escape a DUI charge, but because they couldn't physically tie the men to the car, they dropped off the men at Caesar's.

Joseph's gun, loaded with one round in the chamber, was in the Mercedes's glove box, along with a full magazine of twenty-five rounds. The troopers, who weren't wearing gloves, removed the single bullet and ran a zip tie through the barrel, then placed the items in the trunk.

Sam Cohen, the car's registered owner, never responded to a voicemail alerting him that the Mercedes had been towed, so it was prepared for sale at auction, during which time the ammunition disappeared, leaving only the holster.

SBCSD detectives went to Las Vegas to collect the gun and process the Mercedes on September 17. The wheelbase measured sixty-nine inches, which didn't match either set of tracks at the gravesite.

In late October, Smith tracked down Cohen, who had lived in Hollywood and Las Vegas, through his son's mother. She and

Cohen were no longer together, but she said he'd sent her a photo with a gun in his mouth, and threatened to kill himself. As a convicted felon, Cohen wasn't allowed to buy or possess a gun, but his ex said he had owned a Mercedes. He claimed he'd been in an accident and she hadn't seen the car since. Cohen denied any knowledge of the Mercedes or the gun, and referred Smith to his former roommate, Matthew Ham.

Ham said he'd sold marijuana and glass paraphernalia at dispensaries in Orange County in 2009 and 2010, and had met Cohen online in a Bong TV chat room. He couldn't recall whether Cohen had taken the gun during a visit, or if Ham had given it to him in a trade, but it was sometime between April and November 2011.

Ham said he and his partner, Tony Scarpine, had originally acquired the gun in a trade with a Hispanic man known as "Big Smoke," who sold glass paraphernalia Ham suspected was stolen. Ham recalled meeting Big Smoke at a dispensary in Garden Grove, in Orange County, but said his cell number had a 626 Los Angeles prefix.

The gun-for-weed trade with Big Smoke and his crew was like a Tupperware party, which Ham and Scarpine left with Joseph's 9-millimeter, as well as several .22 Derringers, a crossbow, and a flak jacket. Big Smoke was with a tall, thin guy with a round face and short spiky hair, and they were driving an older gray car, like a Toyota Corolla. They were between eighteen and twenty-four years old and wore baggy clothes. Scarpine said they looked like "South Siders," and thought they drove a Ford Explorer.

Asked "if anything bad had happened with the guns," Big Smoke called them "burner guns," and said they were "getting rid of the guns for a friend." Ham took that to mean, "You don't know anything about the gun, or you don't know who the owner is."

Shown photos of Joseph and Summer, Merritt, Jarvis, and Kavanaugh, Ham didn't recognize them or their names.

Attorney Raj Maline later said the defense tracked down a "Big Smoke," who was sentenced to five years in prison for distributing marijuana in Colorado, but they couldn't prove it was the same guy or connect him to the murders, Kavanaugh, or Quintero and Schneider, the men who ran the marijuana collective and bought EIP, the latter of whom was arrested with several guns and ammunition in his possession.

Michael McStay told Smith he assumed Joseph's gun was auctioned off with the PODS contents, because Joseph had shown it to him several times, and never said he'd sold it "or did anything else with it."

But Maline said that according to Merritt, Joseph kept his gun in the house, not packed in a POD. "Why would you leave the gun in the POD? They brought stuff in. You're just going to leave it out in your front yard? No," Maline said, pointing out that guns can't legally be auctioned off. "PODS is not going to sell a gun and go to jail."

Merritt's daughter, Taylor Jarvis, now an attorney with the Los Angeles County Public Defender's Office, thought the POD scenario was "just dumb. That's a convenient way not to have to address where it came from. I never understood why it wasn't something that wasn't looked into more. Wherever it came from, it's connected to the [McStay] family."

The defense agreed, arguing in a pre-trial motion that detectives should have continued investigating, because "how the firearm was found and to where and to whom it was traced back is some of the best evidence of whom was involved with the death or disappearance of Joseph McStay."

But without a stronger link to the case, the judge wouldn't allow the defense to present any of this evidence to the jury.

Asked in 2023 why detectives didn't investigate the gun further and if he was satisfied with the PODS-auction explanation, Lieutenant Ryan Smith replied in an email, "We followed all leads relating to Joseph's firearm until they were exhausted."

He acknowledged the Mercedes owner was a convicted felon who wasn't allowed to possess a firearm, but after processing the gun for DNA and fingerprints, and interviewing "all involved parties that could be identified," investigators never found "any link to the McStay family or associates." He also said, "There was never any link the McStays were involved with the marijuana industry."

They did look for Big Smoke, he said, "but were unable to locate him. As you could imagine, that's a somewhat common moniker in the marijuana world."

But the bottom line was "there was never any evidence (other than speculation) a firearm was used or involved in the family's disappearance or murder."

Chapter 31

Closing in on Merritt, detectives obtained warrants for wire intercepts and PEN orders, which are commonly used to catch criminals, such as drug traffickers, who frequently change cell phones to evade police detection.

The warrants allowed detectives to tap Merritt's calls from August through November 2014, hoping to capture incriminating conversations or identify possible associates in the murders. During that time, investigators also put pressure on those close to him, trying to elicit damning information.

One of those people was Cathy Jarvis, whom detectives interviewed on October 10, 2014. They also gave her a polygraph exam, the results of which were "inconclusive."

Insisting she'd been home with Merritt the night of February 4, 2010, the last day anyone saw the McStays, she said she saw Merritt's phone ringing on the kitchen counter at 8:28 p.m., with Joseph's name on the caller ID. But Merritt didn't answer it, saying he'd already seen and talked to Joseph enough that day.

She recalled it was a Friday night, but the detectives told her February 4 was actually a Thursday, and showed her Merritt's phone records, which reflected no such call. Only Joseph's records reflected that call, but they didn't show them to her.

Merritt's records showed that Joseph had called Merritt a

week earlier on Thursday, January 28 at 8:17 p.m. and also at 9:27 p.m. on Friday, January 29, which Merritt didn't answer, either. Seeing this, she acknowledged the call could have been on another night.

The day after this arduous interview, the detectives monitored her call with Merritt. Sounding exhausted, Jarvis said she'd been questioned "for hours" by detectives, "making me think I was remembering things wrong."

"Such as?"

"Pretty much telling me that you did the murders and that I, you know, I helped you in some way, shape, or form." They also showed her "evidence and pictures and things."

"Such as?"

"Such as, dammit, pictures of your utility truck, pictures of the family."

"What's that got to do with anything about Joseph?"

"They're saying, 'If you go to jail, nobody's gonna be taking care of your kids. You want them to be without a mother?' And stuff like that. Mind games."

"Those f***ers," Merritt said. "So, what kind of questions were they asking?"

"Like, 'What happened the night before Joseph disappeared?'"

Then they produced her phone records to prove that she'd repeatedly called Merritt the night of February 4, when she said he was at home.

"Chase wasn't home," they said.

"And I was, like, 'What? That's not possible. That's not what I remember.'"

"You were trying to get a hold of him at the time you saw the phone ringing. Look, there's call after call after call, and he's not answering," they said.

"And I was, like, 'That can't be, because he was home. I remember!' It was crazy. I thought I was going nuts."

"It's not your fault," Merritt said.

"They just kept telling me that you had something to do with it, that you're gonna be accused of the murders. I was like, 'It's just not possible. I know Chase. He's got no reason to do this.'"

The detectives also said Merritt's white truck was seen leaving Joseph's house the night the family disappeared. "I was just, like, 'Am I going crazy? Am I remembering things wrong? What the hell is happening?'"

After she told them, "I suppose it could have happened on another day, but I could have sworn it was on a Friday, and I could have sworn this is what happened," then "they kinda gave up. Fun stuff."

"Yeah, sorry about that."

She didn't know "if they're trying to find evidence to pin this on you," or "if they're telling me a made-up story for my benefit, because I'm involved with you and because it could involve me." But after all that, "I was a total frickin' mess yesterday."

"They're spending an awful lot of energy on me."

"They're just trying to find out who did it," she said. "I think they want to cover a lot of bases. It's just that, Chase, you've made a lot of people angry at you. That's part of the problem. If somebody's going to point fingers, they're gonna point them at you, because you've pissed everybody off at some point in time."

"I don't piss everybody off."

"Think about it."

"Like who?"

"Like everybody that you've come into contact with: customers, business associates. You've pissed everybody off. Because you end up walking away. You don't follow through. You don't finish. And that's what I told the detectives. I said, 'I couldn't take that chance with my family,' because you're too reckless and you don't think about the consequences of things. I thought you were going to piss off the wrong person and they were going to come after you and/or us. I said, 'If anything, it would be Chase who'd be the one who ended up dead. But for him to take somebody else out, that doesn't make sense. Chase doesn't care that much about anything or anyone.'"

"Oh, thanks."

"Well, it's frickin' the truth."

"No, it's not."

"You didn't care enough to keep your family together," she said. "You don't stop doing the bad things that you do. You don't think about the repercussions. You don't listen to other people when they're trying to tell you that you're not doing the right things. I still believe in you. I mean, I still care about you, but you drove me crazy."

There was a pause while Jarvis let that sink in. "Anyway. Are you there?"

When Merritt responded, he sounded dejected. Jarvis said she had to feed their son, and they hung up.

Detectives suspected the killer took Summer's and Joseph's phones, both of which were linked to T-Mobile accounts, but couldn't use them because they were password-protected.

According to Joseph's desktop eMachine logs, someone accessed the internet in the wee hours of February 8—four days after the family was last seen—to look up the address for a T-Mobile store in Fountain Valley, near the 405 in Orange County. Kavanaugh also had a T-Mobile contract, which was cancelled in August 2011 for nonpayment.

That internet search occurred within a two-hour period, starting at 2:05 a.m., when the user pulled down six previous Google searches on the toolbar, including "quickbooks online," "dinosaur train," and "stackstone," all of which Joseph had visited recently. Bachman believed the user was trying "to move suspicious searches down the search query bar and move less pertinent queries up." The internet browser was also opened on Summer's HP desktop, but there was no more computer activity until 3:55 a.m., when the eMachine was manually shut down.

Merritt's location couldn't be determined during that period, because his phone hadn't connected to any towers since 5:17 p.m. the night before, and it didn't connect again until 7:26 a.m., when it pinged his home tower.

Detectives believed this user was the killer, hoping to gain access to the phones by personally visiting the T-Mobile store. But by 2014, the store's surveillance footage had long been erased, and a warrant for customer service records proved no help.

In October, investigators prepared one last round of search warrants, still looking for computers with pertinent financial transactions; any of the McStays' belongings, such as the missing block of bank checks; clothing stained with their blood or bodily fluids; a receipt for the sledgehammer; and the book Merritt said he was writing about the case.

Detectives also did surveillance at the senior mobile home park in Homeland, where Merritt lived with his girlfriend, Mechele Muir, and also at Keene Engineering, his new workplace, to gather vehicle information.

Then they called Merritt to schedule an interview for the same day they planned to serve warrants at his trailer and the motor home in Covina where Cathy Jarvis lived with their kids. Merritt said he was willing to talk, and offered to bring the seven chapters he'd written so far.

In the interim, they served a warrant for his medical records at Arrowhead Regional Medical Center, stating they believed Merritt played up his heart problems to persuade them he wasn't "physically capable of murdering the McStay family." Detectives developed this theory after finding footage on Joseph's video camera of Merritt jumping a fence and climbing the mountain near the house in Fallbrook after the family moved in.

"Investigators believe this video shows Merritt was in relatively healthy condition and Merritt's statements of numerous injuries were exaggerated for investigators," the warrant states. "Typically a suspect of murder conducted by blunt-force trauma would have injuries consistent with a fight with a victim, and in this case there were multiple victims."

But the records didn't provide much useful information after all.

By this point, the detectives believed they had ruled out all people of interest except Chase Merritt. His six calls on February 6, 2010 pinged towers in the High Desert, including one near the gravesites, and he was the only suspect familiar enough with the area to know where to bury the McStay family's bodies. When Smith measured the distance from the graves to Merritt's sister's house in Oro Grande, he clocked it at 8.34 miles of "improved dirt roads, regularly maintained and easily driven in a sedan."

Yet, when Detectives Henke and Bachman finally interviewed Merritt for eight grueling hours, he refused to admit that he, or his phone, had been in the desert on February 6.

"Not possible," he said. "I wasn't there."

When they claimed they had GPS coordinates to prove his phone was at the gravesite, he said if he had been anywhere near there, he would have been visiting one of his siblings.

"You're throwing these things at me like they're facts," he said.

"These are the facts, Chase."

"I really don't recollect being there. Matter of fact, I wasn't there. I wasn't at the desert, and I don't know what to say other than that."

Also, after telling Detective DuGal that he'd never driven the Trooper, he conceded he'd driven it several times.

Merritt didn't bring his book chapters as promised, saying he'd loaned his laptop to a friend and would email the file to them.

While Merritt was being interviewed on October 22, a team of investigators searched his mobile home, his 1984 Chrysler

sedan, his newly purchased Land Rover, and the Volvo and Ply-
mouth sedans that Muir and her daughter drove.

They scoured the trailer for the laptop with his book and any
printed chapters or notes, which they believed would reveal if
Merritt recalled "the events from memory or [was] fabricating
items to cover his involvement in these murders." The computer
would tell them when the document "was last changed or altered, and any websites searched to assist Merritt with fabricating his story."

But they didn't find his manuscript there, or on any device
they seized that day—two laptops, a Kindle Fire reader, a video
recorder, and an iPhone 6—only some handwritten notes, which
they said included "several quotes to do with remorse, forgive-
ness and murder."

"This Book is to attempt to accurately Depict a family and it's
counterparts who have experienced a horrific act of Depravity.
it is for joseph, summer, joseph jR and little gianni, for they are
not here to Defend themselves," one excerpt read.

On his nightstand, they found a blogger's self-published book
about the case and the *People* magazine with the McStay family
on the cover.

A forensic examination of Merritt's iPhone turned up some
interesting searches, all in lowercase letters:

"whats necessary for a search warrant?"

"patented gold claims for sale"

"alaska"

"us borders?"

"can you get to alaska without going through canada?"

Investigators searched Jarvis's motor home that same afternoon. Because Merritt visited their children there, detectives believed they might find some of his belongings, such as the
computer he used to print out the forged checks.

Jarvis told investigators she wanted to give them some business records from her mother's house in Arizona, but they'd been thrown away. Her mom subsequently shipped the detectives an old Hewlett-Packard laptop, to which Merritt had access when the McStays were murdered, but it contained nothing of value.

During a monitored call between Merritt and his girlfriend on November 1, he told her he had to go to the library to access the internet, because he couldn't get on with his Toshiba laptop or iPad.

After examining the devices they'd seized, the detectives realized they didn't have either of those, so they figured his book must be on that laptop, which they never found. Merritt later told the author the missing laptop was in a desk drawer the detectives never opened.

In November, they served a warrant to obtain Facebook records for Merritt, Jarvis, and Muir. They received more than 15,000 documents, photos, private messages, group information and phone numbers, the majority of which came from Muir's account. But none of them tied Merritt to the murders.

Chapter 32

After his work with EIP dried up, Merritt built some water-falls for other clients, but started looking for new ways to make money. He worked with MSM on stainless-steel furni-ture and prototypes he designed for new products, such as a downhill-racing pedal for mountain bikes. But he focused mostly on designing gold mining machines, specifically a dry washer to separate gold from dirt.

In the spring of 2014, he made a prototype for his machine and sold the idea to Keene Engineering, which manufactured and sold it as the Keene 190 Triple Threat. Mark Keene told Detective Hanke they "came to an agreement with Merritt for the purchase of the patents" for this and other product ideas he'd designed.

"They put me on as a design engineer. I designed a lot of dif-ferent things for them," Merritt said in a series of interviews with the author in 2022. He claimed Keene signed an agreement to pay him 5 percent of total sales and that they had a meeting scheduled with an attorney to move forward with a patent appli-cation on the dry washer.

"I assume they finished that," he said. "If they didn't, there probably will be some problems later."

The Keene 190, which was selling online for $1,665, was billed as a machine with "six unique patents" that uses an electrostatic charge to "separate and liberate stubborn gold [from dust and dirt] and create an even flow of material."

However, Keene claimed in 2023 that he and Merritt never put anything in writing or scheduled any meeting with a patent attorney.

"We didn't do any patents, it's too expensive. There's no money in that," he said, admitting that the "six unique patents" claim was a marketing gimmick.

Describing Merritt as "a nice, charming, likable guy," Keene said he allowed Merritt to drive a company truck and sleep at the office overnight. He even let Merritt stay with his girlfriend in Keene's guest house, because they lived several hours away.

When Merritt claimed he'd received a $2,500 ticket in Riverside County, Keene reimbursed him for it. But after comparing the ticket Merritt submitted to Keene with the original citation, Hanke determined Merritt had altered the ticket "to defraud Keene" out of $2,500.

According to Hanke's report, Merritt subsequently moved his belongings out of the office and asked Keene to "buy him out so he could move to Alaska" to mine for gold. However, Keene recently said he didn't recall Merritt talking about Alaska, only that he wanted to go out on the road to sell the dry washer. As an employee, there was nothing to "buy out."

But before Merritt could go anywhere, he was arrested on suspicion of murder at 2 p.m. on November 5, 2014, in front of Keene's office in Chatsworth.

Merritt sat silently in the cruiser during the ninety-minute ride to the West Valley Detention Center in Rancho Cucamonga, where he was booked and held without bail. Footage of him was all over the news across Southern California that night, with his head down, wrists cuffed behind him, and ankles manacled, as deputies walked him from the cruiser into the jail. The news soon went national, then international, as social media buzzed with speculation and opinion.

*   *   *

Although Patrick McStay had gone out of his way to defend Merritt before, he now claimed that he'd always believed Merritt could have been involved. "Chase was always somebody, you know, chasing the dollar," he said, and this case "was all about the money."

But after years of complaining about the SDSD's ineptitude, Patrick seemed to feel validated. "I knew they screwed this thing up," he told NBC 7 in San Diego. "All the rest was just sugar coating to make it look like they really were interested in solving, doing something. They did virtually nothing."

Nonetheless, San Diego County Sheriff Bill Gore stood by his department's efforts. "Trust me, our homicide detectives are very thorough and very experienced," he told NBC 7. "Had there been any signs of bloodstain or blood spatter or dents in walls, those would have been discovered."

Despite public comments by Joseph's family that they doubted he and Summer went to Mexico, Gore contended the family had reinforced that theory and supported Detective DuGal's efforts.

"It's one thing now with twenty-twenty hindsight that we have four bodies that have been found a year ago up in Victorville," Gore said. "That's a whole different type of investigation."

The SDSD's unwillingness to admit mistakes is historic. Combined with its lack of transparency, numerous inmate deaths and acts of agency misconduct have resulted in lawsuits that cost taxpayers at least eighty million dollars since 2019. Along with a growing public mistrust in its investigations and its lack of accountability, these have been campaign issues in the last two elections.

Retired SDSD commander Dave Myers, a 33-year veteran of the department, ran unsuccessfully against Gore in 2018, and also against Gore's chosen successor, Kelly Martinez, in 2022. Both

Myers, a Democrat, and John Hemmerling, a Republican he later endorsed, ran on platforms to change the status quo at the SDSD.

Although Martinez ended up winning the seat, both Myers and Hemmerling saw her as no different from her predecessor, whose problematic top-down approach was colored by a "rush to judgment" and "confirmation bias."

"It's a group-think, where we don't encourage independent thinking, especially our high-level investigators, [or] encourage them to question [when] everything isn't necessarily what it appears," Myers said. "We don't have those in supervision who review or question some of the decisions that are made."

As a result, he said, "the department is just leaving a lot of strings that have not been followed up on or tugged on," which are then pursued by "folks who are not trained investigators" in crime forums online such as Websleuths and Reddit.

The approach "that permeates through the entire organization is, let's just try to get this case over with so we can move on to the next one," Myers said, which "begs the question, how many cases in this organization are not being investigated? I mean, literally, how many people have gotten away with murder?"

Merritt's attorneys argued that Dan Kavanaugh had the same motive that detectives ascribed to their client, and they believed that confirmation bias led investigators to dismiss Kavanaugh as a suspect even after SBCSD took over the investigation.

Politics also played a role in this high-profile case, which became a priority for San Bernardino County's top elected law enforcement officials, who had promised speedy justice for the McStay family in front of the television cameras.

DA Michael Ramos, who aspired to be state attorney general, was criticized for grandstanding and tainting the jury pool by touting how much evidence they'd collected against Merritt.

"This is a cold and callous murder of an entire family," Ramos said at the news conference announcing Merritt's arrest. "We are now at least able to get some justice for the family."

The same day Merritt pleaded "not guilty" at his arraignment to four first-degree murder charges, with a special circumstance allegation of committing multiple murders, Ramos declared Merritt guilty on CNN.

"There was no doubt in our mind [Merritt] was the person that committed the murders," he said. "We know there have been many inconsistencies. His story is all over the place."

Sheriff McMahon, who admitted his department had been on the clock to produce results, said investigators didn't identify any other suspects.

"Less than a year ago, I made a promise to the family that our department would do everything in our power to solve this case, and although we can never bring them back, I hope this provides some level of closure," he said.

But when the SBCSD detectives took this death penalty-eligible case to the DA's office a week short of the one-year anniversary, it was based entirely on circumstantial evidence and left many questions unanswered.

The prosecution team took pieces of the detectives' theories and left others on the table. But they all saw Merritt as a greedy child killer with a gambling problem. A con man with no discipline or control over his finances who was angry Joseph was sidelining him, and scared his fraud and forgery would result in a third-strike conviction that would send him to prison for life.

Detective Smith believed the murders went down like this:

After Joseph figured out that Merritt was embezzling from him, he fired Merritt during their lunch meeting in Rancho Cucamonga.

"I don't know if Joseph told him to follow him back to the house so he could pay him out or finish some unfinished business, or if Merritt just followed him," Smith said, though he leaned toward the former, because "it seems like a far drive to prove your point." But either way, "that's where everything escalated."

Merritt killed Joseph first, which rendered Summer and the boys collateral damage because they could identify him. Smith believes the SDSD would have discovered blood if they had sprayed Bluestar at the house.

After taking the bodies through the garage, Merritt loaded them into the truck he'd backed into the driveway, and drove away. The 8:28 p.m. call from Joseph's phone "was a set-up, quick dial-up, hang it up, just to show it's Joseph trying to call him. Our interpretation is he's essentially trying to alibi himself out."

Although prosecutors didn't argue this at trial, Smith believes Merritt transported the bodies to the desert that night. "It doesn't make sense to me to keep the bodies in your truck or anywhere else. You'd want to get rid of them as quickly as possible, and he had ample time the night of the fourth."

Smith believes Merritt returned to check on the gravesite on February 6, "because there was a lot of rain and flooding. The heavy rains is why we have those tire impressions preserved for three years. If you look at the area of the graves, it's in a natural wash," a dry riverbed where it's soft, "so it's possible that some of it could get unearthed."

Asked about the SketchUp 3D modeling program that was in use on Joseph's computer the night of February 4, even after Merritt allegedly drove away, Smith said, "There was a printed check that was spooled to be printed to 'charles merritt,' at like eight o'clock. As far as SketchUp, I don't recall that striking us in any particular way."

For some observers, however, this unexplained discrepancy negates the prosecution's entire case against Merritt. If he killed Joseph and his family and drove away at 7:47 p.m., then who was at the computer, working on the design? And who did the internet searches in the early hours of February 8?

Over the next nine days, Smith said Merritt had plenty of time to do "an extensive cleanup" before meeting Michael McStay at the house.

"He did a good job. There was fresh paint put on the walls, based on McGyver's statement. I bet the futon cover was removed, and that's what was wrapped around Joseph, although we were never able to conclusively say that."

Smith also believes the killer staged the downstairs area. "If that person removed the futon cover, that person also staged the popcorn. For that to be a breakfast thing, that doesn't make any sense."

In the coming years, there was debate about whose truck was on the surveillance video. Virtually every person of interest in this case drove at least one white SUV or truck.

"We did what we could with video measurement, and even with the best [expert], you can only say it's consistent with Merritt's truck," Smith said. "All we can say is it's not the McStays leaving on their own free will," which for him "is one of the saddest parts" of this case. "If San Diego would have gotten more of that video, I think this would have been an open-and-shut case."

Yet, in spite of all the search warrants they served, the detectives never found any physical evidence tying Merritt to the murders at the McStays' home, at the gravesite, or in Merritt's truck. And despite their best efforts, they had no confession, either.

"It was going to be a difficult case," Britt Imes, a supervising deputy district attorney brought in to help Sean Daugherty, recalled thinking. "Is it likely or possible that [Merritt] had help? Sure."

However, Imes and Daugherty decided they didn't need to answer the *when, where,* or *how* questions in court. All they had to do was convince a jury that Chase Merritt was a bad guy who had stolen money from Joseph, then bludgeoned him, his wife, and their two little boys with a sledgehammer.

Chapter 33

Charles "Chase" Merritt was born on May 2, 1957, in Andrews, Texas, a middle child with five sisters and two brothers. His eighth sibling, a baby girl, died in her crib when she was nine months old.

Andrews was such a small town, "you blink and you've passed it," Merritt said. "The post office, the jail, and the city hall were all one building, no more than two hundred square feet combined."

His father worked as a welder in the oil fields, while his mother took care of the house and kids. The family moved to Hesperia in Southern California's High Desert region when Chase was nine months old. His parents split up about three years later.

As a single mother, Lillie Merritt waited tables at a diner, struggling to pay bills and raise eight children on her own. Her husband had moved to Fontana, disappeared from their lives, and later killed himself, leaving only the legend that he'd lost a leg while trying to jump a train.

Chase's brother Bennett, who was five years older, spent nearly twenty years in the criminal justice system after stealing a golf cart at age twelve. Convicted of grand theft twice in Santa Barbara County, Bennett was behind bars again three months after being released from prison in 1977, when he was arrested in Los Angeles as a suspect in the Hillside Strangler case, and held for forty-two days. That particular arrest, which was broadcast all over the media, was so traumatic it "devastated our family back then," Chase recalled. Three years later, Bennett served a couple more years in prison for receiving stolen property, but he finished high school and took community college classes while incarcerated, and never committed a violent crime.

In 1968, Chase's older sister Juanita made the news for being arrested for petty theft as a juvenile, and then nine months later for being arrested for the "sale of dangerous drugs" by a vice-narcotics detail during simultaneous raids in four desert cities. Juanita went on to become an actress and model in New York before returning to open a Denimite clothing store in Victorville, where Bennett worked after his release from Chino.

Chase had ambitions, too. After attending Apple Valley High School through the eleventh grade, he worked to pay his own way to the San Pasqual Academy, a Seventh-day Adventist boarding school in San Diego County. Merritt said he paid $32,000 for tuition, room, and board during his senior year, graduating in 1975. He wasn't religious, but he wanted to be challenged more.

"I wanted to graduate from a high school that was more accredited," he said. "I was struggling at Apple Valley because I was so bored."

After graduation, he returned to Hesperia, where he launched an iron-railing-manufacturing business called Chasro Ornamental Iron. But he soon followed in his brother's footsteps. Convicted of burglarizing a home in Apple Valley in 1977, he served sixty-six days in jail.

Merritt said he doesn't remember any details of the crime. "None whatsoever, only that I was convicted of it. I try to block out those parts of my life. They're obviously something I'm not proud of."

He said he remembered doing the sixty-six days, though, because his "soon-to-be-wife" came to visit him in jail. He and his now ex-wife Rolinda, whom he met during his junior year, were married for five years, but had no kids.

"It was a bad choice on my part. We were like oil and water," he said. "She was very religious."

Merritt also served sixty days in jail for petty theft in 1977, and a month for criminal trespass in 1978. Sentenced to two years in prison for two burglary charges in November 1978, he served only three months.

Merritt couldn't recall those details, either. "I have a very vague memory of my past transgressions," he said, but it wasn't due to drinking or drugs, because he only drank the occasional half-glass of beer. He said he'd "smoked a little marijuana," but could "count those times on one hand."

Merritt stayed out of trouble until 1987, when he was convicted of receiving stolen property in Contra Costa County.

"I do remember that," he said, explaining that he'd unknowingly bought some stolen equipment. "I ended up being convicted of it, because I did have possession of it, and I couldn't tell them the people I'd bought it from because I didn't know their name, and because of my record, it was just kind of a slam-dunk."

He spent some time in jail and eight months in prison before his release in September 1987, returning for four and a half more months for violating parole in 1988.

The following year, he started a steel sculpture fabrication business in Covina in Los Angeles County, where he was convicted of receiving stolen property again. After a couple weeks in jail, he got off with three years' probation.

In 2001, he admitted to stealing $32,000 in equipment from an iron works shop in Monrovia, which landed him in jail for six months for grand theft. This charge, Merritt said, resulted from a business partnership that went sour.

"When we parted ways, it was not amicable. I went and took

what I believed was everything that I was owed as far as the partnership goes, he ended up filing charges, and I couldn't prove that it was mine," he said. "I ended up not fighting it. I just pled guilty."

Merritt told the media his criminal history mostly occurred when he was a young man, but records show he was still in trouble with the law in his forties and fifties, though none of his crimes was violent. He repeatedly violated his probation and failed to show up in court, leading to probation extensions and more than seven arrest warrants related to his 2001 conviction. He was also cited several times for driving with a suspended license as far back as 1991, and twice more in 2011.

Merritt grew animated as he explained how he'd chocked up these citations, most of which, he said, were for speeding or failure to stop during the early hours, "prime time" for police on the lookout. However, his surprising but colorful explanation only covered the 1991 suspension, when he was thirty-four.

Back in his twenties, Merritt said he was "healthy" and in good shape, so he worked as a male stripper for the next fifteen or so years, "depending on whether I needed money or not."

"For years, I supplemented my income—and for a while it was my only income—I ran a stripping company" called Fantasy Strippers in Riverside, he said. "I danced, and I also had quite a few girls that did parties, so I'd be driving them to the parties, and I'd be bodyguarding them, [which] paid almost as much as stripping."

Because he was constantly "rushing from party to party," going "a hundred miles per hour down side streets" in his white Corvette, he lost his license, because he had "too many tickets, and I wasn't taking care of them. Even if I had taken care of them, I had way too many tickets, like ten in one year."

But as he got older, he had to give up that life, because his twentysomething customers wanted younger dancers. "I was the oldest stripper in the Los Angeles-Riverside-San Bernardino

County area," he said. "I think I still looked fine, I was just older."

Merritt's personal life wasn't typical, either. When he met Catherine "Cathy" Jarvis in 1993, he was thirty-six, and she was twenty-three. He'd recently started a new business selling his metal sculptures and wall hangings, but he'd been playing pool tournaments on the Southern California circuit since the early 1980s. They were winner-take-all, and he said he won three out of five, earning anywhere from $75 to $700 a night.

He was getting a feel for the tables before a tournament at In Cahoots, a country-western bar in Fullerton, when he accidentally hit Jarvis with his pool cue.

"She thought I was an asshole," he said, but he didn't even know he'd hit her.

Jarvis, who worked for a water utility company, was there by herself that night. As he watched her on the dance floor, he thought she was "exceptional," so he asked her to dance.

"We hit it off after that," he said.

They didn't win, but they talked for a while before he walked her to her car. After they started dating, he moved into her place within a couple of weeks, and she got pregnant "almost immediately."

"It's all history from there," he said.

But it wasn't that simple. They started arguing about money and unpaid rent, split up about six months into the pregnancy, and Jarvis asked him not to contact her. By the time their daughter, Sara "Taylor" Jarvis, was born in August 1994, Merritt had moved to Covina.

When Taylor was five, Merritt ran into them at a shopping center at lunchtime. After he and Cathy talked for a while, he took them to see his business. From there, Jarvis said, they started "communicating again, having dinner, going to the movies and stuff. . . . [Taylor] actually started calling him dad before I told her" Merritt was her father. He charmed his way into moving in with them soon afterward.

Taylor's sister Jaye was born in December 2000. Around this same time, Merritt was mountain biking in Big Bear and didn't feel right. He took himself to the hospital, where he learned he'd had a heart attack and was diagnosed with coronary heart disease. In January 2005, Merritt and Jarvis had a son, Alexander "Ray" Merritt, who, like Taylor, went by his middle name.

With three children together, Merritt often called Jarvis his "wife" in public, even though they never got married. "Neither one of us cared whether we were married or not," he said. "We were together, and we had kids. It was just kind of assumed that we were going to be staying together, taking care of the kids."

Jarvis said she started out wanting a conventional relationship and marriage with Merritt, but she came to realize that his money-management issues, which ultimately forced her to declare bankruptcy, would continue to cause her problems. So, she decided she didn't want to marry him even after he presented her with an engagement ring. "I knew that if I stayed with him, I'd never have a stable life," she said. "Life with him was just too chaotic."

Once they moved into a house, Merritt started building wall-hanging waterfalls in an enclosed porch and sold them at home and garden shows. As his business grew, he moved his operation into a shop. Jarvis initially took care of the finances, but stopped after they argued over how to handle customers and sales.

Historically, Merritt seemed to care more about his designs and creations than client relations and money, which caused conflicts with customers, landlords, and eventually with Jarvis.

Taylor Jarvis said she remembers moving a lot growing up, but as she admitted, she had only a child's view of her father's business affairs. "Sometimes we had money, sometimes we had less money. Sometimes we'd have to move because of his work."

Cathy Jarvis attributed the moves, which usually came with starting a new business, to Merritt's "money mismanagement." Badlands Steel, for example, which he operated in Brea and San Dimas, grew to employ about eight workers from 1998 to 2003, but ran into trouble with the state Economic Development De-partment. His other businesses included Chase Merritt Designs, Waterfalls by Chase, I Design, WBC Corporation, and IDesign4U.

Although Merritt wasn't a good money manager or people person, records show he did pay off some of his debts. An SDSD background check on February 17, 2010 showed he'd paid off more than $50,000 in tax liens, though he still had tens of thousands in liens, small claims, and civil judgments hanging over him.

Merritt and Jarvis contend his relationship with Joseph was different. They not only worked well together, they actually be-came close friends.

As Merritt did more work for EIP in 2007 and 2008, he moved his operation from Claremont to Pomona. When his fam-ily moved into a rental home in Rancho Cucamonga in 2009, Jarvis was hoping to buy it, so they could stay in one place and gain some stability. Merritt didn't spend that much time with her and the kids, which became a sticking point.

"My family is not super tight-knit," Taylor Jarvis said in 2022. "My dad worked a lot, because he was always running his own businesses."

Money also was an issue. "My dad would take the money he made and put it back into the business," Taylor recalled. "He al-ways had newer, bigger ideas for bigger waterfalls and better things. Instead of giving my mom money for the bills or what-ever, he'd get a new work truck, a new cell phone that he could use for work, or something like that."

Taylor said she didn't know how to reconcile her image of her "very disorganized" father with the reports from previous busi-ness partners and clients that he failed to complete projects, used their money for other purposes, or flat-out stole money or equipment.

"I don't know what his intentions ever were," she said. "He's just not good at keeping track of what he's doing. He's always

on to the next thing, and he's not good at sort of keeping his promises necessarily. I don't think he was ever good with [money]."

Although Merritt quit playing pool tournaments after reunit-
ing with Cathy Jarvis, he picked up a new side hustle in 2007:
competitive poker tournaments.

It all started when a guy who made a "pretty decent living" at
it told him, "You should learn how to do it." Merritt bought
some books, and studied the game for eight to ten months before
entering his first tournament.

He played until he lost, which meant he could be gone for
hours—or an entire day—at a time, which became another problem for Jarvis.

Merritt said players could double the sixty- or seventy-dollar
entry fee even if they came in tenth place, and make as much as
$24,000 if they ranked in the top three in a bigger tournament.
So he kept at it, claiming he "was getting into the money most
of the time."

But "all I really played was tournaments," he said. "I didn't
play cash games, because I didn't feel comfortable" risking bigger losses. "And that's where the prosecution got it all wrong.
Virtually every single time I went to the casino, you will note on
my bank records a specific charge" that could be used as a tax
write-off, "because I was doing it professionally."

His bank statements did show casino expenditures here and there
in 2009, but there were far more ATM withdrawals or purchases of
$100, $200, or $500, sometimes multiple times in one day.

While the prosecution accused him of using that cash to gamble, he claimed he often used it to buy building materials. "I
paid cash for virtually everything in my business at that time,"
he said.

Multiple transactions at a casino in the same day or week, he
said, were to re-up the entry fee for tournaments that ran several
days. But after initially claiming he mostly used his debit card

for those fees, he also admitted to using cash. According to Beastsofpoker.com, some tournaments allow players to "re-buy" a set of chips after losing the initial allotment.

Investigators used his bank records to track these transactions, determining that he had a gambling problem, because he made seventy-three ATM withdrawals at casinos throughout Southern California between February 2009 and February 2010.

An independent tally by this author identified eighty-four transactions at casinos on thirty-six days—with $8,239 in purchases and $10,532 in ATM withdrawals—from January through August 2009. Although he made no casino visits in September or October, he was overdrawn by $389 after racking up overdraft and returned-check fees and loans from Speedy Cash, resulting in the forced closure of his bank account on November 5, 2009.

"I was struggling," he conceded. The business with Joseph was going well, "but I was way overextended. My basic nut at home was $67,000-plus a month," including the slip fee and maintenance for his boat, rent on his workshop, payroll, and liability insurance.

He had no bank account until he opened a new one at Bank of America on February 3, 2010, with a $100 handwritten check from Joseph, and $100 more from cashing a $2,495 printed check from Joseph on February 2.

Pressed to detail his poker winnings, he estimated he made $8,000 to $10,000 in 2009, averaging fifteen to twenty dollars an hour, and "that's above and beyond any money I paid for the tournament itself." He acknowledged, however, that he couldn't prove this from behind bars, because he had no records of his winnings, which were paid in cash.

Cathy Jarvis testified that the time he spent away from home to play poker increased tensions in their relationship. However, she backed Merritt's claim that the family usually made purchases with cash.

"At that point, I'd already had a bankruptcy," she said. "We didn't have a lot of credit, so we paid cash for practically everything."

Jarvis also told investigators Merritt had signed at least twelve checks in her name without her authorization, prompting her to remove his name from a joint account. However, the judge precluded prosecutors from presenting that information to the jury.

After Merritt found the space at MSM in October 2009, he moved his family once again. Unable to purchase the rental house in San Dimas, they moved into the Homecoming apartment complex in Rancho Cucamonga, which had nice amenities, but wasn't *theirs*, as Jarvis had hoped.

The apartment had no Wi-Fi, so Merritt often walked to the nearby community room to watch movies and use the internet, printer, and fax machine. But the cell phone reception was terrible there, which resulted in dropped calls between him and Jarvis.

Joseph had dinner with Merritt's wife and children monthly. "They were more than business partners," Jarvis testified. She recalled one dinner in 2007, when "Joseph was being very open about being very nervous about having a second child with Summer."

In late January 2010, she said, they all had dinner at Charlie's restaurant in La Verne, where Joseph was "almost giddy" about the pending Saudi Arabia job. But he and Merritt were even more excited about a new client in London, where they talked about taking both families "and making a vacation out of it."

"This waterfall in London was supposed to be in the millions of dollars," she said, so Joseph was optimistic about what this could mean for the company and for his family.

These big jobs were important to Jarvis, too, after fighting with Merritt over their finances for so long.

"I felt we weren't putting enough money aside for savings,

for the future. Chase was more of the live-in-the-now sort of person. That got frustrating for me, trying to plan for my family and my children, going to school and everything. We moved a lot with Chase, and it was really difficult."

So, with these big jobs on the horizon, she started feeling more optimistic, too. "I kind of felt like maybe all this frustration was worth waiting for," she said, and once they had "enough established business, we might have a house and things might settle down."

Michael McStay said Joseph had helped out Merritt's family by giving money to Jarvis for groceries while Merritt was in jail, and had also given Merritt money to replace tools he claimed had been stolen.

Merritt claimed none of this was true, although Cathy Jarvis testified that Joseph did advance Merritt money sometimes, such as the $3,000 check he wrote in November 2008, with "For Chase SOS!" on the memo line, at a time when Merritt's rent was $2,500 a month.

But when Joseph disappeared, so did Merritt's income. Merritt and Jarvis were sued in civil court for nearly $11,000, including $7,500 in unpaid rent, resulting in a default judgment against the couple in April 2011. As these dominoes fell, the "marriage" died, and Jarvis left Merritt.

Merritt met Mechele Muir on the internet dating site Date Hookup.com sometime in 2012. They met in person at the Gator Bar, accompanied by Muir's best friend, Barbara Oglesby.

Muir, a divorcée with a daughter, was attracted to Merritt and let him move into her apartment soon after they met. She knew he had debts, but she wanted to give him a chance. Then she fell in love with him.

Merritt and Muir often hung out with Oglesby and her boyfriend, who lived in the same apartment complex. In 2013, Merritt mentioned the McStay case to Oglesby, saying he had nothing to do with the family's disappearance, but she had her doubts. He claimed he'd passed a polygraph, saying anyone could do it if they remained calm.

Detective Smith said Merritt's polygraph questions by the SDSD "were kind of soft. When you do polygraphs, you generally eliminate the person from the crime you're investigating. They didn't do that. There were better questions to be asked," such as "Were you involved in the McStay murder?"

"The reason they gave him a pass was because it didn't show 'glaring deceptive,' it was 'inconclusive deceptive,'" he said.

Oglesby told detectives she hadn't liked Merritt from the start, because she didn't trust him—with good reason. He told her he was going on a hiking field trip in the mountains with his son's class and was thinking of sandblasting the face of Jesus behind a waterfall in advance, so he could make some money by "discovering" it.

Oglesby said she stopped hanging out with Merritt and Muir after they moved. He didn't have a car of his own, so he'd borrow Muir's and leave at odd times of the night. This made Oglesby feel like he was using Muir, who had gotten "wrapped up in his life."

Chapter 34

Soon after his arrest, Merritt was in contact with one of LA's most respected criminal defense attorneys, Tony Brooklier, who had represented Heidi Fleiss, actor Jeff Conaway, drug kingpins, corrupt businessmen, and Brooklier's own father, the Sicilian-born Godfather of the LA Mafia's La Cosa Nostra, who died in prison.

After Merritt was deemed indigent, Brooklier considered taking Merritt's case pro bono, and asked Riverside defense attorney Rajan "Raj" Maline to join him as an advisory assistant.

Brooklier was at Merritt's arraignment on November 7, 2014, when he asked for a continuance "to determine whether counsel will be retained." His presence—and his business card, stapled to the court file—reignited the theory that drug cartels and underworld figures were involved in the McStay family's murder.

Brooklier "believed in my innocence," Merritt said, but because he was a one-man shop, he soon realized that taking on this massive, complicated case for free could bankrupt him.

In the end, that was for the best, because Brooklier took his own life two years later, still distraught after his son's suicide a year earlier.

Instead, Merritt hired Robert Ponce, who had defended him back in 1991 for driving with a suspended license.

After Merritt pleaded "not guilty" to four counts of first-degree murder, the case was assigned to Superior Court Judge Michael A. Smith, who had presided over the court's most complex homicide trials, including numerous death penalty cases, since he was elected to the bench in 1986.

Smith had announced his retirement in 2010, when his salary was nearly $179,000, but he was called back into duty due to a judge shortage, which was later exacerbated by the COVID-19 pandemic.

The son of a quality-control aviation inspector and a dress shop owner who also sold insurance, Smith grew up watching *Perry Mason* in Commerce and suburban Monterey Park. After graduating from the University of San Diego School of Law in 1974, he applied to DA's offices in San Bernardino, San Diego, Santa Barbara, and Ventura. San Bernardino was the first to offer him a job, so he took it.

He'd intended to spend only three years as a prosecutor before going into private practice, but he ended up staying for twelve. A judgeship wasn't in his sights, either, but the longer he was a prosecutor, the more of "a logical progression" it became. Smith ran for an open seat in 1986, and beat his opponent by two percentage points.

He enjoyed making rulings, rather than being subject to them, but there were trials, and then there were *trials*. Feeling the pressure to move things along, he often spent nights and weekends reviewing complicated motions for death penalty cases. After all, he'd earned his bachelor's in political science in only three years at California State University, Los Angeles, and clerked at two personal injury firms during law school.

But he had no idea how prolonged and acrimonious the McStay case would become.

Robert Ponce didn't last long as Merritt's attorney. Ponce was moving too slowly for Merritt, who fired him after only two months. Claiming he had six to eight months to live because of his heart condition, Merritt asked the court for permission to represent himself "pro per" in an expedited trial, contending he could handle it with a high school diploma and two years of college.

Describing the request as "historically unwise," Smith granted it pending a doctor's note that Merritt was physically capable. He appointed attorney David Call as "advisory counsel" and David Farrell as an investigator, at taxpayers' expense.

Ponce was ordered to turn over the 10,000 pages of discovery materials, which Merritt planned to keep in his cell while consulting books in the jail's law library. As the paperwork crowded his cell, Merritt soon realized the library books were missing pages.

On May 19, the day of his scheduled preliminary hearing, he came to court with attorney Jimmy Mettias, but said they had a few things to work out before deciding whether Mettias would represent him.

Mettias, who had been admitted to the bar five years earlier, had been suspended from practicing law until July 31 after knowingly making misrepresentations to two married clients. After that, he would be on probation for a year. So, he not only lacked a working law license, he also was not qualified to represent clients in death penalty cases on his own.

On May 22, Merritt announced he'd hired Mettias as part of a legal team with Jim Terrell, Sharon Brunner, and David Askander. Smith gave them just a few weeks to review discovery materials before the preliminary hearing on June 15.

"We'll be ready on the fifteenth," Terrell said confidently. "We've gotten evidence, we know what we're facing, and we're looking forward to it."

Investigator David Farrell stayed on to assist, and attorney Raj Maline helped behind the scenes. But death penalty cases routinely take years, not weeks, to prepare, a deficiency that became apparent at the prelim.

"I quickly realized that they were in big trouble, based on what they had promised Chase," Maline said.

Chapter 35

On the morning of the preliminary hearing, Michael McStay led his mother by the hand through the crowded hallway to their front-row seats in the courtroom, where they hoped to attain justice for their loved ones.

Journalists from all over Southern California, including this author, filed into the crowded jury box, eager to hear how and why the McStay family had vanished so mysteriously more than five years ago.

Dressed in a long-sleeved gray shirt and tie, Chase Merritt was at the defense table, surrounded by his new legal team, while Britt Imes and Sean Daugherty sat at the prosecution table with Detective Edward Bachman.

When Bachman took the stand, aspects of his testimony, like his warrant affidavits and case summary, didn't match evidence presented later at trial. He even misstated Joey Jr.'s age. But the defense made few objections and did no cross-examination of the eight investigators, who presented the bare minimum of evidence to support the prosecution's case.

The detectives described how the family's skeletal remains were discovered in the desert, outlining the brutal physical injuries in straight, but shocking, detail. This was the first time it was revealed that the family had been repeatedly bludgeoned with a sledgehammer.

Bachman testified that four-year-old Gianni was hit in the head "at least seven times," and the injuries were "pre-mortem," which means the victim was alive. That differed from the pathologist's testimony at trial that Gianni was hit at least six times and the injuries were actually "perimortem," meaning either slightly before or after death. Whatever the case, this horrific image was so unthinkable, it wasn't mentioned in news stories the following day.

The rest of the hearing was filled with a mind-numbing series of numbers: dates and times of cell phone calls and bank checks, made out to Merritt in lowercase letters, allegedly for the first time since Joseph had started using QuickBooks.

Other detectives, whose testimony was also peppered by misstatements, apologies, and corrections, stated that signatures on six of those checks didn't match Joseph's. Merritt cashed or deposited four of them from February 2 through February 9, 2010, hand-delivering the other two to MSM.

No witness presented the total sum Merritt cashed or deposited—and prosecutors declined to answer questions until after the trial—but the amount came to $20,000.

"Did you show him the checks that were created on February fifth and backdated to February fourth?" Daugherty asked Detective Hanke.

"Yes, I did."

"Did he tell you he wrote those checks?"

"I don't believe he said he—I believe he said Joseph wrote the checks."

"Did he deny backdating any of those checks?"

"He did not deny. He did not offer any explanations."

Nor, Hanke said, did Merritt explain why his phone was off, out of range, or in airplane mode for several windows of time between February 4 and 9. Asked why his phone was in the Victorville area on February 6, he said Merritt "told me he was not in the High Desert on that day."

Prosecutors worked in the gambling angle as well, saying Merritt withdrew $3,500 from ATMs at casinos from February 9 to March 12.

Furthermore, investigators said the seventy-three-inch wheel diameter on Merritt's truck was consistent with one of two sets of tire tracks at the gravesite, where it had been raining heavily enough on February 6 to leave an impression.

Bachman testified Merritt was a "match" for DNA found on the steering wheel of the Trooper, which he claimed he'd never driven, and that Merritt was a "trace contributor" to the gearshift, though the lab report actually called him a "possible trace contributor."

Although Merritt told detectives he'd left voicemail messages for Joseph, they said they didn't find a single one from Merritt on Joseph's phone. They also quoted his statement to CNN that "I was definitely the last person [Joseph] saw."

After five hours of testimony by prosecution witnesses, the defense argued that the state hadn't met its burden, and moved for a dismissal.

"Your Honor, we, obviously, have been listening to this testimony all day long, and the important fact is that there hasn't been anything, not one shred of evidence, that has pointed to Mr. Merritt having committed these murders," Mettias said. "We didn't hear that he was in the Fallbrook area any time when these people went missing, or any DNA evidence that has linked Mr. Merritt to these crimes."

Daugherty countered that the defendant "lied about his last experiences with the victim on February fourth," and the checks he supposedly collected from Joseph that day weren't even created until he did so himself the next day. Noting that Merritt's DNA was found in the McStays' vehicle, he said, "to say there's no DNA is flabbergasting."

To a neutral observer, the evidence against Merritt sounded damning due to the sheer volume of numbers presented that day.

But even if Merritt liked to gamble his money away, was $20,000 truly enough motive for a career thief with no history of violence to smash the heads of his best friend's entire family with a sledgehammer?

It was enough for Judge Smith to bind Merritt over for trial, saying the evidence "creates a strong inference, and definitely supports, at a minimum, a probable cause determination that the defendant was a participant in the homicide."

Outside the courthouse, reporters lined up their mics to hear from Joseph's family.

"I was impressed, really impressed, with what they put together," Michael McStay told them. "The healing process started when they found the bodies." After grieving their loss, he was "ready for some closure today," and now "I feel like I can move forward. I just needed to know they had the right person." But "there's more to be shown."

He said it was difficult to watch Merritt being "so nonchalant" and "smug," but hearing the prosecution's evidence today "was enough" that he didn't feel he needed to attend the entire trial. He wasn't opposed to the death penalty, but for anyone who killed two children like this, they could use a lethal injection with "a rusty needle for all I care."

Susan Blake, who appeared emotionally overwhelmed, said it had been a "really hard day" for her. "It's just a lot to take in."

Stepping up to the mics next, Merritt's attorneys shrugged off the judge's ruling, saying they hadn't begun to fight.

"We didn't [put up] a defense today because we believe we can rebut all this at trial," Jimmy Mettias said. "The burden of proof for the DA is very low."

"You only heard one side of the story so far," Jim Terrell said. "We believe our client is innocent. They have a crime scene they don't want to talk about."

As for the check-writing evidence against his client, "there is a reason for that," he said. "There is nothing nefarious. At best, they put on an embezzlement case today. We're here for a murder case."

"Are you admitting embezzlement?" a reporter asked.

"No, no, no," Terrell said. "We don't have one piece of evidence from the FBI."

Some court-watchers deemed Merritt a sociopath, child killer, and liar. But with two sets of tire tracks, others wondered if there was more to this story, and if someone else, or even a drug cartel, was involved. The defense told the media they'd seen similar executions by the Mexican Los Zetas crime syndicate, using sledgehammers. If Merritt was stealing money for himself, why would he pay one of Joseph's vendors with forged checks?

Champing at the bit, the DA's office filed notice two weeks later that it would seek the death penalty if Merritt was convicted.

Jimmy Mettias attempted to downplay the announcement as if it was no surprise. "This is a serious crime, and the people responsible for these heinous acts should be held accountable," he said. "This, however, underscores why it is imperative everyone withhold judgment until the evidence is presented. Mr. Merritt is innocent, and the evidence will eventually prove that."

Realizing, once again, that his attorneys weren't up to the task, Merritt wanted to fire Mettias and retain Raj Maline. But Maline wasn't death-penalty-qualified either, so he couldn't do it alone.

Merritt waited until January 2016 to fire his defense team, dodging another bullet by terminating Mettias, whose law license was suspended again in 2017 after another complaint was filed, with more than seven counts of misconduct. Found guilty of "grossly negligently misappropriating" $110,711 owed to a client, he lost his license for good a year later.

In February 2016, Merritt asked Judge Smith if he could represent himself again. Smith agreed.

Meanwhile, Maline was still waiting in the wings. After graduating from the University of La Verne College of Law in 1997,
he'd worked three years with the Riverside County Public Defender's Office before opening his own practice.

Maline approached James McGee, a local lawyer he respected, to see if he wanted to team up. McGee, who had started
a solo practice in October 2014, was death penalty qualified after
working as a prosecutor in San Bernardino County for twelve
years. McGee agreed, and they officially became Merritt's new
defense team in March. They also formed a law firm together,
Maline & McGee.

But now that Merritt was on his third set of attorneys, Judge
Smith said he wouldn't grant any more requests to change
lawyers, because Merritt had blown through six of them in the
past sixteen months.

"You're both on notice that you're kind of on for the duration
at this point," Smith cautioned—for all the good that would do.

Rather than collect fees from a state fund that pays attorneys
to represent indigent defendants facing death sentences, McGee
and Maline made an unusual arrangement with their new client.

They each agreed to forego $500,000 in payment in exchange
for acquiring the rights to his story for a book and TV/film documentary in what Maline called a "media rights exploitation
contract."

According to Merritt, it was originally drafted to give 60 percent of any proceeds to the attorneys and 40 percent to him, and
was subsequently amended to an even split of 25 percent between Merritt, Maline, McGee, and Robert Wallace, who was
hired to write a book and serve as their "media liaison."

Jacob Guerard, a law student who had worked for McGee
since 2015, assisted on the case, but wasn't part of the deal. The
defense also brought on Gary Robertson, a retired homicide
sergeant formerly with the San Bernardino Police Department,
and Suzanne Sederly as investigators.

After Wallace introduced Merritt's legal team to a production group that wanted to create a ninety-minute documentary through the defense's lens, the producers formed TSG Documentary LLC, short for *Two Shallow Graves* (TSG), and began shooting interviews with the attorneys, Merritt, his partner, and their daughter. Prosecutors, the McStay family, and law enforcement refused to cooperate, because it was a defense-based project.

Taxpayers still had to cover the cost of hiring expert witnesses, because Merritt was indigent. Like the Casey Anthony murder case in Florida, this one was solely based on circumstantial evidence, so Maline anticipated needing a lot of them.

However, their names and payment requests were filed under seal, so prosecutors couldn't figure out the defense's case or witnesses until they had to be disclosed closer to trial. Afterward, Maline estimated the total bill for defense experts and investigators approached one million dollars, if not more.

Allegations of misconduct began to fly back and forth almost immediately, setting the tone for the rest of the proceedings.

On March 8, Merritt's former investigator, David Farrell, called prosecutor Sean Daugherty about a piece of white fabric he'd found near the gravesite five months earlier.

Saying their "conversation never happened," Farrell said he disliked the defense's "involvement with media, and movie and book deals," because he believed "no one was in it for the right reasons."

Although the transcript of the subsequent motion hearing was sealed, the minutes state that Smith said the defense could test the fabric before turning it over to the prosecution, amid "further discussion" of the defense's "accusations of misconduct and unethical behavior on the part of the prosecution."

Chapter 36

The defense team knew right away that this wasn't just a case of a family murdered. It was, as McGee put it, "a case where somebody wanted this family to disappear."

By obtaining aerial photos of the gravesite, dated February 12, 2010, they got a bird's-eye view of the tire tracks. A weather check showed it had rained 1.1 inches there on February 6, and 0.03 inches on February 7. But for the tires to make such deep and lasting impressions, they figured the ground had to firm up a bit, meaning the tracks were probably made closer to the date of the photos than to February 6, when the prosecution said Merritt's phone had pinged a cell tower near there.

As the defense delved into the discovery materials, they saw Dan Kavanaugh as a more likely suspect, a shady character with a similar, if not greater, financial motive to kill the McStays. And unlike their client, Kavanaugh's criminal record involved violence and drugs. In addition to his two domestic violence convictions, court records show that he also admitted to having an alcohol problem, requiring him to attend classes as part of his probation.

His first offense occurred at 2:44 a.m. in August 2011, when police were called to an apartment near Crown Point because a neighbor heard a woman screaming. Lauren Forest-Knowles, the girlfriend who had provided Kavanaugh's alibi for the murders, cried as she told police he'd "pulled her out of the car and onto the ground," scraping her knees. She subsequently obtained a restraining order against him.

By pleading guilty to one battery charge and admitting he "did unlawfully use force against my ex-girlfriend," Kavanaugh got off with three years' probation, which he violated for non-compliance and a second domestic-violence arrest two years later.

Another girlfriend obtained a restraining order against Kavanaugh after an incident in July 2013, when police responded to a similar 911 call, prompted by screams from a woman's apartment. When officers arrived, Kavanaugh ran to the balcony, where they found "scratch marks on his neck and chest and a scrape to the right side of his face."

The victim told authorities she'd moved there "to get away from the defendant after an earlier incident. She said he found her and started appearing at her door. She started dating him again. She said it was easier to date him than try to leave." They were arguing after a night of partying in Pacific Beach, when he "grabbed her by the wrists and dragged her from the elevator, through the hall, to her apartment." When she yelled for help, he covered her mouth and pinned her down on the bed, but she broke free and ran to the kitchen, where she "grabbed a knife and fork. She pointed the knife at the defendant, but he grabbed it away from her."

Kavanaugh told police she was having "a bad trip," which made her "rowdy and physically violent" and punch him in the face. He admitted to consuming alcohol, but denied taking drugs, insisting he was just "trying to make sure she was safe." Police arrested him and took him to jail.

Asked by email to be interviewed for this book, Kavanaugh initially agreed to "chat" by phone, but then balked at not getting paid for what he considered a commercial endeavor. Told this was his chance to give his side of the story and defend himself against the claims made against him in this case, he wrote, "good luck with all that but i'm not interested . . . i can tell it's a waste of my time." All in lowercase letters.

In character-reference letters that Kavanaugh's defense attorney rallied his family, friends, and former clients to write, his mother, Tamara Lyn Terry, described him—one of four sons she'd raised as a single mother—in glowing terms, stating, he "hasn't got a mean bone in his body." Terry said she lived in Texas, and because Kavanaugh's father wasn't around when he was growing up, her father, John A. Pugsley, helped raise him. Pugsley, a *New York Times* bestselling author, had lived in Carlsbad in San Diego County sometime before he died in April 2011.

Nonetheless, Kavanaugh's probation was revoked in January 2014, and he was sent to jail for several months.

But as Merritt's attorneys learned, Kavanaugh not only attacked his girlfriends. He was accused of threatening men, too, and not just Joseph McStay.

On November 23, 2013, eight days after the authorities announced the family's remains had been found in the High Desert, Kavanaugh allegedly threatened another male client, Roger Martinez.

He and Martinez had made a barter deal: Kavanaugh would design a website for Martinez's aquarium business in exchange for an aquarium. Kavanaugh apparently held up his end, but didn't answer his phone for a week, which prevented Martinez from gathering the necessary specs to complete the project. When Kavanaugh did pick up, Martinez said he sounded "extremely angry and possibly on drugs," and showed up at Martinez's shop five minutes later.

Martinez was so upset by what happened next, he reported the incident to his neighbor, a San Diego County sheriff's deputy, who filed a report that was eventually turned over to the

SBCSD: Kavanaugh "looked high and was sweating profusely. He said he had not slept in several days." He told Martinez "he had been done dirty" and knew "how to make people disappear, and if anything happens again, they will find [Martinez's] bones in the desert," like the other people who had gone against him in business deals.

But more to the point, Kavanaugh had apparently bragged about killing the McStays to other people, as well.

On November 15, 2013, a tip came to the SBCSD through multiple sources, including "Mark," who posted a comment on a KCBS-TV story in Los Angeles with the headline, "The McStay Murders: Who Could Be Responsible for Such a Heinous Crime?": "It was Dan kavanaugh [sic], he has been bragging for years around San Diego how he killed that family. Look at the evidence too. Can't believe the police missed it."

Detective Smith reviewed this tip, as well as one that came in to Crime Stoppers, on August 13, 2014, which referred to conflated reports of evidence from an internet search by an unknown user that had yet to be released publicly: Kavanaugh "conducted the internet searches on the McStay computer and lured Joseph and his family away the night they disappeared, killing them and burying their bodies. The tipster claims to have reported this information in February of 2010 and that the tipster's ex-girlfriend reported the same."

Smith's report, dated August 14, 2014, simply acknowledges reviewing these tips, stating, "Dan Kavanaugh has been interviewed multiple times" by the SDSD and SBCSD, even though Kavanaugh wasn't interviewed by San Bernardino detectives for another month.

Merritt's attorneys believed the motive for murdering Joseph McStay had a strong financial basis, so they subpoenaed records detectives never tried to obtain, comparing them with those investigators had in hand.

Elluma Discovery, a forensic computer analysis firm, was hired to evaluate what was going on in the McStay family's lives at the time they disappeared. Bryan La Rock took "forensic images" of digital files and browser activity logs from the approximately thirty computers and other devices collected during the investigation, and cross-checked them with emails, bank statements, phone records, sheriff's investigative reports, and witness interviews.

As La Rock tracked Kavanaugh's location by his internet and phone use, he found a text Kavanaugh sent to Joseph on the morning of January 5, 2010, asking if he could leave his BMW, which had been Joseph's, at the Fallbrook house:

Is there any way I can park the beemer at ur crib while I'm gone?

In March 2017, the defense obtained Kavanaugh's PayPal log-in and transaction records, which showed he was using an IP address in Hawaii when he logged in January 14, 2010. However, after a twelve-day hiatus, he logged in on January 26 to establish three "merchant-initiated payments relationships" from an IP address in San Diego. He conducted thirty different transactions from that same IP address until February 17, the day he claimed to have returned from Hawaii. He didn't meet face-to-face with SDSD detectives until February 22.

Noting Joseph's multiple calls to Merritt after their lunch on February 4, La Rock cross-checked Joseph's computer records with his 4:18 p.m. call to Merritt from his "home tower" in Fallbrook. Joseph made that call eight minutes after he opened Google SketchUp, and the related Google 3D Warehouse, on his desktop eMachine.

This series of events supported Merritt's claim that the two men were collaborating on a design, which they wouldn't be doing if Joseph had just fired Merritt for embezzling money. La Rock found this also fit with a pre-established pattern of teamwork behavior, where Joseph would do something on his computer, then contact Merritt to discuss it.

On the night of January 31, for example, Joseph used Sketch-Up for forty minutes to design a water feature project labeled "fred," in lowercase letters, which referenced Merritt. Joseph called Merritt in the middle of the session, at 8:47 p.m., then texted him a photo at 9:56 p.m.

Similarly, Joseph's eMachine was used to log into his Quick-Books custom account at 7:56 p.m. on February 4 and create a $4,000 check to "charles merritt," which was then sent to an "alignment page" at 7:59 p.m. to go to Joseph's Epson printer. La Rock found this transaction in a print spool file the sheriff's computer analyst said he couldn't read because it was garbled. La Rock said the check was never actually printed, so it was apparently a test.

La Rock said Joseph's subsequent call to Merritt at 8:28 p.m., while the SketchUp program was still in use, also fit a related pattern of calling Merritt right after writing him a check via QuickBooks, as he'd done on February 1. Joseph called Merritt that day a few minutes after adding "charles merritt" as a vendor in lowercase letters on his eMachine.

So, if Merritt was driving away from the house at 7:47 p.m. after killing the family, then who was working with the Sketch-Up program, creating a check, sending it to the print alignment page at 7:59, and calling Merritt at 8:28?

The defense hired forensic accountant Dennis Shogren's team to do a similar analysis using financial records to determine earnings and losses related to Joseph's business, and custom jobs in particular. Shogren was also asked to compare the financial ups and downs for Kavanaugh and Merritt before and after the family went missing.

Based on the documents, Shogren believed it was in Joseph's and Merritt's best interests to maintain a working relationship, because they made good money together. Their custom jobs brought in $330,376 in 2007, of which Merritt was paid the bulk, $204,667. That income rose to $342,099 in 2008, when

Merritt earned an even higher percentage. After adjusting the payment split in 2009, Merritt still earned $158,000.

After Joseph disappeared, Merritt lost his business, while Kavanaugh fared much better financially. In January 2010, Kavanaugh's bank account was overdrawn by $40. Then, on February 2—while Joseph was still alive and handling all sales and bill collection for EIP—Kavanaugh sent a $12,750 invoice to Geis Construction for two waterfalls, asking for half upfront by credit card to his personal PayPal account, which was linked to his personal Gmail address.

The defense argued in a pre-trial motion that the Geis invoice "could be construed as circumstantial evidence that Mr. Kavanaugh expected the McStay family to not be around to object in the near future to these inappropriate transaction[s]," and also supported "the notion that Mr. Kavanaugh had previous knowledge of their future murder and was involved in the planning or execution of their murders."

In March, when Kavanaugh was still working with Michael McStay and Susan Blake, he received a $16,839 wire transfer for the Saudi job. That same month, he sent Heather McFadden $1,000 for Elijah's support, paid $10,000 to MSM, and sent $800 to Adagio Water Feature. Yet he still ran out of money, after making repeated charges at the Hard Rock Café and racking up overdraft fees. By April, he was overdrawn by $1,247, prompting closure of his account.

Once Kavanaugh had successfully sidelined Merritt from the business, he opened the new EIP account at Bank of America with a $3,600 deposit in June, spending only $2,100 on waterfall-related business that month.

In the months that followed, Shogren said Kavanaugh's profit margin was much higher than Joseph's, and he also spent far more of his business income on personal expenses. His bank statements, which were part of the court record, show numerous line items, for hundreds of dollars each, at bars and nightclubs in San Diego's downtown Gaslamp Quarter, including Hooters,

Voyeur, Fluxx, Zanzibar Café, Whiskey Girl, and Hard Rock Café. In August, for example, he deposited $12,199 from EIP clients, but after numerous charges to Guitar Center, his favorite sushi restaurant, and several other bars—and transferring $8,000 to his personal account—his business account had a balance of only $126.

Shogren calculated that by year's end, Kavanaugh had raked in more than $206,000 in business income, only $58,677 of which went to produce waterfalls. Shogren couldn't evaluate earnings in 2011, because he didn't have those records.

The defense also approached this case from a DNA angle, hiring forensic analyst Suzanna Ryan to collect samples from items pulled from the gravesite with the hope of identifying other suspects.

In March 2018, Ryan sent ten samples she collected to the Bode Cellmark lab in Virginia, now known as Bode Technology Group, four of which "showed DNA at some level." However, before sending the samples to Bode, the defense team allegedly made a decision to "forego the CODIS upload" referring to the database that contains DNA from convicted criminals nationwide, and didn't agree or ask to have the test results run automatically through such "comparative databases."

Because the DNA levels were still below Bode's threshold for detection, Ryan subsequently sent Bode's raw digital data to Cybergenetics in Pittsburgh to interpret with its proprietary "probabilistic genotyping" technology, known as TrueAllele.

Cybergenetics interprets DNA data that's deemed "inconclusive" by other labs, when the levels are too low or too mixed with others to be detected by traditional tests. By separating these DNA mixtures into genotypes, this technology can determine "how strongly evidence matches a person or even other evidence" in an "automated and objective" fashion and produce partial profiles.

San Bernardino County's CODIS administrator ultimately

claimed this early decision by the defense to "forego the CODIS upload" effectively precluded her from running through the national database the partial profiles that Cybergenetics produced months later.

But Maline characterized this as "another example of the prosecution twisting nonsense." He said the defense didn't answer that question on the standard form either way, because it "doesn't pertain to non-law enforcement submissions. We can't ask them to do that; we're not a law enforcement agency. The defense does not have access to CODIS."

The vast majority of clients using TrueAllele technology are prosecutors, including the Kern County DA's office, which has been presenting this evidence since 2013. Cybergenetics helped identify the remains of victims after the 9/11 disaster in 2001, and the FBI approved its technology for use with CODIS in 2006.

Chapter 37

Based on promising data from Bode, the defense met with prosecutors and Judge Smith in chambers on July 13, 2018, revealing that the preliminary DNA findings showed several genetic markers, two males and a female, had been found on items in or next to the gravesite—none of which matched Chase Merritt or the McStay family.

The defense asked prosecutors to drop the case against Merritt based on this and other exculpatory evidence, or at least take the death penalty off the table. But prosecutors wouldn't budge. Like their ambitious boss, Michael Ramos, who by this time was in a political hot mess, they had dug their heels into this high-profile case.

"They just laughed at us," Maline recalled. "They were going to make their mark, stake their place in history, no matter what."

Elected in 2002, Ramos didn't like letting go of a case, even when he was losing it. In the Colonies corruption case, which ultimately brought him down, Ramos spent nine years pursuing convictions against a developer and three former San Bernardino officials.

The Colonies trial in 2017, which was also before Judge Smith, resulted in three acquittals and a hung jury for the fourth defendant, former assistant assessor Jim Erwin, whom Maline represented. Erwin's charges were subsequently dismissed. Developer Jeff Burum, one of the acquitted, subsequently sued Ramos and the county for falsifying evidence and malicious prosecution in federal court.

Not long after the Colonies trial began, Ramos pulled out of the state attorney general's race to run for re-election as DA in 2018. After the local newspaper endorsed him in the primary, law professor Lara Bazelon blasted him in an op-ed for his "win-at-all-costs" mentality, saying his victims included "the wrongfully accused, the wrongfully convicted, and the survivors of crime and their families who are revictimized when the real perpetrator goes free. They deserve the truth, they deserve a fair process, and when a mistake has been made, they deserve a remedy." Four days later, Ramos lost his bid for DA to one of his former prosecutors, who won 52 percent of the vote after raising twice as much in campaign funds.

In March 2020, a federal judge ruled Ramos had acted "in bad faith" when he destroyed "evidence of his nefarious conduct"—by deleting text messages and emails—after the Colonies jury began deliberating.

The county ultimately settled two lawsuits filed by Burum and his Colonies Partners group for $69 million in November 2020. However, the county's insurance company refused to pay the settlement, claiming it "arose out of the willful or intentional acts" of Ramos and his prosecutors.

Supervising Deputy District Attorney Britt Imes was hired by the San Bernardino County DA's office in 1998 after graduating from McGeorge School of Law in Sacramento. He worked juvenile prosecutions and led the gang unit for several years at a time when the county had the nation's third highest number of gang members. Many of his convictions came out of the county's biggest gang case ever, in which sixty-one members and associates of East Side Victoria entered pre-trial guilty pleas for crimes ranging from drug and gun sales to robbery, burglary, assault, conspiracy, funneling money to the Mexican mafia, and murder.

Imes joined the Merritt case after Sean Daugherty developed scheduling issues amid delays caused by the defendant's attorney-switching antics. Daugherty came to the DA's office in 2001, right out of Western State College of Law. He was promoted to supervising deputy district attorney in March 2017.

Melissa Rodriguez, an ambitious junior prosecutor, asked to join the team sometime after the preliminary hearing in 2015. She'd been with the DA's office since 2007, after two years with the city attorney's office in San Diego, where she attended California Western School of Law while raising three sons.

The three of them split duties according to their specialty areas: Rodriguez's husband used QuickBooks in his business, so she took on that aspect of the case, as well as Merritt's spending, gambling, and criminal background. Daugherty, who has a bachelor's degree in biology, focused on the DNA and scientific issues. Imes picked up the computer and cell phone components, saying, "Let's go to town. I call it dumb luck, and I'm glad we had it because it worked out very well."

Daugherty and Rodriguez declined to be interviewed for this book.

In October 2018, James McGee and Raj Maline dissolved their firm and returned to practicing solo. Jacob Guerard went with McGee, but they all continued to work the case together, anticipating proceeds from the documentary deal.

After Maline's experience with the Colonies case, he and McGee believed the DA's office had wrongly targeted their client, as well. They set their sights on a third-party culpability defense, focusing on Dan Kavanaugh as the more likely killer. Such a defense, however, requires the judge's approval before trial.

But before the defense could submit a formal request, the prosecution filed a preemptive motion, based on discovery materials and the defense's witness list, on November 14, 2018. Among the witnesses they asked to preclude were those who had been revealed in discovery materials, including Matthew Schneider, Joaquin Quintero, Michael McFadden, Dan Kavanaugh, Tina and Tracey Riccobene, and any witnesses "related to the arrest of multiple persons for the sale of marijuana and any other narcotics," or "to the recovery of Joseph McStay's gun."

"Evidence that another person has mere motive or opportunity to commit the crime, without more, will not suffice to raise a reasonable doubt about a defendant's guilt: there must be direct or circumstantial evidence linking the third person to the actual perpetration of the crime," the prosecution argued.

"The discovery provided by the defense serves merely to confuse and convolute the issues related to the murders of the McStay family. Many of the acts and people the defense will allude to as having potentially been involved in the murders are based upon speculation and innuendo. Furthermore, the majority of the evidence presented by defense counsel post-dates the commission of the crimes by years."

The defense countered with a number of points they wanted to present, including the alleged threat against Roger Martinez, arguing, "Here, Daniel Kavanaugh recited specific facts which described the nature of this crime, and the manner in which the McStay family was killed and buried."

They also argued the jury should hear that Kavanaugh had Googled the Fifth Amendment privilege against self-incrimination on November 29, 2013: "Why would someone be concerned with asserting this privilege unless they thought it was a very real possibility they might be implicated in this crime?"

But Judge Smith said no to both, also throwing out Kavanaugh's threatening messages to Joseph in January 2009, and anything about Kavanaugh's character or criminal record.

After the defense argued Kavanaugh was "withdrawing or accessing funds from the McStay business accounts impermissibly," Smith ruled they could discuss money transfers to Kavanaugh and the general financial workings of EIP after Joseph disappeared. "If there is evidence that Mr. Kavanaugh was doing that as well, seems to me that that is admissible, and I would permit that."

The defense tried to get Joseph's banking and business records thrown out, claiming that only he could validate the prosecution's analysis of them, but Smith said no to that, as well.

They also tried, unsuccessfully, to throw out Merritt's cell phone records due to what they alleged was an erroneous and overreaching search warrant, based on a lack of probable cause. They cited Kavanaugh's remark to San Diego probation officers about "the business partner who lived in Victorville owed Joseph $30,000," which showed up in the warrant as a $30,000 *gambling* debt, saying "there is no statement anywhere in discovery" to support that claim.

Chapter 38

With the trial fast approaching, a young woman named Tracey Riccobene burst onto the case with a groundbreaking confession to authorities, only it wasn't her own. She contended her best friend of ten years, Dan Kavanaugh, had hinted around, then finally confessed two weeks earlier, that he'd killed the McStay family.

Worried that Kavanaugh would retaliate, Riccobene said she was too scared to come forward initially, but her mother, Tina, called the FBI and said Tracey had information about the case. When law enforcement officers showed up at Riccobene's apartment in San Diego, she sent them away, saying she needed more time.

Jury selection had already begun when they met with Riccobene on October 30, 2018. As she sat in a SDPD police interrogation room, she answered questions from investigators who took turns for the defense and the prosecution, while the attorneys from both sides watched from outside the room.

"We're just really glad you're here, Tracey," the first investigator said. "We want you to tell the truth in reference to this information, okay?"

"Well, I think you guys have the wrong man," she said.

"And that's what we're here to talk to you about. Did you

ever hear Dan mention the name of the individual in custody, Charles Merritt?"

"Not until two weeks ago when he told me how he framed him."

Tracey said the questions grew more combative from there. "How do you know Dan? Are you making this up just to get attention?"

"I would not make this up," she replied.

"They didn't take me seriously," she said later. "Dan was [the prosecution's] witness, they'd validated him, and to admit they'd all been manipulated six weeks before trial, it was way too late. I just stood up and said, 'This is ridiculous.' They were attacking me the whole time."

It seemed to her that Raj Maline, who met later with Tracey and her mother, didn't take her seriously, either.

"They didn't want me to testify," Tracey said. "What can I do? The truth is still the truth, either way."

Riccobene said she met Kavanaugh in the summer of 2010, when she was a twenty-year-old student at San Diego City College. After he invited her to be his web-design intern rather than transfer to San Diego State University, she helped him design websites. Riccobene said she also drove Kavanaugh to the court-ordered classes after his domestic-violence conviction in 2011.

While Riccobene was working with Kavanaugh, she claimed he sexually harassed her. After complaining to a female executive in 2017, Riccobene submitted a formal complaint to the state Department of Fair Employment and Housing, contending she was harassed, retaliated against, and "forced into early termination." Although she was issued "right to sue" letters in 2017 and 2018, she never filed a lawsuit. She did, however, apply for a restraining order against Kavanaugh in December 2017.

Kavanaugh "repeatedly [sic] shows up at my home 5+ times after I asked him not to. Serious threats to me and my livelihood, defamation of my character and carrer [sic] and gross

mistreatment. Daniel is a repeat DV offender and murder suspect," she wrote in her application, which was denied for insufficient information after neither of them showed up for the
hearing.

Several months before Riccobene came forward in the
McStay case, she said, Kavanaugh showed up again, and this
time, he went into detail about how he raped Summer and then
killed the McStays with two Mexican men he'd hired. Her statement to a defense investigator didn't mention anyone helping
him, nor were they alluded to in court papers or at trial.

"Tracey stated that Kavanaugh told her how he took one of
the small children hostage at knifepoint, corralled the family
into their vehicle, and then ordered them to drive towards the
high desert," a defense motion stated. "Tracey then described
how Kavanaugh raped Summer McStay at knifepoint before
killing her."

In November 2018, Larry Haynes, whose place in Hawaii
Kavanaugh claimed to have stayed with his girlfriend in 2010,
talked to the prosecution's investigator, Jesse Moon. Haynes
said he'd never met Lauren Forest-Knowles, didn't recognize
her photo, and said she'd never been to his house. He also said
that his dogs were still alive when Kavanaugh last stayed with
him, and they died in 2009. Asked at trial whether Haynes had
dogs at the time of their visit, Forest-Knowles said no.

However, prosecutors didn't notify Merritt's attorneys of this
interview until after the first of two hearings on the third-party
culpability defense in late November 2018.

In light of the new potentially exculpatory information by
Haynes and Riccobene, the defense asked the judge to recon-
sider his previous rejection of the third-party culpability defense, focusing on Kavanaugh.

"The fact that the evidence surrounding the discovery of the
bodies links with the story Kavanaugh gave on how they could

have disappeared is clear circumstantial evidence that he knew of and was involved in the McStay family's disappearance," the defense argued.

"Based on Inv[estigator] Moon's recently provided reports, it is clear the version of events Lauren has provided to law enforcement over the years regarding Kavanaugh's alibi is now more suspect than ever," the motion stated. "We see that there is at least a strong likelihood that Lauren is attempting to cover up Kavanaugh's whereabouts by giving him an alibi."

The defense argued the reconsideration motion before Smith on December 19, a day after alerting the prosecution of all the evidence they were going to lay out, including their DNA profiles from the gravesite.

The judge denied the overall motion, but he did allow a narrow band of evidence, which the defense pushed at every chance over the next five months, amid constant objections that were only occasionally overruled.

Despite objections by prosecutor Melissa Rodriguez that Riccobene had "severe credibility issues," Smith ruled she could testify about Kavanaugh's alleged confession. He also threw out the prosecution's claim that Merritt sold his tools to MSM owner David "Joe" Sequeida, then reported them as stolen to Azusa police.

However, that still fell far short of the defense's hopes. Kavanaugh "not only stole money, he had the party of the century in 2010," Maline said recently. He bought champagne for his friends at nightclubs and bought himself DJ equipment, as EIP went upside down, but "we couldn't get in any of this stuff [at trial]."

The day after the hearing, then-Sergeant Ryan Smith showed up at Chase Merritt's sister's property at 7:30 p.m. with a team of investigators and a warrant to collect DNA from Chase's brother Bennett.

They said they believed Bennett had assisted Chase in killing and burying the McStay family, because DNA had been found in the desert gravesite, and they were going to match it to Bennett's.

Bennett started to feel unwell, so the investigators said they would come back to question him. Chase's sister Juanita, who had her own history of health problems, didn't feel well, either, and she drove them both to a nearby emergency room, where she was treated and Bennett was admitted.

Sergeant Smith had already interviewed Bennett, Juanita, and her longtime boyfriend in 2014, following up on Merritt's claim that his phone would only have pinged in the desert if he was visiting one of them.

At that time, Smith asked Juanita when she'd last seen Chase. She replied, "In five years I haven't seen him. He works 24/7."

James McGill, Juanita's boyfriend, told Smith he didn't believe Merritt had come to see them around the time of the McStays' disappearance, and that Juanita also hadn't picked up Chase in San Diego or near the Mexican border.

"I'm not crazy about her brother," he said. "I don't even like the guy. I just try to smile and pretend."

In 2014, Bennett told Smith that he didn't even hear about the McStay family's disappearance until a British reporter came to his gate after the bodies were discovered. He said he couldn't imagine who would kill a family with young children.

"You've got to have a twisted mind is all I can say," he said. As he'd already told another detective by phone, they were "barking up the wrong tree" by suspecting Chase, because he "would never do something like that."

Bennett said he'd never met the McStays, didn't know what happened to them, and hadn't picked up Chase or Cathy Jarvis from San Diego or near the border. He didn't even have a driver's license.

With DNA samples from Chase and Bennett Merritt now in hand, Detective Smith decided to have the sledgehammer re-tested for DNA right before trial, since technology had improved since 2013.

This time, the samples were sent to a private out-of-state lab, DNA Solutions in Oklahoma City. When the results came back on January 11, 2019, however, the outcome was the same: "no quantifiable amount of DNA was detected" on the sledgehammer, so they had nothing to compare to the Merritt brothers' DNA.

Because the warrant for Bennett's DNA was filed under seal, the source that gave investigators probable cause was hidden from the defense. With opening statements fast approaching, the defense filed a motion to unseal it so they could prepare to cross-examine that person.

"It appears the People have changed tactics and now believe Charles Merritt's brother Bennett was somehow complicit in the McStay murders, given the discovery of unique DNA by the defense," the defense argued.

The prosecution fought the motion, alleging in bold italicized print that it was "*based on self-aggrandized speculation*," and refused to reveal their source publicly.

"The defense would like to have this court believe that an investigation ends upon the filing of criminal charges," Britt Imes wrote. "They also would like this court to speculate that they have some truly exculpatory evidence upon which their motion and defense is based and was the instigator of any further investigation of this case. *Both are far from the truth*."

Before Judge Smith could act, however, the defense withdrew its motion after prosecutors conceded the information came from a confidential informant who wasn't going to testify.

Still, many had speculated—including attorneys on both sides—that the killer may have had accomplices, which would have made it easier to separate Joseph, Summer, and the boys, and to drive and bury them in the desert. Investigators clearly saw Bennett Merritt as a natural choice.

In addition to his nonviolent record, Bennett had gotten caught up in a homicide case before, forty-one years earlier. Bennett told the story to the Victorville *Daily Press* in 1978 after this painful historic chapter of criminal injustice was over, fore-shadowing what his younger brother would claim in his own murder case:

Fresh out of prison and still on parole, the incident began after Bennett drove his mother's Cadillac to LA for a swap meet with his cousin, and rented a motel room in Hollywood. While he was cruising the strip to buy beer, he said, a sex worker got into his car and propositioned him.

After he declined, she got out. But the car stalled, and by the time he got it running again, she'd gotten a good look at his car, which was gray with a white top.

In the past month, ten young women, ranging from twelve to twenty-eight years old, had been found dead in the Hollywood Boulevard area—naked, strangled, and most of them raped. The first victim was a twenty-year-old sex worker who was a friend of the woman who got into Bennett's car. Witnesses told police that they saw the tenth victim "being taken" by two men in a big dark car with a light-colored top, which police thought sounded like Bennett's car.

When the woman who propositioned Bennett was arrested a week later, she learned there was $115,000 in reward money in the Hillside Strangler case. She accused Bennett of raping and robbing her after police showed her a composite drawing of the Strangler, which resembled Bennett.

After Los Angeles police drove to Victorville to arrest Bennett at his sister Juanita's store, they found women's clothing in the family's Cadillac. Although Juanita said the clothing was hers and that she had asked Bennett to take it to the dry cleaners, he was charged with robbery, and the sex worker was released.

Although Bennett's accuser eventually confessed by phone that he hadn't harmed her, police couldn't find her to confirm that in court. In the meantime, Bennett's name was all over the TV news as the prime suspect in the Strangler case, while he was held on $20,000 bail for forty-two days in two different jails.

Nicknamed "Strangler," he was subjected to lineups, interrogations, and solitary confinement. He also feared being poisoned by a guard who said, "Your dinner will have something in it tonight," because he knew what Bennett had done. As a result, Bennett lost fifteen pounds.

Although police concluded within days that he wasn't connected to the slayings, it took nearly two weeks for the robbery charge to be dismissed, and even longer for Bennett to fight the parole violation that came from being arrested. After a hearing where Bennett said the authorities tried to "manufacture a case" against him, the violation was dismissed, and he was free to go.

Because San Bernardino County spans 1,730 square miles of mountains and desert, the attorneys debated what areas should be excluded from the jury pool so jurors didn't have to drive three hours round trip every day to carry out their civic duty.

Although the High Desert could be an hour's drive to court each way, the prosecution pushed to include that region, because the McStay family's remains were unearthed there.

Early on, the attorneys estimated the trial would last "close to three months" and, as the judge put it, "a lot shorter" if Merritt was found not guilty. As the trial grew closer, the estimate grew to four months, which was important in terms of availability due to planned vacations or summer jobs. But no one foresaw the trial dragging on longer than that.

Chapter 39

On January 7, 2019, the courtroom was packed, and the air was electric with anticipation for the long-awaited opening statements.

Joseph's and Summer's family and friends sat on the left side of the gallery. Merritt's people were on the right, behind the defense table. Reporters grabbed seats where they could, in what prosecutors described as a "circus atmosphere."

Before the openings started, the attorneys debated whether the proceedings should be videotaped and livestreamed by the Law&Crime network. Judge Smith, who is no relation to the prosecution's investigating officer, then-Sergeant Ryan Smith, agreed to let the cameras roll over the objections from the prosecution, who seemed primarily concerned about the TSG documentary. Their argument that coverage should be limited so it didn't "become so pervasive as to deprive a defendant of due process" came back to haunt them, when the cameras captured their team smirking, talking, laughing, and texting.

After the jury of eight women, four men, and six alternates, was seated, prosecutor Sean Daugherty delivered seventy minutes of inflammatory rhetoric, with the first of many references to an emotionally powerful image that couldn't be argued or forgotten—the monster who had hammered two little boys to death.

"How does this family of four disappear off of the face of the earth?" Daugherty asked, promising to explain "not only the how, but the why, and especially the who" of this case.

He introduced the McStay family, first with photos of them alive and smiling, then as brutally graphic collections of bones and fragments, with circular holes in their skulls. He noted four-year-old Gianni, and Joey Jr., who had just turned three, were "beaten about the head and face until they died," then were driven to and buried in the desert, where their remains were ripped apart and scattered by creatures until they were just "a set of a few bones."

"The why boils down to greed, and greed's child, fraud," he said. "The who is sitting here in court today, Charles Merritt," a man who claimed to be Joseph's best friend and yet didn't call authorities to report him missing.

Instead, he forged checks, "putting his hands in the cookie jar, [then] desperately tried to cover his tracks after the murders. He misled investigators, he talked in circles, and he played the victim for almost four years."

Daugherty detailed items pulled from the graves, the stains on the sweatpants that looked like bleach, and remnants of bath towels, which seemed to come from the house. And, of course, the sledgehammer.

He also recited a mishmash of financial transactions, check amounts, cell phone calls, times, and locations, as he outlined a complicated, but incriminating, timeline of Merritt's activities, which the defense would spend the next five months trying to disprove. It was an overwhelming volume of numbers to process, but perhaps that was the strategy, because it sure sounded bad, as if the prosecution had done its homework.

Daugherty laid out how Merritt had fraudulently collected money from Joseph by printing, then backdating and deleting, checks using Joseph's QuickBooks program, noting many involved a laptop computer that investigators didn't find at the Fallbrook house.

Because Daugherty didn't disclose that investigators never found the laptop Joseph used for many financial transactions, the inference was that Merritt had done them. After all, Merritt's name was entered into the QuickBooks Custom account for the first time using lowercase letters on February 1, an hour before he received Joseph's email about the $42,845 he owed.

The next day, Daugherty said, Joseph gave Merritt a handwritten check for $100, which he used to open a bank account on February 3. But Merritt also deposited $100 from a printed check for $2,495 from Joseph's account that had been created, printed, and deleted on QuickBooks the day before. And so on.

Daugherty also described the long periods of inactivity on Merritt's phone, which he said was purposely turned off or put into airplane mode so it couldn't connect with any towers, sending calls to voicemail as Merritt carried out the murder and subsequent cover-up. The hypocrisy of his ATM withdrawals at casinos across Southern California while telling detectives he didn't have enough money for rent. And so forth.

But most important, Daugherty said, as he showed the jury a photo of the mountaintop Quartzite cell tower overlooking the gravesite, were Merritt's calls that pinged in the desert between 10:46 a.m. and 1:30 p.m. on February 6, two days after the murders.

Daugherty glossed over the SDSD's failures and mistakes, Susan Blake's kitchen cleanup, the computer that Michael McStay believed he had permission to take, and the video of the truck leaving the McStays, which the SDSD thought was the family's Isuzu Trooper.

"They were given a certain set of facts, and those facts boxed them in," Daugherty simply said.

The prosecutor also played up the small amount of Merritt's

DNA that investigators found in the Trooper, saying the chance of finding it randomly was "one in eight hundred and fifty million."

Although he hinted that Merritt may have had an accomplice, he said prosecutors were going to ask the jury to "hold him accountable" for the murders.

The defense used equally inflammatory language in their two-part statement—as James McGee countered the prosecution's characterization of the evidence and Raj Maline detailed the defense's version of events.

McGee offered benign, rational explanations for many of Merritt's actions and statements, accusing the prosecution of attacking Merritt's character and refusing to consider evidence that pointed to his innocence. Portraying Merritt as wrongly accused, he said the prosecution's entire case was based on confirmation bias.

"That's when you decide what conclusion you want and look for facts that support it, and that's what this whole investigation is," McGee said. "We want Chase Merritt, so let's just twist our necks, do gymnastics with logic, and figure out how do we build a case against him."

Rather than admit "such severe head trauma" would "leave large pools [of blood] everywhere in the house," investigators first said it wasn't a crime scene, because they couldn't find "a trace, not a speck" of it. Then, later, detectives conveniently said the opposite, that "it had to happen there because that's our theory."

Because the dogs were outside and the family appeared to have been eating breakfast, McGee said it seemed more likely that the family was still alive until the morning of February 5. "They were not killed in that house on the fourth."

If Merritt left his apartment as soon as his cell phone pinged in Rancho Cucamonga at 5:48 p.m. on February 4, he still had to drive through sluggish commuter traffic to arrive at the Mc-

Stays' house before the Mitchley video started at seven o'clock. A trip that would normally take an hour and twenty-three minutes at that hour, give or take, he said, would have had to take less than one hour and twelve minutes "*in the rain*."

McGee listed the inconsistencies between the truck in the video and Merritt's actual truck, such as the location of taillights, parking lights, headlights, and tailpipes. "If it's not his truck in the video," which left the house at 7:47 p.m., he said, "then there is zero evidence that he drove down there on the fourth."

But if he did kill the family there that night and bury them in the desert two days later, as the prosecution alleged, then why didn't investigators or the cadaver dogs find any trace of them at the house?

"For you to believe their story, their theory of the case, the family was killed in the house with no trace [of blood]. Nothing."

Alternatively, if Merritt kept the bodies in his truck for two days, why didn't any of his neighbors at the apartment complex complain about the smell?

"We know blood spatter would be all over the assailant from crushing those heads with the sledgehammer," McGee said. "Blood would drip out of the back of the truck when you are driving around for two days."

Detectives didn't properly photograph or document the location of each item found outside the graves, he said, so the defense had to obtain aerial shots of the tire tracks from the county Department of Public Works.

Based on these photos, McGee suggested multiple murderers were working in "two teams that are far enough apart so they don't hit each other. They are working at the same time. It's not Chase by himself, then the theory is gone. But confirmation bias. Let's ignore that fact."

Because Joseph was wrapped and tied up, with a vehicle key in his pocket, McGee suggested he was killed elsewhere. The fact that Summer and the boys' remains weren't wrapped, her jaw was broken, her bra was cut in half, and her pants and underwear were above her head, indicated "she was raped at knifepoint. That means there are two murder weapons at the scene."

McGee said he'd been asking the prosecution for over a year, but they still "refuse to see if this [vehicle] key works" in the Trooper. If it did, then "how did the truck get anywhere unless Joseph drove it there? What are they hiding? Why aren't they looking?" (A week after McGee's statement, the detectives did determine this was a working key to the Trooper.)

Then McGee dropped the first bombshell: the defense had discovered several DNA profiles on items from the gravesite, which had yet to be linked to specific people, but did exclude Chase Merritt and the McStay family.

"That's correct. Nobody knows this but us. So, apparently, Chase killed this family, buried them and put someone else's DNA on everything and not his own," he said, pausing dramatically and lowering his voice for emphasis. "And we are still going to trial."

McGee saved Merritt's potentially damning cell phone activity for last, alleging that the prosecution's expert, FBI agent Kevin Boles, "has no technical training" or engineering education in cell tower systems "or how they actually work."

According to maps and pie-graph analysis Boles created, McGee said, Merritt "was able to dig graves, rape Summer, kill Summer and the two boys, bury their bodies, and clean up so he doesn't have any blood in his truck and get back into Victorville," all within twenty-two minutes on February 6.

However, the defense's cell phone expert, Vlad Jovanovic, would dispute that. His substantive thirty-nine-page report showed Merritt's phone had long delays before connecting with various AT&T towers, whose poor performance issues were known within the industry at that time.

"It's reaching, because it can't find what it's supposed to do," or what tower to connect to, he said. "You will find all during that time on the sixth [of February], that's what Chase's phone was doing. You don't know where it was. Clearly, the cell phone wasn't at the graves."

Raj Maline followed up by underscoring the "huge missteps" by investigators, starting with the bumbling SDSD.

"You don't allow family access to the home, you seal it," he said. "You don't allow family members to take property out of the house, you seal it."

Instead, the SDSD allowed this, insisting it was a missing persons case, which caused many investigative opportunities to be lost. They also treated the McStays' neighbor with surveillance footage "with kid gloves," rather than forcing the issue by obtaining a search warrant. So, all they got was a one-hour snippet of video from a camera that shot the McStay house diagonally from across the street.

Those detectives, he said, failed to secure footage of the Trooper entering the San Ysidro mall parking lot as well, even though the surrounding restaurants, gyms, and stores all had cameras.

"How is that possible?"

Later in the case, he said, SBCSD detectives compounded these blunders by failing to apply common sense, by using outdated techniques to gather and test evidence for DNA, and locking in "on what they thought was their smoking gun"—Merritt's calls on February 6.

Echoing McGee's claims of confirmation bias, he said detectives failed to look at Dan Kavanaugh as a suspect, even though he, too, "was broke," and his bank account overdrawn by forty dollars, in December 2009. They ignored that he started transferring money from Joseph's PayPal account, which he'd never done before, "swiping" $7,900 before the family had even been reported missing.

"The only way he'd do that is if he knew Joseph wasn't coming back," Maline said, noting that Kavanaugh told Detective DuGal that he was "seeking investors" for EIP, only to sell the business the very next day.

"It wasn't his to sell. It never was," he said, though he collected $20,000, plus 20 percent of net profits for a year, and cancelled a $100,000 debt in the process. "What was the debt, you ask? We don't know, because San Diego never asked."

After Joseph bought Kavanaugh out of EIP for $30,000, Maline said, he knew he had to keep "Hacker Dan" out of his online QuickBooks account. So, he and Merritt agreed to switch over to the desktop version, QuickBooks Pro, and to delete checks from the online custom account "to hide the activity" from Kavanaugh.

When detectives interviewed Kavanaugh twice in February 2010, he only showed them his online reservation for a flight departing San Diego on January 7, returning from Hawaii on February 17. He didn't show them a used boarding pass, let alone a used ticket or manifest showing when he actually sat on the plane.

"What did San Diego do to check out whether he was actually in Hawaii or not during that period in February? Right. Nothing. They accepted his word."

Later, when the SBCSD did check it out, he said, the detectives wrote "in a sworn affidavit" that Kavanaugh didn't leave for Hawaii until February 6. And Kavanaugh's landlord in Hawaii told them he hadn't seen Kavanaugh since 2009.

"So where is this alibi going now? Remember, blinders are on, and no one is asking questions. Nobody."

Maline went on to drop their other bombshell: Tracey Riccobene, the woman who called Dan Kavanaugh her best friend, said he'd confessed to killing the McStay family, information she'd relayed to the FBI, prosecution, and defense in San Diego in October 2018. After hinting around, Kavanaugh described to her in detail how he'd forced the family out of the house by holding one of the boys at knifepoint. He took them to the desert, where he raped Summer, "because he wanted revenge for the alienation of the custom [fountain] business." Then he killed the family, burying the sledgehammer with their bodies. Afterward, he went back to their house for some time, possibly overnight, and "lived a life of pretending to be Joseph."

"She's terrified of him," Maline said. "He has no empathy for others, and that's how he's capable of killing babies."

Although Riccobene had asked prosecutors "to give her some type of witness protection," she was denied. "What follow-up do you think they did?" Maline asked rhetorically. "Right. Nothing. They didn't believe her. Even though she was able to tell facts to all of us, as you will see, that were not known to the public."

Reinforcing the gravity of the defense's groundbreaking DNA profiles from the gravesite, Maline said, "Those are the killers."

Chapter 40

The prosecution's case lasted for nine weeks, with twenty-eight days of testimony by thirty-five witnesses, many of whom were recalled by the defense.

As the first witness, Susan Blake's memory was even foggier nine years after the fact, but her feelings were clear: Merritt had stolen from her and killed her son's family.

After writing $5,000 in checks to Merritt to finish the pending fountain jobs, she said, she expected to be reimbursed.

"It was agreed that I would, you know, receive my funds back, especially from some of the bigger fountains. Money would come in, but I never saw any," she said, even after the Saudi Arabia job, for which she heard Merritt got paid something like $17,000.

Prompted by prosecutor Melissa Rodriguez, Susan testified Joseph had told her, "Chase had a gambling problem, and he had paid him some money to get him out of a scramble or debts or whatever." On cross, Susan said the total loan amount was $20,000 for "things that were not business-related."

But overall, her testimony varied, depending on which side was asking the questions. She often answered "correct" to confirm whatever point the prosecution was trying to make, such as her initial testimony that the walls of Joseph's house looked freshly painted. On cross-examination by the defense, however, she contradicted her previous testimony, saying the walls looked prepped for painting.

"So, certainly the house didn't smell freshly painted?" Maline asked.

"Uh-huh," she said.

By bringing out these conflicting statements, Maline illustrated that her perceptions seemed based more on emotional memory than actual facts. And like her son's subsequent testimony, her answers in court and previous statements to detectives were cited later by Merritt and his attorneys as being manipulated to fit the prosecution's narrative.

"So, when Chase asked for money, did you know what he was asking for?" Maline asked.

"He was asking for money to complete some fountains, but received money also prior to that, and [was] asking for more money."

"But you didn't know which jobs he received that money for, did you?"

"I didn't know," she said.

Shown a $3,300 check she'd written to Merritt in April 2010 that bounced, she said she didn't remember that happening, nor did she review any of Joseph's bank or PayPal statements. After Michael opened the Chase Bank account for EIP, she said she was only involved in the business for seven weeks tops, "so I only saw the checkbook."

"To your knowledge, there was no money coming in, at least you didn't learn of any coming in?" Maline asked.

"Correct, yeah," she said, she never monitored if clients were sending money to the PayPal account, or knew if Kavanaugh had "full access" to it, because she'd stopped speaking to both of them.

"Did you ever wonder what was happening with all of that money?" Maline asked. Multiple objections.

"I was just trying to help. My mind wasn't all into the circumstances," she said.

"Are you aware that that money, that seventeen thousand dollars [for the Saudi Arabia job] went into Dan Kavanaugh's personal account?" More objections. "You were left to believe all these years it was Chase that got the seventeen thousand dollars?"

Susan finally admitted she didn't know where that money went. She also confirmed that Joseph was trying to get rid of Kavanaugh and add a couple of other welders besides Merritt.

Britt Imes called Michael McStay to paint a picture of his relationship with his brother, the events before and after his missing persons report, and his brief efforts to keep EIP going.

Asked if he recalled telling Deputy Tingley that Merritt had hacked into Joseph's email and PayPal account, Michael paused, then said, "I must have if it's in the document, sir."

As Imes went over the timeline of Michael's trips to Joseph's house, he skipped over the portion of Tingley's report that quoted Michael saying that he drove by on February 4 or 6, fast-forwarding to Michael's trip there with Merritt on February 13.

"The defendant told you he didn't want to go into that house because he had a prior record?" Imes asked. Objection. Overruled.

"Um, he had some trouble with the law, and he didn't want to go in," Michael said.

This exchange led McGee to complain to Judge Smith during the break that Imes, "in flagrant disregard for any due process rights," had brought out Merritt's criminal history, and "character evidence to attack his credibility."

Imes retorted that the defense had opened the door during Maline's opening statement, saying Merritt "had a felony warrant."

If the defense was "lodging a formal accusation of prosecutorial misconduct, I'm entitled to a hearing," he said. "A false allegation of misconduct is a maliciously false allegation, subject to discipline by the state bar." He would repeat this statement throughout the trial as the attorneys flung accusations of impropriety at each other on an almost daily basis during sidebars and hearings outside the jury's presence.

"I don't think it's misconduct," Smith said, agreeing that the defense never moved to exclude Merritt's criminal history.

Maline said it was actually McGee who referred to Merritt's record in his opening, but the bigger issue was that Imes used the police report to elicit a purely speculative statement from Michael. The defense didn't object to it so as not to look to the jury "as if we are hiding."

Back in session, Maline got Michael to confirm that he had, in fact, driven past Joseph's house on February 4 or 6. Asked why, Michael said the family or "someone had been talking about not being able to get ahold of them."

Maline asked what prompted him to do this several days before his father asked him to go on February 9, when he refused.

"I'm not sure, to be honest," Michael said, but he thought "it was in the daytime, and I might have been in my work truck." This left the inference it could have been Michael's white truck on the Mitchley video.

Reminding him that he'd previously testified that he'd never been to the house before Merritt took him there February 13, Maline asked how he knew where to go.

"I don't remember the dates, but I know it was the week before," Michael said. "I'm not sure how I knew the address. Maybe my brother told me or something. I'm not really sure what I meant that I had been there or been inside. I don't recall going there, honestly."

"Yet you remember that my client is standing twenty feet away from you in the backyard?"

"Yes, sir."

Maline showed him DuGal's report, which quoted Michael as saying that Merritt had, in fact, come into the house, contrary to his earlier testimony.

"You did let Chase in, right?"

"I remember opening the slider. If he went in or not, I don't recall. I don't believe he did, but if that report says—I'm not really sure."

Troy DuGal, who had since become a cold case detective for the SDSD, testified for parts of three days.

As Sean Daugherty walked him through his investigation, DuGal described his partner's call with Merritt to set up the interview in Rancho Cucamonga.

"Did he say it would be an hour and twenty-three minutes [from Fallbrook], give or take some time, or did he say that it would take an hour?"

"Exactly an hour."

DuGal said he'd caught maybe five hours of sleep between the evening of February 15 and his interview with Merritt on the 17th, because he and his team were busy with other cases, including a nationally publicized missing persons case that turned into a double-homicide involving two San Diego–area teenagers, Chelsea King and Amber Dubois.

"That pretty much took everybody away from me," he said.

If so, it wasn't for long. Chelsea didn't go missing until February 25. Then, a few days after her body was discovered on March 2, sexual predator John Gardner also admitted to killing Amber. Detectives spent six weeks trying to find independent evidence to make their case, and when they failed, Gardner made a plea deal sparing him the death penalty.

After DuGal detailed all the items in the McStay house that Susan Blake either cleaned up or moved, Daugherty zoomed in on a photo of the dining room table.

Asked if he'd seen blood spatter in other cases, DuGal said yes, but he couldn't say that's what was pictured in the photo.

"It's a horrible moment where I don't know what it is. I did not see it with my naked eyes when I was in the residence at all. And now that the district attorney zoomed it in, it puts a pit in my stomach, but I can't say it's blood, I can't say it isn't blood."

"Can you say that in your experience as a homicide detective, at least it was consistent with blood?"

"It could be blood," DuGal said. But "several of us sat at this table, and that was not seen."

On cross, Maline asked DuGal if he'd questioned Kavanaugh about the transfers made from Joseph's PayPal account to his own, which started only a few days after the family was last seen.

"I'm sure I did," DuGal said.

"What did you ask?"

"If he had a legal right to be involved in the business finances," DuGal replied.

"And what did Dan Kavanaugh tell you?"

"Yes, he had access," he said.

"So, Dan Kavanaugh told you that he could go into Joseph's PayPal account and transfer money?"

"I don't think he told me those exact words, but he said he had access to the business financial records," DuGal said, adding that Merritt said he had access, too.

DuGal confirmed Kavanaugh had emailed him a purported summary of PayPal transactions. However, he acknowledged he didn't compare them with the actual PayPal records, question their legality, or investigate the accuracy of Kavanaugh's claims by asking to see his banking records, because he didn't want to interfere with the family's efforts to keep EIP operations going. By the same token, he didn't try to obtain Merritt's banking information, either.

"Without Joseph's words, it was just what it was on face

value," DuGal said, reiterating that he couldn't get search warrants to dig any deeper. "All I had was Earth Inspired Products and Joseph. I had no probable cause to reach out and start to look at any other citizen in America."

Still, Maline's questions made it sound like DuGal had essentially thrown up his hands and looked the other way.

"Did you ask Mr. Kavanaugh if he had a right to transfer EIP's PayPal account [to himself]?" Maline asked.

"Both business partners said they had a legal right. They were running the business, they were continuing to manufacture and distribute water features, and there would be money flow occurring, and the family members were trying to take over the business to make sure the business didn't fail," he said. "Although I, for sure, was suspicious of the money flow, there was no way to prove, without Joseph's words, the money flow was illegal."

As Maline tried to press DuGal harder on Kavanaugh, the prosecution repeatedly objected, citing pre-trial rulings on the third-party culpability defense. Judge Smith sustained most of them.

For example, Maline was unable to ask DuGal about his queries about John Pugsley, whose credit card kept Joseph's QuickBooks account active through 2011, maintaining Kavanaugh's access to the EIP records he needed to sell the business.

"I want to critique his investigation of this, because he never bothered to look to see this was Dan Kavanaugh's grandfather," Maline said in a sidebar.

"You're not going to ask him those kinds of questions until there is competent evidence that that's the fact," Smith said.

However, Maline was able to ask DuGal about the information that Patrick McStay had forwarded to him, which DuGal characterized as "beliefs," not facts.

"Oh, I used it," he said. "I would follow up on it, and in every instance, it was disproved."

Maline turned that around by asking if Patrick had tipped him to the advertised sale of EIP, and suggested he look into it—which Patrick, in fact, did. But DuGal didn't have to answer. Objection. Sustained.

DuGal claimed he had no animosity toward Patrick, alleging that the private investigator he'd hired was only interested in grabbing media attention, because none of his leads proved legitimate. But, in fact, DuGal was confused; he was referring to Susan Blake's investigator.

Back on redirect, DuGal complained to Daugherty that he was experiencing "Monday-morning quarterbacking" with so many defense questions about why he didn't do a homicide investigation when he had no proof the family had been murdered.

Britt Imes questioned forensic tech Denys Williams next, asking her to discuss her reaction a week earlier, when prosecutors had showed her the same photo of the dining room table.

"When I saw it, I was horrified," she said.

"Why?"

"Because I thought it was something I missed. I know I didn't see it that day."

Based on her experience with the color and pattern of blood stains and spatter, she said, "It looked to me like it very well could be blood, and it would have been something that would have been very good to know then instead of last week." However, she couldn't say definitively what it was, either, because she'd never swabbed or tested the table.

For the next couple of weeks, prosecutors presented witnesses who were involved in the discovery, excavation, and forensic examination of the family's remains. During graphic testimony that was difficult to stomach, the jury viewed photos of the gravesites, tire tracks, and investigators retrieving bones and other evidence.

Photos of the human remains and mud-caked clothing, laid out on paper sheets, were displayed as the pathologist conveyed disturbing details about the victims' fractures and shattered skulls. Perhaps the most horrifying—and unforgettable—was the picture of Joseph's skull in a yellow body bag, still largely intact, with his jaws open in what looked like a silent scream.

On January 29, the prosecution called Elva Fonseca, who worked as Merritt's administrative assistant in Pomona for eight months in 2007.

She started by answering phones and managing his calendar, then moved into bookkeeping and "quality control." Her testimony indicated, tellingly, that Merritt used QuickBooks for his business, illustrating his pre-existing familiarity with the program.

She said Joseph routinely bought pumps for the EIP projects, at least one of which Merritt used for another client's waterfall. He also told Joseph he'd finished a job when he hadn't so he could make payroll at a time he was also behind on rent.

"Did you ever have an opportunity to tell Joseph McStay that the defendant was doing that?" Rodriguez asked.

"Yes," Fonseca said, she'd told Joseph about both situations, but all he did was step up to help Merritt pay his employees.

Detective Joseph Steers took the stand to talk about his visits to the former McStay home to collect paint chips in August 2014. The new occupants had replaced the downstairs linoleum and removed carpeting, but hadn't repainted the kitchen.

Steers acknowledged he'd returned to the house to look for signs of a crime the SDSD had missed. But of the several stains he found and tested, none was positive for blood.

On cross, James McGee underscored the SBCSD's determination to stick with the theory that the murders had been committed in the house.

"Is there anything in that house that you found, you have read, or you have seen, that tells you those murders happened in the Fallbrook house?"

"In totality, I do believe they occurred in the house," Steers said.

"That's not my question, sir," McGee said. "I didn't ask what you believe. I said, 'Did you see any evidence that shows you the crime happened in that house?'"

"No."

"But you believe it did."

"Yes."

"Without evidence," McGee said. Objection. Sustained. "Isn't it true that if you can't find evidence that makes that murder happen in the house, you can't prove a case against my client?"

"You can save those [points] for your closing argument, Mr. McGee," Judge Smith said.

After the jury was excused in the afternoon, the attorneys dove into another round of bickering about misrepresentations and discovery violations by the other side, pleading with the judge to restore order.

McGee asked Smith to admonish prosecutor Britt Imes, contending that he would seek sanctions for Imes's negative comments, "because his unprofessionalism has been the highest I have ever seen."

"And I would do the same," Imes retorted.

By this point, the judge's typically calm demeanor seemed to reach a breaking point. "The unprofessional conduct, I think, is equal on both sides," he said. "The level of speaking objections, the level of arguments with objections, the disrespect to the court in the arguments on both sides, is at least unparalleled in my thirty-three years. I am trying to exercise patience and not starting to cite counsel for misconduct in front of the jury, but my patience is wearing thin."

* * *

The prosecution called Carmen Garcia to ask about the signatures on the two checks Merritt brought to Metro Sheet Metal on February 8, which she said looked "odd or different."

Garcia conceded that although Merritt was a friendly guy, "later, I did become quite uncomfortable around him, yes." But she said it was Dan Kavanaugh, Michael McStay, and Joseph McStay who had payment-related disputes with her boss, with whom Merritt continued to have a working relationship until 2011.

On cross, Maline tried to blow holes in the prosecution's timeline that gave Merritt enough time to drop the Trooper at the San Ysidro mall and still make it back for his phone to ping his "home tower" with a 1:54 p.m. call that Monday.

When Maline asked Garcia to pinpoint when she spoke with Merritt at MSM as they chatted about "not being able to get in touch with Joseph," Garcia initially said she couldn't be sure. She thought it was nine or ten o'clock, and finally settled on "mid-morning." She also confirmed Joseph started submitting mostly typewritten, rather than handwritten, checks in December 2009.

After McGee wrote, "Carmen Garcia saw Chase at Metro mid-morning" on the display calendar for the jury, prosecutor Melissa Rodriguez wrote "unsure" next to it to indicate the time was squishy.

The prosecution's forensic photogrammetry expert, Leonid Rudin, was called to speak at an evidentiary hearing on February 5 to discuss his upcoming testimony comparing Merritt's truck with the one in the Mitchley video.

Rudin said he'd used his proprietary software to analyze "a three-dimensional world captured in photographs or flat videos." However, even science had its limits, so all he could say at this point was, "we could reject" the idea it was Merritt's truck on the video.

Asked for clarification by the judge, he said, "I cannot eliminate that model."

"But you also cannot make an identification and say it definitely is the truck?"

"You are correct, Your Honor," Rudin said, adding that he also couldn't use the term "consistent," which would require additional points of comparison to match up. "At this point, we would not call it consistent or inconsistent."

On cross, McGee asked Rudin if he'd also informed the prosecution "that the wheelbase measurement didn't match."

Rudin replied obliquely that he had "delete[d] some files" from his PowerPoint, but "I never said the measurements were off. I just indicated the measurement error."

The next morning, McGee told Judge Smith the defense had concerns about Rudin's wheel-base measurement, which "sounds like it excludes this vehicle." They also had discovery issues, he said, given that Rudin "did other examinations that he deleted [from his PowerPoint presentation] because he found them not to be relevant. That's also a huge problem for the defense," because it would result in "cross-examination on the fly."

Britt Imes explained that Rudin, "being the quirky mathematician genius that he is," had continued to refine his measurements, which created new data. But Imes said he'd shared the new information with McGee as soon as he got it.

The judge agreed to give the defense more time to discuss Rudin's testimony with their expert and scheduled him to testify on February 19.

Meanwhile, Rudin told Imes privately that he still didn't think his measurements were precise enough, so he wanted to do a 3D laser scan of the McStays' street and a "live reprojection validation experiment."

Imes said that wasn't necessary, so Rudin took it upon himself to do more 3D modeling analysis and computations. Within a week of the hearing, Rudin had determined the running light on Merritt's truck was 5.17 feet from the ground versus 4.37 feet for the truck in the Mitchley video. For them to be the same truck, Merritt's back tires would have to be underground.

He called Imes to explain his change of thinking and renew his call for the validation experiment, but he was driving in the mountains at the time and wasn't sure if Imes understood what he was saying, because Imes kept asking, "Are you sure?"

But Imes had heard enough. Deciding to cut Rudin loose as an expert witness, Imes emailed him at 10:17 a.m. on February 15 to stop work on the case.

Rudin, who was offering his services pro bono, was left confused. "I have never seen anything like that before in my thirty-year career as a forensic scientist, being basically told to stand down, when, in fact, I could have continued working," he said at a hearing several months later.

Imes subsequently informed McGee by email at 10:44 a.m. that Rudin wouldn't be called as a witness "in our case in chief," though he still might be called as a rebuttal witness.

Imes told McGee the defense was welcome to call Rudin to follow up, because Imes didn't understand all the technical information involved.

"I only have a rudimentary understanding of this," Imes wrote.

Forty minutes after receiving the stop-work email, Rudin compiled his thoughts into a text, providing a more detailed explanation for his new conclusion. He sent it to Imes, but got no response.

Because Imes had already notified the defense by email, he later claimed he either didn't pay attention to Rudin's text, or didn't see the need to forward it. At some point, Imes deleted the text. He said later he had no recollection of receiving or deleting it, but it was his regular practice to clear out data so it didn't bog down the memory on his phone.

However, to the defense, this was reminiscent of the email deletion by his boss, Michael Ramos, which led to the federal judicial finding that Ramos had acted "in bad faith" in the Colonies case. Was this an accepted practice in the DA's office?

In the first half of February, the jury heard testimony about the activity on Joseph's QuickBooks account starting February 1, 2010, when vendors were added and checks were printed, backdated, deleted, cashed, or deposited. They also heard about Merritt's calls to QuickBooks, as he tried to set up the desktop Pro version on Joseph's account and delete the online version.

Detective Hanke testified that he viewed these activities as suspicious. Most of them happened after Joseph disappeared, and no checks were written on that account before February 1, when Joseph had historically typed names using capital letters.

On cross, McGee led Hanke through a cross-comparison of QuickBooks and phone records, which indicated Joseph and Merritt had discussed similar transactions by phone in real time before he disappeared.

The calls came "right after all the checks were adjusted and deleted and everything, correct?" McGee asked.

Pausing before answering, Hanke said he was confused from going back and forth between the various records and reports. "Correct," he finally said.

"Did you note all of that in your report?"

"I didn't."

"Did you even notice it?" McGee asked.

"I did not analyze the phone records," Hanke said.

"Make it seem a little less suspicious now since there is communication?" McGee asked, reminding him that Joseph's statement to his friend McGyver McCargar that he'd finished buying out Kavanaugh coincided with this new activity on Quickbooks.

"As part of your investigation, were you aware that Dan Kavanaugh was violent?" McGee asked. Objection. Sustained.

Although this unanswered question hung in the air, McGee was unable to explore Kavanaugh's criminal history due to repeated objections and a ruling that morning by the judge. McGee had asked for permission to question Hanke about Kavanaugh's threats to Roger Martinez for "doing him dirty," because Kavanaugh had used those same words when he told the detective that he'd taken over Joseph's QuickBooks account after Joseph had "done [him] dirty," too.

"The fact is, they are making this a financial crime, saying [Merritt] stole twenty thousand dollars," McGee told Smith. "Mr. Kavanaugh profited a quarter million dollars after they disappeared."

"You've already argued that," Judge Smith said. "I've already ruled on it. Your record is made."

But at that point, Smith was expecting the defense to call Kavanaugh as a witness. "After Mr. Kavanaugh testifies, [that] may be a different story," he said, adding, "it might be more relevant on a number of bases."

Next, the prosecution called forensic accountant Scott Weitzman to testify about Merritt's financial activity, based solely on his bank statements. Weitzman said he'd asked for checks, but never got them.

The statements indicated Merritt made a habit of cashing, rather than depositing, checks, he said. They also reflected a general pattern of financial mismanagement, with closed and overdrawn accounts, and dozens of ATM withdrawals at banks and casinos, resulting in numerous fees. Although Merritt's statements showed $147,189 in earnings from January 2009 to May 2010 (excluding the three months he had no bank account), he still ended up being overdrawn or close to it.

Imes then recalled Sergeant Smith to outline how much time Merritt spent at casinos, judging by his bank and cell phone tower records. The obvious inference was that Merritt had spent much of his income gambling with cash.

FBI Special Agent Kevin Boles spent parts of three days reconstructing Merritt's activities and locations from his cell phone records.

He said he'd cross-checked Merritt's and Joseph's phone records with FBI lists of locations for AT&T's and T-Mobile's respective cell towers in 2010, then used mapping software to create a "very rough estimate" of where Merritt's phone "had moved" on relevant dates and times.

It's the phones or the network, not the user, that chooses a tower to connect to, he said, based on signal strength and how many other phones are already using it, and it's not necessarily the closest one. A tower's altitude, the proximity and line of sight between towers, and the angle or direction of its antennae, also factor in. When calls are dropped, it's due to a poor "handoff" from one tower to another, but even if the user isn't traveling, the towers that start and end a call might be different.

After that prelude, Imes walked Boles through a tediously long series of maps, laying out the initiating tower locations for many of the calls Merritt made after Joseph was last seen and before he was officially reported missing.

When Merritt's phone didn't connect with any tower for nearly four hours on the evening of February 4, Boles said, "The phone could be off, off the network, in airplane mode, any one of those." However, he acknowledged the records didn't distinguish between a phone being off and a weak tower signal. "With these records, you can't tell."

When Merritt's phone connected again at 9:32 p.m., he said, it was with a tower near Interstate 15, not the usual one near his apartment, where he claimed to be.

On the morning of February 6, when the prosecution claimed Merritt was burying the bodies, his calls registered at towers in and around Victorville, Oro Grande, Hesperia, then back in Oro Grande.

"That area you are describing as Oro Grande is quite a large area on that map, is it not?" Imes asked.

"Yes, that particular cell tower is on top of a very large mountain," Boles said, referring to the Quartzite tower, which reaches 4,552 feet in altitude.

Historically, the only other time Merritt's phone hit that tower, he said, was on July 12, 2009, though it had connected with the antenna pointing in the opposite direction, "more to the west," where Merritt's sister lived.

"Were you made aware of statements by the defendant about his activity in the desert [in that] timeframe?" Imes asked.

"Yes. I was told there were statements that he had not been up there," Boles said.

On February 8, Merritt's phone didn't connect with any towers for six hours until 1:31 p.m., when he was in Corona, heading north on Interstate 91, and then it pinged in Rancho Cucamonga during a 1:54 p.m. call.

Out of the jury's earshot, McGee complained to the judge that Boles had admitted to analyzing FBI lists of tower locations and directional antennae that were never shared with the defense. Merritt's attorneys wanted to review those lists, because they'd "found errors throughout" the AT&T records.

"We want to see if they have correct ones, because [the antennae] are pointing in the wrong direction," he said.

Judge Smith agreed, issuing a court order for the FBI to hand them over, and gave the defense time to review them. However, he rejected the defense's request to tell the jury this delay stemmed from a late-discovery violation by the prosecution.

Maline objected, calling this "a trial by ambush." But by now, such objections were becoming accusatory white noise.

Back on cross, McGee asked Boles a few questions about data sources and technical training, with which the FBI agent said he wasn't familiar. When this cross-examination was placed under a microscope later, McGee said he stopped there because it was obvious that more technological questions would go over Boles's head.

McGee's main thrust was that the towers listed on Merritt's phone records from AT&T couldn't be used effectively by the prosecution to place him in any exact location at a given time.

For example, his call at 12:38 p.m. on February 10 hit a tower in the Lake Matthews area of Riverside County, whereas a call he'd made one minute earlier had hit a tower nineteen miles away in Rancho Cucamonga.

"Based on the azimuth, is it fair to conclude that he, reasonably, could have been at or near his home?" McGee asked.

"Yes," Boles replied, describing this type of call as a "flyer."

McGee asked Boles similar questions about Merritt's 9:32 p.m. call the night he was accused of killing the family in Fallbrook, which hit a tower about twelve miles from Merritt's apartment.

Boles said he couldn't "specify where the phone was when the call was made, so, yes," McGee's scenario—that the call was a "another flyer," and Merritt could have been home at the time—was possible, because Merritt had to be "somewhere in the coverage area of that tower."

McGee also presented a tediously lengthy series of examples to illustrate that no one could determine from the AT&T records whether Merritt had purposely turned off his phone that night, because, as Boles admitted, they showed that no tower connection was made numerous times when Merritt was actually on another call.

"This appears it's possible that the phone was on, but for some reason wasn't registering the [incoming] cell tower," Boles said. "But I don't have an answer for every single one of these."

Later in the trial, David Lipnitsky, an AT&T records custodian, acknowledged that if the phone rings but the caller hangs up before leaving a voicemail, "it may not show on these particular records."

Boles also conceded the records couldn't definitively show whether Merritt was stationary or moving when his phone connected with a different antenna on the same tower, as it did on February 6, when he was accused of burying the family in the desert.

"It's reasonable to say it's stationary, and it's reasonable to say it's movement?" McGee asked.

"Yes, I think they both would apply in this situation."

In fact, his calls that day also bounced back and forth between separate towers, as they did during four of his calls to Cathy Jarvis, which were less than thirty seconds each. Boles said they took a long time to connect, then lasted only a few seconds more; some didn't register an ending tower, indicating the call was lost or dropped.

"Is it fair to say, with just the limited information that you have, that it would be too speculative to try to pinpoint [the location of] a phone?" McGee asked.

"Correct."

"Is it also fair to conclude that the only reasonable opinion or conclusion you could make from this data is that the cell phone was in the High Desert area?"

"Yes, I believe that's a fair assessment."

"Did any of the sheriff's detectives that you spoke to ever ask you if you could say that this cell phone was at the gravesite?"

Boles couldn't recall if they asked that specifically, but indicated he wouldn't have answered in the affirmative. "I would have said that the data doesn't allow that kind of precision."

The defense's cell phone expert, Vlad Jovanovic, was in the gallery for much of Boles's testimony, and had been scheduled to take the stand as a defense witness, out of order, as soon as Boles stepped down.

But McGee had decided not to call him. As he explained to Maline and Jovanovic, he'd already gotten Boles to admit he couldn't definitively pinpoint Merritt's location with the AT&T

records, so McGee believed they had nothing to gain by putting Jovanovic on the stand. The jury already had enough information to create reasonable doubt. However, McGee didn't inform his client of this.

When Merritt turned around and realized Jovanovic was gone, he tapped Maline on the shoulder. "Where's Vlad?"

"He's not testifying," Maline replied.

Merritt was furious, because in his mind, their "entire case was based on Vlad." He was already angry McGee hadn't cross-examined Boles further about the calls allegedly made near the gravesite, and now, McGee was compounding that omission by preventing Jovanovic from explaining the fatal flaws of the records that supposedly placed Merritt there.

Merritt had analyzed those records himself, and he and Jovanovic were both insistent the expert should explain to the jury that two antennae on the Quartzite tower were "cross-connecting"—falsely registering Merritt's location near the gravesite, rather than on the west side of the tower where his sister lived, as he'd claimed. The AT&T records were also in conflict with the FBI records.

"Chase figured it out on his own; that to me was pretty extraordinary," Maline said. "It was extraordinary to Vlad as well."

Also, because the Quartzite tower was at such a high altitude, it could be accessed by many areas across the High Desert, where reception could drop and bounce, making it impossible to get a signal or complete a call, all of which meant that Merritt could have been miles away from the gravesite that day.

Although Maline said he was surprised by McGee's decision, he confirmed McGee's assertion that it was a strategic decision to "leave it alone because we thought we were in a good place."

Next, the prosecution called Edward Bachman, who was now a sergeant, to describe the Google searches on Merritt's phone, which indicated to them that he was contemplating fleeing to Alaska.

On cross, however, Maline got Bachman to acknowledge that the same search session included "California gold mines for sale," and more general searches such as "gold mine claims for sale" and "patented gold claims for sale."

It was unclear whether Bachman was purposely or innocently ignorant about Merritt's job at Keene Engineering, where he was arrested.

"And that's a gold mining equipment company, is that correct?"

"I don't recall specifically what they do, but they build machines that are for basically excavation type of equipment."

"Do you know if Mr. Merritt was involved in testing the gold mining equipment for Keene Engineering?"

"I think he had something to do with testing some of the equipment there."

Recalled to piggyback on that testimony, Sergeant Smith described several other questionable items recovered from Merritt's phone: a screenshot of a search for "how to change your identity" from December 17, 2013; a photo of the tire tracks taken at the gravesite three days later, and one of Merritt posing with Joseph's cross there; and thirty-five screenshots of a blog discussing Joseph's phone records.

On cross, Maline suggested benign reasons for Merritt's having these items, which Smith acknowledged had been sent to Merritt's phone. One came from an iPad, for example, though no one mentioned that an iPad was seized from Merritt's trailer.

"You came to learn in your investigation that Mr. Merritt was writing a book, is that correct?" Maline asked, implying these were research materials.

"Yes."

The jury heard about twenty minutes of excerpts from Merritt's eight-hour interview with Detectives Bachman and Hanke from October 16, 2014, during which he calmly and consistently refused to say he'd been at the gravesites on February 6, 2010. Judge Smith advised the jury that detectives are allowed to lie to suspects as an interrogation technique, "to see what their reaction is."

On cross, Maline grilled Bachman about the cell phone records and GPS coordinates he told Merritt had put him squarely at the gravesite.

"Is it your understanding that these records give the location of the cell phone?" Maline asked, just one day after Boles testified he never told detectives that.

"My understanding, or my belief, is that there were GPS coordinates in the call detail records," Bachman said.

After Maline pressed him, noting Boles had specifically testified that the records didn't include GPS coordinates, Bachman backed off.

"I don't recall what my understanding of the records were," he admitted, but "it was our understanding that his phone showed [he was] out at the gravesite or out in the area of the gravesite."

Maline pointed out that Bachman, when he was the case agent, had written a summary indicating that Merritt "had turned off his cell phone so he could evade his location."

"That was my belief, yes."

To underscore the inconsistent logic, Maline noted Bachman's summary also indicated "his phone was on during the time that he's burying the bodies in the desert, correct?" Objection. Sustained.

"And no matter how many times you asked him, he said he wasn't there, is that accurate?"

"Yeah, he didn't admit to being at the gravesites."

Melissa Rodriguez then called Merritt's sister, Juanita, to confront her about the statement to then-Detective Smith in 2014 that she hadn't seen Merritt in five years.

"I don't remember saying anything like that," Juanita said. "I saw my brother all the time."

"So, if the transcript says that, that would be incorrect?" Rodriguez asked.

"I wasn't even in my right mind when I talked to a detective. I could hardly talk when he was there," she said, noting she'd recently had her ninth surgery—this time for an embolism in her lungs—was taking narcotic pain meds, and was "drooling out of my mouth."

"I remember some things, but just trying to put them in the correct chronological order is almost impossible," she said.

Juanita said she didn't recognize Sergeant Smith in court, recalling the investigator she spoke to as being "much younger."

So, Rodriguez recalled Smith to testify about Juanita's cognitive condition during that interview.

"It was fine, she was very talkative," he said, though she did mention "she had several strokes and that timelines were difficult for her." She indicated she talked to Merritt about every six months, but she "did not see him, 'because he works 24/7' is how she described it."

And, no, he said, she wasn't drooling. "She told me her dog's name. We talked about recent events in the Victor Valley area. She was coherent."

Now that Leonid Rudin was out as the prosecution's photogrammetry expert, they scrambled to find a replacement who would testify that the truck in the Mitchley video was "consistent" with Merritt's.

In the meantime, they recalled Sergeant Smith to testify about his own unscientific study, involving a comparison of "screen captures" from the Mitchley video with a Faro 3D laser scan of Merritt's truck.

He said the still images showed the relative positions of the "low-hanging tailpipe," where the rear brake lights hit the ground, and also the bright area on Merritt's truck, which Smith said was a latch, reflecting Mitchley's porch light.

On cross, Smith acknowledged that the latch on Merritt's truck had a flat metal surface, not shiny chrome, underneath the white paint that covered the original gray. He didn't explain how a nonreflective surface could have produced the bright light seen on the video.

"You are not offering an opinion as to whether or not that's my client's truck, right?" McGee said.

"My testimony is that it's consistent with his truck, yes."

"So, you can't see the light that is on, but you can see the reflection of light that you don't know where it is, off a metal surface that's not chrome?" McGee asked. Objection.

Moving on, McGee asked Smith about the keys found in Joseph's pocket.

"If you have house keys and car keys in the pocket of your clothes, is it not a reasonable inference to look at from an investigative standpoint [and ask], did Joseph drive that car to San Diego, where it was found?" McGee asked.

The Trooper key was "clearly a copy," Smith said, and "it was abundantly clear they didn't drive themselves to the desert, and then drive that car down to San Diego."

McGee asked if detectives eliminated the possibility that the McStays drove the car to San Ysidro, and were taken to the desert from there, but the prosecution objected. Sustained.

"Did that become part of your investigation that maybe they were taken outside the house?" McGee asked.

"Absolutely, that was part of the investigation from the time the McStays were missing," Smith said, adding that his team also concluded that the people in the grainy video of the border crossing wasn't the family after all, noting Summer's Ugg boots were still at the house and Gianni's leashed backpack was in the Dodge truck.

The next day, the prosecution took jurors on a field trip to Victor Valley to examine the gravesite for themselves.

The following day, Sergeant Smith was back on the stand, being grilled by McGee about the tips he'd received and ignored: the one claiming that Dan Kavanaugh had "lured Joseph and the family out of the house, killed them, and buried the bodies," and others that Kavanaugh was bragging to people in San Diego about killing the family. Smith acknowledged he hadn't pursued any of them.

Next, the prosecution played a forty-seven-second excerpt of Merritt's CNN interview, which the defense had tried to keep out, arguing that his statement about being the last person to see Joseph wasn't an admission.

"They're attempting to misrepresent facts to the jury," McGee argued.

Judge Smith agreed that because the excerpt was taken out of context from a two-and-a-half-hour interview, he would advise the jury that CNN was only required to turn over footage that aired on TV.

In the excerpt, CNN's Randi Kaye is talking with Merritt, who is wearing a cowboy hat.

"So, you say you cooperated a great deal with the authorities," Kaye said. "You were questioned by the detectives. What did they ask you?"

"Do I know anything about them disappearing? Did I have anything to do with it? Just the standard questions, you know, they probably asked everybody."

"As far as you know, you were the last person or one of the last people to see him, right?"

"Yeah, yeah," Merritt said. "When he left Rancho Cucamonga, nobody else—although I think somebody, there was another person or two that he talked to, I'm not sure—"

"But you were the last person he saw," Kaye said.

"I'm definitely the last person he saw," Merritt said, nodding in agreement.

With that, the prosecution conditionally rested its case, with one last possible witness to come.

Once the jury was excused, the judge ruled on the defense's motion to dismiss the case against Merritt for lack of sufficient evidence, which is standard.

"They have zero direct evidence," McGee argued. "There is no evidence of a murder occurring inside the home. No evidence of cleanup. There is nothing in the home that supports the theory that the family was killed inside the home on the night of the fourth. If it happened on any other day, they can't put our client anywhere near the home."

After Imes opposed the motion, Judge Smith ran through what he viewed as the prosecution's strongest evidence, emphasizing the importance of Susan Blake's testimony, and in particular that Joseph was planning to "phase out" both Dan Kavanaugh and Chase Merritt, even though she'd contradicted the statement on cross.

Nonetheless, Smith cited her testimony and Merritt's bank records to further extrapolate that Joseph wanted to sideline Merritt for several reasons: Merritt had money problems, partly due to his gambling habit; he hadn't repaid a loan from Joseph; and he had a pattern of claiming he needed money to finish a project, only to use it for other purposes.

Smith also cited the presence of Merritt's DNA in the Trooper; the absence of voicemails from Merritt on Joseph's phone after February 4; the checks Merritt cashed after deleting them from the QuickBooks ledger; his calls to QuickBooks; and the calls he made near the gravesites on February 6, which "becomes more significant given the geography of that area," as it's "mostly open desert."

Although he conceded the murders could have occurred "either the evening of February the fourth or early morning hours of February the fifth," he said, "the court finds if the jury accepted the prosecution's evidence, arguments and conclusions, and returned a verdict of guilty, that there is substantial evidence to support such a finding."

Motion denied.

On March 12, the prosecution called its last witness: Eugene Liscio, a photogrammetry expert from Toronto.

His analysis, based on a 3D computer model and comparison of digital photos of surface components of Merritt's truck with the Mitchley video, deemed the headlamps, tailpipe, brake lights, certain shadow and glare patterns, and other measurements of the two trucks "consistent."

"It's not going to be one hundred percent perfect," Liscio said. "There's some little tiny things that are different, but the overall shape, scale, and measurement is consistent with the outline and what is actually documented on the truck."

Although he acknowledged he didn't do a formal analysis on the "bright spot" on both trucks, he said it "happens to coincide with a latch, which is on the side of [Merritt's] vehicle."

During more than three hours of cross-examination, McGee got Liscio to admit he didn't know the latch was made of non-reflective metal. He also elicited a key admission that Liscio didn't consider the side-camera footage in his analysis, only the one from the front porch.

Despite being confronted with components that didn't fit into his model, however, Liscio wouldn't budge from his position. "What I have done right now is just shown you a number of features that align, and they're within a reasonable margin of error," he said.

McGee asked Liscio if he was falling prey to confirmation bias when he refused to agree, for example, that a light on the video taken from the side camera, which he showed Liscio, was from the truck's taillight.

"Why won't you say this is a taillight?" McGee asked.

"It's not about what I can say or can't say, it's about what the evidence can show," he replied. "It behaves differently in the other video."

They also butted heads over the latch. "So, you're just going to find whatever evidence matches the theory that you want to reach, and you're going to say that's a latch, it's not a light, right?" McGee asked.

"I don't know. I know you want me to say maybe it's one or the other."

"To be clear, if that's an actual taillight, that's not my client's vehicle, right?"

"I'm not saying that this is your client's vehicle," Liscio said. "All I'm saying is that the vehicle in question is consistent with my report. If there's another vehicle that looks similar, that is possible."

Perhaps unknowingly, Liscio also gave testimony conflicting with the prosecution's contention that Merritt's wheelbase matched one set of tire tracks at the gravesite.

"You also measured the outside wheel width and from one edge of the tire to the other edge of the tire, correct?" McGee asked.

"Yes," Liscio said.

"And what was the distance there?"

"The outer was seventy-one and a half."

"Not seventy-three?" McGee asked, referring to the official measurement of Merritt's wheelbase and the first set of tracks.

"If somebody took it from the edge of the tire and it was flatter or had less air, then it could expand another inch or whatever."

"Not seventy-six?" McGee asked, reminding the jury of the width of the second set of tracks.

"We roughly got seventy-one and a half, so that's what I have."

* * *

Meanwhile, as Leonid Rudin listened to Liscio's testimony on YouTube, he grew concerned enough to call the defense.

As Maline put it, Rudin said, essentially, "I told the prosecution it wasn't your guy's truck and therefore I had to tell you. They should have told you on their own."

Chapter 41

The defense started its ten-week case on March 13, the day after Governor Newsom instituted a moratorium on the death penalty, to last as long as he held office.

"My intent is to tell the jurors that, number one, that has no effect, whatsoever, on this phase of the trial, the guilt phase," Judge Smith told the attorneys.

But if Merritt was found guilty, the jury would still have to decide if he should get a death sentence, because, as both sides agreed, "It's still the law here."

The defense continued their mission to undermine the prosecution's timeline and circumstantial evidence with their twenty-three witnesses, a third of whom were recalled in an attempt to impeach their earlier testimony. But the defense got off to a rocky start.

First up was Merritt's daughter, Taylor Jarvis, who was now twenty-four and preparing to enter Loyola Law School, McGee's alma mater, in the fall.

As Raj Maline questioned her about the night of February 4, 2010, Taylor said she remembered her parents arguing after Merritt didn't answer Joseph's call, which became an ongoing "topic of conversation" when Merritt couldn't get hold of him in the coming days.

"Why didn't you pick up your phone?" Taylor quoted her mother, Cathy Jarvis, as saying. "That's why I can never get a hold of you. You just ignore calls when you don't feel like taking them."

On cross, Melissa Rodriguez asked if Taylor had discussed evidence presented at trial during jail visits with her father. Jarvis said yes.

"And your dad talked to you about what he wanted you to testify to, right?"

"No, not that I recall."

After Rodriguez handed Taylor the transcript of a jailhouse conversation that she and Merritt hadn't known was being recorded, Taylor admitted they stopped talking about the trial once they learned they were being taped.

Despite Rodriguez's aggressive questioning style, Taylor didn't get emotional or let the prosecutor rile her up. On redirect, however, Maline's questions brought her to tears.

"In the entire four-and-a-half-year period that you have been visiting your dad, has he ever once told you to lie for him?" he asked.

"No," she said. "He's actually been really specific. He said, 'If you don't remember something, don't say it.' I don't have any reason to lie for him."

Before Cathy Jarvis was called to testify, the defense tried to keep the prosecution from playing recordings from some of her jail visits and calls with Merritt. Jarvis was on the prosecution's witness list but was never called.

At an evidentiary hearing, Sergeant Smith explained that while monitoring Merritt's phone conversations after the trial started, he noticed Merritt stopped visitors from talking about certain topics before coming to see him, saying, "We'll talk about it on Friday."

Once they were in the visitor's booth, Merritt had them speak loudly through the glass instead of using the jailhouse phone, which he knew was being recorded. So, in early February, Smith started showing up before scheduled visits to hide a digital tape recorder in the booth.

"His conversations provided important evidence" relevant to the case, Smith said.

James McGee accused the prosecution of bad faith by waiting to disclose these recordings to the defense "for tactical purposes," to prevent the defense from telling their client, "as we told him many a time, stop talking about the case."

Prosecutors, in turn, accused Merritt of attempting to "engage in witness tampering, to sway the testimony of one or more witnesses" and "to fabricate evidence," by telling Jarvis "what to say when she's asked certain questions and telling her background that she doesn't necessarily remember."

"We have evidence of police doing the same thing," McGee countered. "We can go down that road and spend two months doing that," noting detectives tried to influence Jarvis's testimony with the "threat of arrest" during interviews. Even so, McGee said, Jarvis simply repeated the same story she'd been telling all along, so Merritt didn't cause her to say anything different.

During Maline's gentle direct examination, Cathy Jarvis painted a benign portrait of Merritt, characterizing him as "very artistic" and "very creative. He could build anything, he was a hard worker, and that's what he spent most of his time doing."

Jarvis described Merritt's business relationship and friendship with Joseph as unusually good before he disappeared, because they were both excited about their new lucrative projects.

She confirmed that Merritt sometimes came home with blank checks from Joseph so Merritt could buy materials and pay vendors, but said the family mostly used cash.

Asked about his interest in poker, Jarvis said Merritt started playing competitively in 2007, continuing for "approximately" a year.

"The thing with Chase is he gets these little itches, he gets ideas, and he gets super intensely focused on certain things," she said. "He got it in his head that he was going to try his hand at poker."

This sympathetic treatment on the stand ended when Rodriguez began her cross-examination, which was often combative. Jarvis sounded agitated at times, flustered at others, sighing and pausing throughout her grueling day and a half of testimony.

Showing Jarvis her own bank statements, Rodriguez forced her to acknowledge that Merritt's gambling continued through 2010. But even then, Jarvis insisted it must have stopped and started again.

Jarvis admitted she wasn't aware of how much money or time Merritt spent at casinos, because she didn't necessarily know when he was going to one. But the couple of times she accompanied him, she scolded him about making ATM withdrawals, because the fees were so high.

Rodriguez asked why Merritt had moved his workshop to different cities so many times. "Part of that was because of his business dealings with people, right?"

"It was mostly because of his money mismanagement," Jarvis said.

"Because he made people mad, right?"

"No, it was because he didn't manage his money well."

Rodriguez reminded Jarvis of her statement to detectives, "'that he's pissed everybody off because he ends up walking away and not following through.' Do you recall saying that?"

"I think that's taken out of context," Jarvis said. "I didn't actually mean 'everyone.'"

Jarvis still wouldn't admit what she'd said, even after Rodriguez asked her to review a transcript of her interview with detectives on October 10, 2014.

"That doesn't sound like the way I talk," Jarvis said. "I don't know if I used those exact words."

So, Rodriguez played Jarvis's taped phone call with Merritt the next day, when Jarvis recounted making those same comments to detectives. This was one of the recordings the defense had tried, unsuccessfully, to prevent the prosecution from playing for the jury, along with her jailhouse conversation with Merritt on Super Bowl Sunday.

As the grilling went on, Jarvis seemed to be on the verge of tears, as she was compelled to publicly reveal her long-held frustrations and problems with Merritt. She was also visibly and audibly upset about her treatment, first by detectives and now by the prosecutor, likely influenced by Merritt's belief that he was wrongly accused and the truth was being manipulated at every turn.

However, as much as she tried to support her children's father, whom she maintained was innocent of murder, she repeatedly minimized the same behaviors that ultimately broke up their "marriage."

When Maline asked her about the night of February 4, Jarvis seemed to genuinely believe she'd seen Merritt's phone on the counter when Joseph called at 8:28 p.m.

Although she'd conceded her memory could be faulty when detectives showed her Merritt's phone records, which reflected no such call, she stuck to her original story under cross-examination.

"We proceeded to get into a little bit of an argument about him not answering his phone," she recalled.

"What was the reason?" Rodriguez asked.

Jarvis said Merritt told her, "I already saw him. I talked to him a million times today. I'll call him tomorrow."

Rodriguez proceeded to play the jailhouse tape, so the jury could hear Merritt telling Jarvis how to describe what happened that night. The obvious conflict between Jarvis's testimony and her taped conversation with Merritt brought Rodriguez's point home.

On the tape, Merritt correctly predicts she'll be asked at trial why she repeatedly called him if they were both "home" that night. So, he reminds her to mention their history of bad reception, dropped calls, and calls that wouldn't connect when she was in the apartment and he was in the clubhouse nearby.

"You're going to be talking about that," he says, reminding her of their dropped calls during his interview with Detectives DuGal and Fiske in the clubhouse, when he called to ask if she remembered where he was on February 8.

More specifically, he predicts they will ask why she called him six times the night of February 4, and gives her a practice question: "You wouldn't be trying to call him if he was home, would you?"

"At the time, obviously you're being confronted by two detectives, and you're flustered anyway," he says. "Don't hesitate to say that on the stand if that's the case, because I know for a fact, now that I go back over everything, I was home."

"Yeah, I know, that's what I testified to begin with," she says.

"'Kay, well, you haven't testified yet."

Walking her through that night again, he says he probably took "one or other of the kids, or I was in the computer room [in the clubhouse] or something. You were trying to reach me. For a time, I came back to the house. Laid my phone on the counter. Phone rang, you saw it. Obviously, I never remembered that phone call. Ever. I still don't to this day."

"You remember when I pointed it out to you?" Jarvis asks. "I know we had a discussion about it that night."

"I'm sure we did, but I don't remember the call, and I don't remember the discussion," he says, adding that he had no reason to be in Mira Loma, where his 9:32 p.m. call pinged.

Merritt also tells Jarvis that "we need you to remember" the details about the Provecho restaurant debacle.

"Why?" she asks.

"Because that's the only way we can get a picture of it to the jury," he says.

When she says she vaguely remembers it, he replies, "Okay, you need to remember—re-remember it. Because when you get on the stand, they're gonna ask you, 'Do you remember this waterfall?' 'Yes.' And Joseph got stiffed for the $32,000, and he was doing a lawsuit against them, but him and I had decided that if he lost, or if he didn't get the money back, that him and I would eat [that]. I was supposed to give him back $19,000 over a period of time. I know you've got to remember that."

Rodriguez asked Jarvis what she meant by her earlier testimony that her words were "taken out of context."

After a long pause, Jarvis said, "I have a long history with Chase, and I have built up frustrations with our relationship together. I get angry and start spilling out and overexaggerating things that happened."

"So, it's your testimony that this was an overexaggeration?"

"Yes."

Rodriguez pressed harder, suggesting that Merritt had coached her how to testify. "In fact, he didn't ask you to lie, he told you what you needed to remember, right?"

"He told me to tell the truth," Jarvis said.

Handing Jarvis the transcript of the jailhouse conversation, Rodriguez asked her to review it and "tell me where it says for you to tell the truth."

After a long wait, Rodriguez asked, "It's not there, right?"

Jarvis had to admit it wasn't.

"Are you familiar with the term 'confirmation bias'?" Rodriguez asked. "Do you know what that means?"

"No," Jarvis said.

"Nothing further."

On redirect, Maline tried to salvage the testimony of his client's primary alibi witness by allowing her to say she still supported Merritt and had visited him weekly for more than four years.

"Is that one of the things he told you, to tell the truth?" Maline asked.

"Yes," she replied.

"Did he ask you to lie?"

"No."

"Nothing further."

Free to step down, Jarvis whispered, "Wow," loud enough for the mic to pick up.

After watching his daughter and her mother get hammered by the prosecution, Merritt felt in his gut that he was going to get convicted.

As the trial headed into its third month, the defense recalled Susan Blake.

While prosecutors had used Susan's testimony to try to prove Merritt had taken thousands of dollars, first from Joseph, and then from her, the defense now tried to show she'd written herself checks to profit from Joseph's business, and that she was so laissez-faire—or oblivious—that she allowed Dan Kavanaugh to tank EIP, all while blaming Merritt.

Maline's questions implied that Susan would say anything to support the prosecution's case, even when confronted with contradictory evidence, just as the prosecution tried to prove Taylor and Cathy Jarvis would say anything to support Merritt.

Returning to the topic of Joseph's expansion plan, Maline tried to get Susan to repeat what she'd already testified. "Did he want to get rid of Chase and replace him with other welders, was that your understanding?" he asked. "Or add welders to keep Chase and just add additional welders?"

"No, he wanted to get rid of him," Susan said flatly.

Maline tried to read aloud a portion of her interview with Detectives Hanke and Steers where she said the latter, but prosecutors blocked him.

After repeated objections, Maline gave up and asked her to silently read the transcript, which quoted her saying, "He didn't say as much about Chase, wanting to get Chase out. He wanted to get more Dan out. Because he acted as if he could just flip the switch and shut his whole business down. And Joey couldn't get it back and up."

But even after she read her own words on the page, she refused to admit to the jury what she'd told detectives.

"In other words, you knew about Dan's threat to shut down the business, correct?" he asked.

After a flurry of sustained objections, Maline asked, "Do you know why Joseph didn't want to take Dan with him and wanted to buy him out instead?"

"I don't know why," she said defiantly.

After another objection, Maline was forced to leave the jury with Susan's response that Joseph had "wanted to get rid" of Merritt.

Switching topics, Maline asked Susan about the transactions in the Chase Bank account her son Michael had opened in March 2010, challenging her to recall the purpose of her purchases, cash withdrawals, fund transfers, and checks she'd written to herself and Dan Kavanaugh. But she couldn't.

"What did you do with the four-thousand-dollar [withdrawal]?"

"It would have been used for the business."

"Do you know who you gave it to?"

"I don't remember that far back."

Maline also showed her a number of credit card charges—for gas, a store called Giggles and Hugs, and a Sprint phone bill—which she said weren't hers.

"So that [charge] could potentially be your son [Michael]'s as well?"

"It's not mine."

"None of these card purchases were yours, correct?"

"Correct."

The implication was that Susan and Michael had done exactly what the prosecution accused Merritt of doing—spending Joseph's money for their own personal use, while claiming they were keeping his business afloat until he came home.

"You've seen these checks. I have totaled them, and the total comes to $20,450," Maline said, referring to checks she'd mostly written to herself, with a few to Kavanaugh. "You don't have an answer as to what you did with that money, is that correct?"

"That money would have went back to Chase for everything towards the business."

"Well, it's funny that you mentioned that, because in this statement, there's several checks made to Chase for waterfalls," he said, challenging her recollection that she gave Merritt cash on top of writing him checks.

"Yes, I have given him cash," she said.

As Maline asked her to explain how Joseph and Merritt split up payments on the custom jobs, she was under the impression that once Merritt was paid by the client, "the funds should have went back, all of it, into Joey's account." But that was never her son's arrangement with Merritt.

On cross, prosecutor Melissa Rodriguez gave Susan a way to explain her notable lack of recall. "Would it be fair to say that when this [Chase Bank] account was opened, that was a fairly traumatic time period for you?"

"Most definitely."

"And would you agree that this was by far the most difficult thing that you ever had to deal with in your life?"

"The worst. Devastating."

"And so, during that time, when you're experiencing this extreme devastation, you're trying to run a business and keep a business afloat for your son, right?"

"Trying."

Rodriguez asked Susan about her conversations with Merritt, when he said he needed money, then she showed Susan a series of checks she'd written to Merritt, which, including the $5,000 she'd paid him from her personal checking account, totaled $15,900. "So, it seems that you gave him a significant amount more of money then you believed you did, right?"

"Correct."

"And to your knowledge, the reason that the defendant didn't have access to [Joseph's] bank accounts was because Joey had paid off some gambling debts for him, right?"

"Correct."

McGee objected, citing speculation and a lack of foundation. Although the judge sustained the objection, Rodriguez used this same unsupported claim during her closing argument.

On cross, Rodriguez returned to Susan's interview with detectives in 2014. "And did you tell Detective Steers that Joey was going to buy Dan and Chase out?"

"Yes," Susan said.

"You haven't profited in any way from the disappearance of your son and his family, is that right?"

"That is correct."

On redirect, Maline continued to imply Susan's memory was selectively biased against Merritt by asking her about the deposits to the Chase Bank account for EIP, which they hadn't discussed yet.

"I know you don't want to add up the total deposits for the account. I'll let you know, it's $36,000. Do you recall depositing or receiving funds in that account? Do you know how much total funds that you received?"

"Honestly, I do not. I wasn't in the right frame of mind."

After the jury was excused, the prosecution complained to Judge Smith that Maline kept bringing up Kavanaugh, despite the court's third-party culpability ruling. The judge reiterated that the buyout and sale of the business were admissible, however, he scolded Maline for joking about objections and the court's ruling on them.

"I understand that it's a tactic to try to perhaps ingratiate yourself to the jury or to make it sound like it's not a big deal, but it's improper and it's unprofessional, and I'm warning you now, if it happens again, I will hold you in contempt for it," Smith said.

"I agree," Maline said. "You will only have to tell me once, Your Honor."

"I hope that's true."

But, Maline said, "At the same time, this type of conduct goes on constantly with these prosecutors."

"Both sides have been guilty of that and that also is improper," Smith said. "But, you know, my ability to control that has been demonstrated to be not very good."

On March 19, McGee called Detective Steers, intending to impeach his testimony based on "past acts of untruthfulness and trustworthiness" in various aspects of the investigation, such as alleged misrepresentations in search warrants and reports.

While detectives were compiling the timeline of Merritt's activities, Steers wrote in a report that he drove the 68.3 miles from Merritt's apartment to the McStay house to time the trip. Leaving at 8:31 a.m., he arrived in an hour after driving in "moderate traffic," at seventy to seventy-five miles per hour.

"Why didn't you drive from 5:30 [p.m.] from Rancho Cucamonga to see how long it took you, at that time, under the same conditions?" McGee asked.

"I don't know," Steers said.

Steers also timed the 60.6 miles from the house in Fallbrook to the San Ysidro mall at 10:49 a.m. in October 2014, which took him fifty minutes.

Steers's report stated that he scanned the mall parking lot until he found a pay phone, hoping Merritt had used it to call for a taxi or to ask Cathy Jarvis to pick him up. However, the number didn't turn up when he checked her phone records, and no taxi service he called could document any customer trip from the mall to Fallbrook or Rancho Cucamonga.

Trying to portray as benign the periods when Merritt's cell phone lost contact with cell towers in February 2010, McGee got Steers to acknowledge he documented this same pattern numerous times—for as long as fourteen hours straight—while they were monitoring Merritt's cell phone in September and October 2014.

"Did he ever talk to anybody, saying something about the investigation or something about the murders with an unknown party?" McGee asked.

"No," Steers said, admitting he only noted the losses of phone contact he thought were "nefarious," as McGee put it, such as when Merritt's phone pinged near a casino.

"Because those are the only things, at the time for this portion of the report, I felt were pertinent," Steers said, acknowledging Merritt's casino visits weren't illegal.

Recalling Michael McStay on April 3, Maline asked if he'd taken Joseph's laptop the same night he took the desktop eMachine and SIM card. Michael said no.

Reminding Michael of his testimony that he'd had "little, if nothing, to do with EIP prior" to Joseph going missing, Maline brought up a false claim Michael made in 2007, which resulted in a lawsuit three years later, accusing him of fraud.

"Did you ever apply for a loan, indicating that you were the owner of Earth Inspired Products?"

"I don't believe so," Michael said.

When Maline handed him the legal documents Heritage Pacific Financial (HPF) had filed against him, prosecutors objected, saying they weren't in discovery as Maline stated, and were also irrelevant and "extremely misleading." Overruled.

HPF accused Michael of defrauding the mortgage lender by misrepresenting his employment information on an application for a thirty-year home loan for $67,500, claiming he was the self-employed owner of EIP.

"These representations were materially false," the lawsuit stated, alleging Michael knew he wouldn't otherwise qualify for the loan.

Records show Michael defaulted on the loan, then failed to appear in court for the lawsuit, so a default judgment was entered against him in November 2010. HPF didn't respond to a query as to why the complaint was dismissed without prejudice in April 2011.

Shown a copy of his false statement on the witness stand, Michael admitted he'd submitted it to HPF.

"You told the bank that you were the owner of Earth Inspired Products?" Maline asked.

"I believe that was with my brother's approval," Michael said. "I wouldn't have signed for something unless I talked to him first."

"That [statement] was not true, was it?"

"I was not the owner, no."

"And you're aware when you signed that application to the bank that it was under penalty of perjury?"

"I don't know. Is it? You would know. I wouldn't."

Maline asked if something had happened with the loan that prompted him to go to Joseph's house on February 4 or 6, 2010, as he'd testified.

"This loan wasn't even on the radar," Michael said. "I have no idea why you are even asking this question. I didn't talk to him about this loan or whatever you are implying."

Imes objected again, arguing in a sidebar that the court had already ruled against a third-party culpability case. Sustained.

McGee argued that the defense had recalled Michael to impeach his testimony, based on past misrepresentations of fact, but Judge Smith held fast.

So Maline asked Michael about his white Chevy 3500 truck. "[It's] the same exact model as Chase's truck, correct?"

"No, it's not," Michael said, listing several different features.

Referring to the white truck seen leaving the McStays in the Mitchley video the night of February 4, Maline asked, "Is that your truck?"

"Is what my truck?"

When Maline wouldn't let him off the hook, Michael contradicted his earlier testimony. "That's not my vehicle on the fourth. I was never there on the fourth," he said.

Maline also brought up Michael's comment to *The Orange County Register* in March 2010, describing the fear that he was "looking for two adult shallow graves and . . . my two nephews' crosses."

"Yes," Michael said, "before they were found, right. Because that was my fear—that I wasn't looking for a missing persons case, but rather a possible homicide."

"You were very specific," Maline said, segueing to Michael's falling-out with Summer.

Despite Britt Imes's objections, Maline got Michael to confirm his remark to detectives that Summer had driven "a wedge between Joseph and his son" Elijah, and that she had "divided your family," as if this were a possible motive for murder.

On cross, Imes tried to undo the damage of these implications, starting by listing all the differences between Michael's and Merritt's trucks. McGee objected, saying, "counsel is testifying." Sustained.

So Imes moved on to directly address "the elephant in the room."

"Did you kill your brother?" Imes asked, in a tone that implied the notion was not only offensive, but ridiculous, for the defense to suggest.

"Absolutely not, no way," Michael said, characterizing the inference as "more mudslinging from the defense."

The next portion of the defense's case centered on the three unidentified DNA profiles from the gravesites. Much of this testimony was quite technical and may have been difficult for the jury to grasp, which made the witnesses' credibility subject to the tone of voice and brinksmanship by prosecutors.

Forensic DNA consultant Suzanna Ryan explained that she'd chosen ten evidence items for testing, then demonstrated how she'd used the MVAC to collect the samples. An MVAC is a wet vacuum that can gather as much as two hundred times more DNA and is far more sensitive than the swabs used by the SDSD and SBCSD. It's also especially good in cracks and crevices.

She said she selected items from inside and outside the graves, to which she suspected the killer might have "applied pressure or friction." Among those were the two white cords wrapped around Joseph's neck, at least one of which was tied into a knot; the red tie-down straps; both halves of Summer's cut bra; her sweatpants; and her underwear.

Some of these items had already been swabbed by the crime lab's DNA analyst, Donald Jones, but had produced zero DNA or insufficient levels to analyze. Jones, who testified for the prosecution, said he didn't test the other items because they had been in the dirt for nearly four years.

"My opinion was that it would have been a futile effort," Jones said.

Ryan disagreed. Although DNA can degrade with time and exposure to the elements, she said, it can still be detected if it's been separated from the fluids decomposing bodies produce.

Because Merritt's DNA was detected in comparatively minuscule amounts on the Trooper's steering wheel and gearshift, the defense suggested this was likely the result of a handshake between him and Joseph after lunch at Chick-fil-A, though Merritt had also been a passenger six weeks before. Ryan confirmed that secondary transfer of DNA was possible if two people shook hands, then one of them touched an object.

If a mix of contributors is found, she said, the person who touched the object the longest and most directly would leave the highest level, especially if that person touched it after someone else. Asked specifically about a mix of contributors on a steering wheel, she said, "If someone drove a car for ninety minutes, the expectation would be that they would be more of a major contributor." In this case, Joseph was the major contributor, not Merritt.

Ryan agreed with Jones's earlier testimony that secondary transfer was a "possible" and "reasonable" explanation for why Merritt's DNA was found on the steering wheel, but she noted DNA can get transferred by a criminalist who brushes areas for fingerprints before swabbing them for DNA. Samples can also become contaminated if swabs taken from different areas are examined on the same microscope plate.

On cross, prosecutor Sean Daugherty got Ryan to say the interior of the Trooper could have been wiped down, such as the driver's-side door handle, because it showed such low levels of measurable DNA. But she said the presence of even low levels of DNA didn't support that scenario.

"There's also low-level DNA, comparatively speaking, on the steering wheel, right?" he asked.

"It's a low level, but it's not unusual to find a lower amount of DNA from a touched object," she said, noting the driver's-side door "was ten times lower."

She reiterated that the person who last drove the vehicle for ninety minutes would be a major contributor on the steering wheel, "based upon the studies that were citied, and the fact that it's a harder surface, not cloth, for example," which is more porous.

"And an assumption the person didn't wear gloves, right?"

"Sure, yeah."

As they revisited the items she sent to Bode, Daugherty put the Stanley sledgehammer in front of her. "Did you request that item [be tested]?"

"No, I did not," she said, noting the MVAC is more effective on porous items or those with ridges.

"There are ridges on the handle," Daugherty said.

"There are some ridges on the handle, yes."

Circling back to the Cybergenetics results, Daugherty pointed out that one of the bra cups that produced a partial DNA profile was outside of the grave, exposed to the elements. Hypothetically speaking, he asked, if it "would be odd" if test results from items found underneath a decomposing body actually excluded the victims' DNA?

Ryan said, rather, it "might be surprising."

When Daugherty claimed few law enforcement agencies use Cybergenetics or probabilistic genotyping technology, Ryan countered that it was "more common for both TrueAllele and STRmix to be used in criminal laboratories" for the prosecution side of cases. She also noted that the San Diego Police Department "routinely uploads multiple complex mixtures," obtained with this technology, to CODIS to identify suspects.

Refuting the prosecution's characterization of probabilistic genotyping as junk science, Maline emphasized later that San Bernardino County routinely uses STRmix-generated profiles, "their version of Cybergenetics," in DNA comparisons submitted to CODIS.

The two technologies are similar enough that Cybergenetics filed a federal lawsuit in 2019, alleging that the STRmix software infringed on two of their patents.

* * *

Suzanna Ryan left the details of Bode's lab results to senior analyst Christina Nash, who testified that Bode had started using probabilistic genotyping software in January 2019, indicating its gain in popularity.

Nash said the ten samples she received from Ryan on March 12, 2018, either detected no DNA or levels below the lab's threshold on Summer's panties, her sweatpants, and the red strap found outside the graves. However, she did find partial profiles on each of Summer's bra cups, a red strap, and one of the white cords. Because the DNA levels were below Bode's detection threshold, which was "consistent" with being exposed to the elements over time, the lab sent the raw digital DNA data to Cybergenetics on December 10, 2018.

Daugherty's cross-examination was peppered by objections by McGee, who claimed the prosecutor's "whole line of questioning is inappropriate and irrelevant" because he kept asking Nash about hypothetical comparisons that didn't apply to this case.

The judge overruled McGee's repeated objections until he finally relented. Nonetheless, the gist of Daugherty's line of questioning was likely communicated to the jury via somewhat patronizing queries such as:

"So, if you don't have any good data, you can't just make up a profile?"

"Correct. You can't just plug in numbers into a little table and make comparisons," Nash said.

"Do you have to have a full profile to give it to a lab to upload to CODIS?"

"No."

"You don't? You can have a partial profile?"

"We can have partial profiles," she said. However, as she pointed out, the defense "decided to forego the CODIS upload," and because Bode is a private lab, it doesn't have access to CODIS, but it needs to be aware of this in advance of testing.

Once Bode's raw data reached Cybergenetics, forensic analyst Beatriz Pujols inputted the files into the TrueAllele software. After the program was done processing, she testified, she "ask[ed] it to make a comparison to known references," which in this case were the four victims and Chase Merritt.

She ran the analysis several times "to ensure reproducibility of those results." The whole process took about a month, culminating in a final report the defense received in January 2019, after the trial had already started.

Mark Perlin, Cybergenetics' chief scientific and executive officer, took the stand next to interpret those results for the jury.

Perlin, who has a medical degree, PhDs in math and computer science, and holds ten patents, said he developed this software, because 70 percent of evidence items were previously tossed aside as "inconclusive," and analysis of DNA mixtures often gave flawed "match statistics."

"Does the work at Cybergenetics, do they intentionally skew those parameters to try to force a result that you would want?" McGee asked.

"No," Perlin said. "The whole point of TrueAllele is that we don't know. The computer doesn't know or care what the result is. It separates out genotypes from the mixture data."

He said the results in this case statistically excluded or likely excluded Merritt and the McStay family members from the tested items, but most importantly, Cybergenetics produced DNA database search files that could be submitted to CODIS.

If they got a hit in CODIS, he said, they could make a direct comparison with the DNA of the person who was identified via the database search, which would take the probabilities out of it.

"So, theoretically, if I had access to CODIS, I could do a keyboard search, and I could see if there's any possible matches based on just entering these numbers in?" McGee asked.

Yes, Perlin said, it was possible to type in a manual search to see if "one of the fifteen million profiles on CODIS might produce an association for investigation."

On cross, Daugherty's questions suggested Perlin's technology wasn't used by more labs—only 10 out of about 350 nationwide—because it didn't meet accepted scientific standards, and that Perlin was benefitting by being an expert in this case because he could hype his product. Daugherty also challenged Perlin's findings, noting the presence of a particular allele he said was a match for Merritt.

DNA is complicated enough for juries to understand, but probabilistic genotyping requires a logarithmic jump in comprehension. The exchange soon escalated into a rhetorical spat over technical terminology and the validity of Perlin's approach.

"The data's not important?" Daugherty asked rhetorically.

"Your characterization of the alleles as being primary, it's an old way of looking at things," Perlin retorted.

"And it's the way it's accepted in all but what, ten labs that use TrueAllele?" Daugherty said.

"They don't look at the allele approach that you do, no," Perlin replied, explaining that it was the genotype, not the allele, that Cybergenetics uses to calculate the match statistics.

Perlin said the CODIS database only recognizes alleles, so his company has to essentially "retrofit" the data by putting it into a twenty-year-old format the database could understand to do a search.

Daugherty asked Perlin skeptically why an adult body, decomposing on top of an item, would be statistically excluded, while an "unknown, potentially touch-DNA" item outside the grave would be a closer match.

Perlin said the person's DNA could have been "erased through enzymes" within the grave, which are more actively intense than certain bacteria that thrive outside a grave.

The DNA on the white cord, which was wrapped around Joseph's body, for example, was degraded, "but we also know that there was information present. So, there was some DNA, and from more than one person," Perlin said.

"But your data excluded the deceased individual's DNA that was wrapped with that item, right?"

"Correct," Perlin said. "There needn't be any anomaly if there were parts of the cord that were bound up in such a way that they were never exposed" to the elements, enzymes, and bacteria that "chewed" up the DNA.

Asked if it would be reasonable to expect to find the DNA of the bra wearer, Perlin said yes, but as a body decomposes, the fluid actually causes that person's DNA to disappear, so its absence "is not surprising." In fact, it's expected. That's not the case for touch DNA, however, whose chance of surviving in a grave "would depend how protected" it was from contact with those same enzymes and bacteria.

As for the light areas on the sweatpants, which the prosecution suggested was bleach, Perlin said urine breaks down to ammonia, which is a bleaching agent.

Asked if he could say "with any degree of certainty" that the DNA on the tested items was "representative" of the state they were in when they were buried with the family's bodies, Perlin said no. Nor could he tell when the DNA was placed on the items.

Moving on to the financial evidence, the defense called Sarah Kane, records custodian for PayPal, to shed light on Dan Kavanaugh's early attempts to obtain money from Joseph's account.

After making numerous minor purchases in Hawaii in January with a PayPal debit card issued by Joseph's account, Kavanaugh sent him a request for $800 on February 6, 2010.

Four days later, after a weeklong gap since Joseph had sent one of the smaller amounts Kavanaugh had requested in recent weeks, Kane said there was a failed login to Joseph's account, followed by two password changes made over several days.

In the two weeks after the first password reset, the account holder approved this and all subsequent transactions—from Kavanaugh's IP address—for a total of $9,900 in transfers to Kavanaugh's account. Later in the year, Kavanaugh changed the name on his own account to Earth Inspired Products on September 29.

On cross, Imes tried to impeach Kane for not knowing what a "third-party user" was in the PayPal system, noting Summer Martelli was added as one to Joseph's account on February 3.

However, Maline got Kane to point out that Summer's name was added in lowercase letters—before she and Joseph went missing.

Imes then suggested the Excel file of six hundred pages of spreadsheets, which Kane sent to the defense, could have been altered. Although Kane said they were "protected," Imes demonstrated he could delete a line on the spreadsheet, using his laptop.

"At this point, Your Honor, I move to strike her testimony," he said. "She's an incompetent custodian of records." Overruled.

On April 16, the defense called one of its key experts, Bryan La Rock, who offered an entirely benign view of Merritt's working relationship with Joseph. La Rock also introduced what little, but important, evidence the judge allowed the defense to present about Dan Kavanaugh.

As La Rock shared his analysis, he presented examples that contradicted the prosecution's narrative that the murders came as a result of Joseph's discovery of Merritt's embezzlement. Rather, he said, their relationship seemed like more of a collaborative partnership to protect the business from Kavanaugh.

For example, Joseph added MSM and Merritt as vendors to the QuickBooks custom account on January 22, and typed in "day labor" as a new account on January 25—all in lowercase letters—a full week before that same lettering was used on checks to Merritt on February 1 and 2. After also adding check entries for Merritt and MSM on the afternoon of January 22, Joseph called Merritt, who called him right back, and they talked for twenty minutes.

"That's the beginning of a pattern that I noticed," La Rock said. "A phone call was made [from Joseph] to Chase every single time that a check was issued for the QuickBooks online records."

He identified a similar pattern for checks issued with follow-up calls and texts on the morning of February 4, with continued calls to Merritt throughout the day and into the evening, corresponding to the respective SketchUp and QuickBooks activity on Joseph's computer.

Maline also walked La Rock through the Excel spreadsheets on Joseph's computer, which showed he and Merritt had historically "squared away" their debts and payments on the custom jobs by year's end, give or take $200, from 2007 through 2009.

As further proof of their healthy friendship, La Rock offered Joseph's text, wishing Merritt a happy new year, on January 2, 2010: I truly hope it's a very, very good year for us.

This elicited an objection from Britt Imes, who had been making them throughout La Rock's testimony: "They are going to imply that it's a good business relationship based on the truth of those statements." Overruled.

When Maline broached the topic of Kavanaugh's IP address being in San Diego while he claimed to be in Hawaii, Imes objected again, saying the location of the address could have changed since 2010. La Rock assured the court that in his experience, "they have generally been consistent" over time, so Smith let him continue.

La Rock said Kavanaugh's PayPal records listed his IP address as being in Hawaii until January 14, 2010, at 12:31 a.m., and there were no more transactions until January 26 at 4:47 a.m., when he used an IP address registered in San Diego. He used that same address until February 17, when it changed to one associated with Southern California in general.

"That is a mobile device, and often those regions are not as specific as some of the other ones," La Rock said, underscoring that Kavanaugh made the two password changes to Joseph's PayPal account from the San Diego IP address.

During a break, the defense tried again to persuade the judge to let the jury hear evidence of Kavanaugh's incriminating Google searches, as well as the threatening string of instant messages to Joseph in January 2009.

The defense argued this evidence would support their claim it was Joseph, not Merritt, who started creating and deleting checks on QuickBooks on February 1, to hide them from Kavanaugh. But Smith, once again, said no.

Smith did, however, allow them to question La Rock about a document Joseph emailed himself, called "Dan pay off," which showed four payments he made to Kavanaugh in late January and February 2009, totaling $6,300.

On cross, Imes tried to impeach La Rock with sarcasm, suggesting his testimony was self-serving and hyperbolic, and his conclusions were subjective, because his firm had earned $122,000 for work on this case.

"I believe my conclusions are objective," La Rock countered.

Smith overruled the defense's objections that Imes was being argumentative.

After the jury was excused at day's end, the defense asked the judge to admonish Imes as he had Maline. "The unprofessional tone and nature of the questioning to this point is highly objectionable," McGee said, accusing Imes of "really treating this like a joke."

Smith replied he "would treat any attorney the same for similar conduct," but he believed counsel "are entitled to be aggressive" as they cross-examine witnesses. He contended he'd sustained the "majority" of defense objections, which was true: he sustained fifteen, but he also overruled ten others.

"When [Imes] mocks the witness and mocks me in my line of questioning, I think that goes to what is considered aggressive," Maline said, which "demeans the proceedings, it demeans his office." But when the defense tries to point out where the court is not treating both sides equally, he said, the judge only "remind[s] us of our missteps."

The next morning, Imes challenged La Rock's ethics: "Have you been interviewed by the defense documentary team?" he asked, the same question the prosecution posed to other defense experts to imply they were compromised, sometimes adding, "That's good advertising, right?"

After McGee's objection was overruled, La Rock said he'd been questioned five or six times but hadn't received any compensation for doing so.

Imes tried to negate La Rock's testimony about Kavanaugh's San Diego IP address by asking if it was possible that "multiple service providers can be used in that course of conduct, creating a chain of connectivity."

"Generally speaking, when you are connected to the internet via any device, you are using one service provider," La Rock replied, but, yes, it's "possible."

Imes got La Rock to agree that someone with technical computer skills could mask their true IP address or location by using a virtual private network (VPN), which would show the IP address of a centralized network, or by "spoofing" the address using a "plethora of technology" available. But La Rock pointed out that such tactics would require "a different skill level" from someone who was good at building websites and manipulating Google rankings, like Kavanaugh.

La Rock said he actually tried "to ascertain if there was any evidence to show" Kavanaugh had been using a VPN, and "definitely found evidence" to the contrary. Specifically, Kavanaugh logged into Gmail on January 14 from an IP address in Hawaii and on January 26 from an IP address in San Diego, which reaffirmed the addresses in the PayPal records.

Moving on to computer use at the McStay house, La Rock said Joseph primarily used the eMachine until "mid-to-late 2009," when he switched to the Dell laptop that turned up in the eMachine logs as "Giuseppe-lap," indicating that the two devices were interacting. Holiday photos from 2009 featured Joseph and Summer using the Dell two months after another laptop, which was seized from the house, was last used in October. The Dell laptop interacted with the eMachine for the last time on February 3 at 12:26 p.m.

On cross, La Rock confirmed the sheriff's computer analyst's previous testimony that there was no QuickBooks activity on Joseph's eMachine on February 1. Asked if he could point Imes to forensic evidence that proved the Dell laptop was used to create and delete checks on QuickBooks on February 1 and 2, La Rock said he couldn't, because the device wasn't collected from the house by law enforcement. But if it had been, he said, it likely would contain "potentially highly significant" information.

Trying to prove Kavanaugh was in Hawaii as he'd claimed, Imes put Kavanaugh's phone records on the overhead screen, highlighting sixteen of the nineteen calls he made between January 31 and February 1, 2010, to numbers with Hawaii's 808 prefix. La Rock acknowledged he hadn't reviewed those records.

After a couple more sarcastic questions by Imes, the defense complained in a sidebar about the judge's repeated failure to curtail the prosecutor's argumentative tone. Despite the court sustaining the defense's objections, "he continues this tone,"

Maline said. "It doesn't faze him one bit because there is no sanction, no admonishment."

"There is a sanction to all counsel, I think, in the eyes of the jury as to how you are behaving," Smith retorted. "My impression is that all counsel have basically decided to behave as petulant children, arguing on the playground, and have made a conscious decision that it is tactically advantageous to your position. I tried for months to try to dissuade you from that. Nobody was dissuaded. I have given up."

Back before the jury, Imes showed La Rock a portion of Kavanaugh's PayPal account, asking if his IP address jumped from Davis, California, to Redmond, Washington, and then to San Diego, all within an hour and ten minutes, as the records seemed to indicate.

"No," La Rock said, noting "different providers have varying degrees of specificity" in their records.

"So, these records, you are saying, are unreliable?"

"No, that's not what I'm saying," La Rock said. Rather, the provider "did not have a very good understanding as to the location," as evidenced by one example that was "simply listed as the United States of America."

"But you are willing to accept that when it says San Diego?"

Yes, La Rock said, because that's how it was listed by three independent providers.

The defense called crime-scene reconstructionist Randolph Beasley on April 22 to counter the speculative testimony about the tiny reddish splotches in photos of the dining table that the prosecution intimated "could be" blood.

Beasley, who had processed hundreds of bloody scenes during his thirty-year career at the SBCSD's crime lab, explained the "spatters" visible in the photos are commonly seen in wood staining. Covered with polyurethane, the splotches are obscured by the glare when light is shined on them. In fact, he said, he had a similar dining table at home, which he photographed and analyzed for comparison.

"It's not blood that's on the surface," he said. "It's not anything that's on the surface. It's underneath the topcoat, which is why it's not visible."

After studying photos of the McStays' house and garage, Beasley highlighted the importance of what he *didn't* see: blood swipe patterns, transfer stains, and drip stains or trails that would be left if someone "had suffered a blunt-force trauma within the house somewhere," and had been moved from room to room.

He also didn't see blood spatters on the edges or legs of the dining table, around or beneath it on the rug or linoleum floor, on the knit hats or other items on top of the table, or on the surrounding chairs. Nor did he "see any damage to walls or doors or the floor, that could have been the result of a blow with a sledgehammer or any other kind of weapon."

When a person's skull is bashed four to six times, he said, the blood typically goes "everywhere." It would fly at least several feet in a "castoff" pattern, covering the killer "from head to toe," and any vehicle he got into afterward, especially if he'd moved bodies in it.

For investigators not to see even one spot of blood was remarkable, he said, because "it would be a lot to clean up." Also, even if someone had painted over spatter on walls, "shadowing through the paint" would still be visible under an "alternate light source."

On cross, Sean Daugherty asked if Beasley could "say to any degree of certainty that nothing happened in the house," specifically blunt-force trauma.

"It could have happened in the house, but there is no evidence, in my opinion, to support that it did," Beasley said.

"Are you assuming there wasn't sufficient time to clean up?"

No, Beasley said, "I'm just making the opinion there is no evidence to that."

Asked by McGee to elaborate, Beasley said, "Because the cleanup that would be needed, in my opinion, to remove that type of blood spatter and pooling of blood would have been more thorough, so that there would not have been the dirt and dust or whatever other debris that I observed," such as the pine needles from the Christmas tree that were still on the carpet.

Chapter 42

When the trial broke at noon during Randolph Beasley's second day on the stand, Maline thought McGee looked pale and seemed less energetic than usual as they ate lunch at a diner.

"What's wrong?" Maline asked.

"I'm not feeling well," McGee said.

When they got back to the courthouse, McGee decided to go home, leaving Maline to finish questioning Beasley.

McGee was still out the next day, so Maline also had to question their photogrammetry expert, Gregg Stutchman, who had been McGee's witness.

Stutchman said he disagreed with prosecution expert Eugene Liscio that the truck on the Mitchley video was consistent with Merritt's, because it had no side running lights and the headlights were at a different level than Merritt's. The bright spot Liscio said was a reflection on Merritt's truck latch also ran horizontally when the latch was actually positioned vertically.

"So even if this were a reflection, it wouldn't match, is that correct?" Maline asked.

"Right."

Furthermore, they couldn't be the same truck, because the

side light on Merritt's vehicle, which was sixty inches high, wouldn't be visible in the video, because it would be obscured by Mitchley's porch light.

Merritt's truck also had a "very prominent driving light, turn-signal light beneath the headlight and above the reflection," he said, whereas the truck in the video has "no corresponding light there. In fact, there's a dark spot between the bottom of the headlight and the top of the reflection."

The next day, McGee showed up briefly to meet with Judge Smith in chambers. McGee said he didn't know what was med-ically wrong with him, but was waiting for some test results.

"But inside, I knew what was going on," Maline recalled, saying he believed McGee's condition was brought on by the constant conflict with the prosecution. "He was one of the most ethical DAs I ever dealt with. He was having a very difficult time with these prosecutors. A guy like Jim can't deal with stuff like that. I can, and I was stunned by the level of lies and mis-representation by the prosecution."

The defense had planned to call Leonid Rudin, the prosecu-tion's former photogrammetry expert, next. But because he was now McGee's witness—and a key one for the defense—Smith agreed to delay his testimony. Still, the judge told the jury opti-mistically that the defense hoped to rest its case the following week.

As the days went on, Maline handled what witnesses he could on his own. When Merritt asked what was going on with McGee, Maline said he "was having equilibrium problems and he couldn't think."

McGee didn't talk specifics about his illness at the time, but he conceded later on the TSG documentary that "I had to have a neurologist get into it. I literally sat there in a daze and I had no thoughts going on in my head. I was in a quiet room 24/7. If you'd asked me my address, I wouldn't have been able to have told you. All I can say is I didn't know if I'd ever practice law again."

After a couple of weeks had gone by, Merritt asked Jacob Guerard how his boss was doing. "When's he coming back?"

Guerard, who had passed the bar by then, said McGee was taking it one day at a time, working from home as he could. Guerard had taken over McGee's court appearances with other clients, which put most of the Merritt case on Maline, leaving them all wondering if he'd have to finish the trial on his own.

"We were all concerned because we didn't know what was going on with Jim," Guerard said. "We were taking it day by day, basically."

In the meantime, Maline called their forensic accounting expert to the stand. Dennis Shogren told the jury he'd analyzed "a truckload of data," including Joseph's QuickBooks ledgers, which he'd only just received, to understand the workings of EIP and to assess Joseph's relationships with Merritt and Kavanaugh.

EIP was a "project-based business," he said, so materials wouldn't be purchased until customers paid a 50 percent deposit, with the balance paid upon completion. The spreadsheets were updated as jobs were finished, which "changes the math of what's owed back and forth" between Joseph and Merritt. The final reconciliation, or "zeroing out," didn't happen until the year's end.

"Would it be accurate to say that at any given time in the year 2008, or any year for that matter, picking any date you want, there could be an amount owing to Chase or an amount overpaid to Chase, which means an amount owing to Joseph?" Maline asked.

"That's correct," Shogren said.

Breaking down Joseph's email about the $42,845 Merritt

"owed" him, he said the amount was still in flux when Joseph disappeared, because Merritt still hadn't received his $26,000 share of the deposits for the Paul Mitchell and Saudi Arabia jobs in January—so it wasn't truly a "debt."

"At any given point in time, that number is going to change, depending on what the most recent payment received, or payment owed, would be," Shogren said, pointing out that Joseph had owed $23,251 to Merritt in January 2009.

When Melissa Rodriguez challenged the accountant's assessment that Joseph didn't consider the $42,845 a debt, Shogren replied, "I have not seen any evidence of a demand for payment or settlement," only a boxed note to the side on the spreadsheet.

"So, if Mr. McStay actually intended this document to mean that the defendant owed $42,845, and Mr. McStay was gone, I guess that debt disappears, right?" she asked.

Shogren contended that any "debt" for jobs gone wrong, such as Provecho, would have been the responsibility of EIP, not Merritt. If Joseph had meant for it to be in the "overpaid" column of the ledger, "he would have put it there."

Asked by the judge if the email was meant more as a notice from Joseph that this was "something that we need to talk about," Shogren replied, "Yes, that's correct."

Retracing Joseph's PayPal history with Kavanaugh, Shogren said Kavanaugh had submitted payment requests since July 2005. Once they were accepted, Joseph transferred the money to him. Starting on February 10, 2010, however, when Joseph's password was reset, Kavanaugh stopped sending requests, yet the transfers continued.

"Is that what you meant by 'hacking in'?" Maline asked. Objection. Sustained.

After Joseph disappeared, Shogren said, EIP customers began sending payments for waterfalls "to a Kavanaugh account," and by year's end, he'd taken in more than $206,000, including wire transfers, PayPal payments, and deposits to the EIP bank account he opened in June.

But each time Maline tried to ask Shogren how much of this income went to Kavanaugh's personal expenses, such as the "tens of thousands of dollars spent in nightclubs," he was interrupted by a cascade of objections, which Smith sustained.

Asked if Kavanaugh benefited financially from Joseph's disappearance, Shogren said yes. "For the last year or so, he'd earned significantly less money than he had previously, and then almost immediately after the disappearance, his income from Earth Inspired Products went up significantly. So, under the parameters we were working with, I called that a gain."

Merritt's company, on the other hand, went under in May 2010, because his main source of income, from EIP, had dried up.

Asked if any of the $147,000 in Kavanaugh's business profits went to the McStay family, Shogren said, "No, I don't recall seeing anything given to [them]," other than the $6,250 that Geis Construction sent directly to Susan Blake.

On cross, Shogren acknowledged only one page in his nine-page report involved Merritt, because most of the records he'd received from the defense concerned Kavanaugh. He also didn't consider Merritt's personal spending, gambling, or ATM withdrawals at casinos.

"I didn't care whether he was buying lunch or a poker chip. It was not what I was looking at," he said, which was only the "income and expenses" associated with EIP business.

"You didn't think that would be important in terms of your financial analysis in this case to look at the defendant's spending history?" Rodriguez asked, challenging the expert's reported impartiality. Objection.

By the end of April, one male juror had stepped down, saying he was unable to concentrate due to panic attacks, and an alternate had taken his place.

Concerned about the impending time crunch, Judge Smith re-called that jurors had been told initially they likely would only have to serve through April. So, if they'd mentioned commit-ments in May and June, "We said, 'Don't worry about it.' Well, those are starting to create problems. And the further we go, the more problems we're going to have where we could start losing jurors."

"That's what happens when we take a month off," Imes quipped.

"Well, we took various times off for various reasons," Smith replied.

Maline felt an added layer of crunch that week as witnesses McGee had prepared to question had to be delayed on the calen-dar and discovery materials came in last minute.

McGee was still undergoing medical tests "to rule out some things," as Guerard put it, but said he would be out at least an-other week.

This "puts us in a place where we have to scramble," Maline told the judge. "These are not my witnesses." He said he'd rather the judge continue the witnesses until McGee's return so the "focus of blame" wasn't on him. "It's not so much me, it's more my concern for my client."

Smith said he didn't "have a problem letting the jury know that," which he did, saying that in McGee's absence, Maline had been "feverishly trying to get prepared to do those witnesses."

"I know it's frustrating, but it certainly is not anybody's fault," Smith said.

Judge Smith welcomed McGee back to the courtroom on May 7. But the attorney didn't stay long after watching Maline's efforts to impeach Sergeant Edward Bachman about his agency's investigative failures. Bachman, who had been promoted since Merritt was arrested, repeatedly said he didn't recall what re-ports he'd reviewed or when.

"Did you ever ask Mr. Kavanaugh, how was it that he was able to sell Joseph's company without Joseph or his family's permission?" Maline asked.

"It didn't look like we confronted him regarding that," Bachman replied. "There were a lot of questions, obviously, because we had never talked to Mr. Kavanaugh before. At that point, we still hadn't even spoken to Mr. Merritt."

After the morning recess, McGee announced he was not well enough to stay. "It's clear I came back too early," he said. "Took me about thirty minutes to figure that out."

The defense asked Smith to further delay Leonid Rudin's testimony, go "dark" the following week, and then reassess the situation.

"It's not like Mr. McGee has a clear set date [to return]," Maline said.

When Smith suggested they come back in two weeks, the prosecution objected, saying they could lose jurors.

"There's been nothing but dark time in this defense case to get ready for whatever was necessary," Daugherty said. Rodriguez chimed in, citing Marsy's Law, the victims' families' right to a speedy trial, and their frustrations with all the delays.

But, as Smith pointed out, "it would be more frustrating for them, in the name of expediency, to go forward if the end result is going to be either a mistrial or reversal, and have to do it over again at a later time."

Maline said he wasn't going to address the prosecution's "insensitive" and "nonsensical" remarks about McGee's condition. "They don't know what they're talking about. They don't know how he's feeling," but "Mr. McGee wants to go forward and would do so even against doctor's wishes if he could."

Smith agreed to revisit the issue in two weeks to ascertain whether McGee was well enough to proceed, or if Maline should step in.

In the meantime, Maline recalled Detective DuGal to present

a number of questions he and his partner had asked Merritt in the past tense, only to use his responses—also in the past tense— against him.

"Would it be fair to say that those are questions in the past tense?" Maline asked.

"I would say, generally, I'm asking in the past tense because I don't know any of these people," DuGal said. "So, yeah, I'm referring to the past."

The next morning, the attorneys debated Maline's request to call the defense's investigator, Gary Robertson, to outline his failed efforts to serve Dan Kavanaugh with a subpoena to testify. Not surprisingly, the prosecution objected, deeming it irrelevant and "an attempt to backdoor third-party culpability."

"There's reasons we didn't call him [as a witness], and those reasons are protected by work product," Daugherty said.

Smith ruled the defense was entitled to present evidence that they'd tried unsuccessfully to locate Kavanaugh, however, they couldn't argue Kavanaugh "prevented the presence of Ms. Riccobene," as Imes put it, or "argue Kavanaugh is hiding, he's running, [or] it's a consciousness of guilt."

This led to another round of accusations between the attorneys and a mounting collective frustration with the judge for not intervening, during which Merritt covered his face with his hands, and shook his head.

The prosecution complained that Merritt's attorneys had repeatedly violated the court's pretrial rulings, but Smith said he would have instructed the jury if that was the case.

"But that's happened already," Rodriguez insisted.

Maline countered that the prosecution had violated court orders "on a daily basis" throughout the trial.

"That's an accusation of misconduct, let's have a hearing," Imes said again.

Sounding like an elementary school teacher, Smith said, "I've

allowed both sides to say things and do things that were improper and making allegations that were either partially true or
not true at all. And we could certainly sidetrack the entire trial
and have a whole trial just on the conduct of counsel. That, of
course, would be to the benefit of the defense, because we would
never finish the trial. So, I'm not going to do that. I'm going to
keep the focus on the trial and let others deal with misconduct of
counsel at a later point," a comment that created a possible
opening for a point of appeal.

But the prosecution wouldn't let go.

"We're going to start losing jurors, and we will end up in a
mistrial," Imes said, complaining that McGee's protracted absence was unduly prolonging the trial.

Imes went so far as to accuse McGee of malingering, saying
he'd seen the allegedly sick lawyer at a weekend social event,
"where he was perfectly fine, drinking, and dancing."

McGee wasn't there to defend himself, but he later told TSG
he had only enough champagne for a toast and danced one song
with his wife, who was holding him up because he felt so un-
steady he thought he might fall.

"These are starting to appear like intentional stall tactics,"
Imes said, adding that the defense's "experts aren't completing
work [and reports] until the night before they testify, even
though they've had the case for three, four, or five years."

Maline threw the same accusation back at the prosecution,
noting Eugene Liscio was hired mid-trial. "Every time we discuss these issues, the three of them get up like cackling school-
girls, and go through this thing, that we're engaging in some
type of misconduct, and the court allows this to occur on a regular basis. So, should we just sit down and not say anything?"

Defense investigator Gary Robertson testified that he'd tried
to serve Kavanaugh with subpoenas at locations all over Southern California. The first time, in August 2017, he was seeking

paperwork. He tried again in 2019, a month before the defense began presenting its case, this time with a subpoena to testify.

Over the course of three months, Robertson went to seven different locations, checked jail database systems and social media, and conducted surveillance. Because Kavanaugh was on the prosecution's witness list, he asked them for a current address, but they gave him one he'd already checked.

"Did it become apparent, at some point, that even though Mr. Kavanaugh was on the prosecution's witness list, that they weren't going to call him?" Maline asked. Multiple objections.

On cross, Melissa Rodriguez asked if Robertson had tried looking in Hawaii or San Francisco, where Kavanaugh's social media said he was. Robertson said no.

Considering that homicide detectives and TSG producers found Kavanaugh (as did this author), some observers questioned how hard the defense actually looked for him.

"It wasn't hard to find Dan," Detective Hanke said on TSG.

Mary Ellen Attridge, who recently retired as a senior supervising attorney from the San Diego County Public Defender's Office, offered two possibilities.

"Possibility one is that Dan is an expert at computers and actually could hide himself digitally," she said. "The other possibility is that there were half-baked attempts to find him, because it's easier to argue with a straw man than a real man."

In other words, it was easier for the defense to name Kavanaugh as a suspect in the McStay murders if he wasn't there to be questioned or cross-examined. But, whatever the reason, neither side called Kavanaugh or Tracey Riccobene.

As Maline told Smith on May 20, in spite of a subpoena to testify, Riccobene "still refuses to come. The court said we could have a warrant issued. She, under no circumstances, even with a warrant, even being arrested, because of her fear of Kavanaugh, will not testify."

Rodriguez, who argued before trial that Riccobene had credibility issues and shouldn't be allowed to testify, dismissed her as "not credible" again on the TSG documentary.

"I'm looking up at her face [on the interview footage] and I can see a lot of marks to me that are indicative of somebody that's using drugs," Rodriguez said. "She was definitely under the influence, so I think it was quite clear that she was very clearly unstable."

Although Riccobene appeared fidgety on the video, she denied being under the influence, and she and Maline both denied she had sores on her face.

Maline said he decided not to call her because "she's a wild card," who wouldn't help his case.

"Her behavior was becoming more erratic, that was the problem, and I just didn't know what she was going to say anymore," he said later. "She would have been destroyed on cross-examination."

But he did believe her story made some key points that weren't publicly known, such as Summer's wedding dress being out of its box and that Kavanaugh had talked about having muddy shoes after returning from burying the family in the desert, which fit with the rainstorm on February 6.

McGee returned to court to help Maline with jury instructions on May 20. Welcomed again by the judge, McGee said he still wasn't feeling "100 percent. I don't know when I'm going to be 100 percent."

In retrospect, Merritt wasn't happy about that. "If he was indeed sick and he couldn't handle my case properly, then the court should have said, 'You shouldn't be dealing with a death penalty case.' But he didn't, he just let him continue."

The night before Leonid Rudin was set to testify, the defense alerted Britt Imes they were alleging he'd committed a Brady violation for not sending them the entire explanation behind Rudin's new conclusions.

A Brady violation is misconduct that occurs when a prosecutor breaks a rule of discovery, established by the U.S. Supreme Court in *Brady v. Maryland* (1963), by failing to alert the defense about exculpatory evidence that might exonerate the defendant.

Once they finished with jury instructions, the defense asked to question Sergeant Bachman further about his interview with Kavanaugh, during which Kavanaugh uttered numerous falsehoods, to underscore the department's investigative failures.

"That money was all swiped from Joseph's account, Joseph's estate, right under the noses of these investigators, who never even bothered to follow up," Maline said. "Then, when they are told these lies in this interview, they just simply gloss over it."

Imes objected, saying Shogren's "numbers were inflated by cash deposits that he couldn't attribute to actual business proceeds, and therefore you can't say those statements are false."

Maline disagreed. Shogren had testified about cash *withdrawals*, he said, not deposits, claiming Kavanaugh had basically stolen $100,000 from Joseph's estate by taking customers' money and spending it in nightclubs.

Nonetheless, Judge Smith sustained the prosecution's objection. "The evidence is already there to support those arguments as to Kavanaugh's motive and reason for potentially being involved as a perpetrator and the failure of the investigators to discover that information and follow up on it," he said.

The defense also asked the court to order the three DNA profiles identified by Cybergenetics to be entered into the CODIS database.

When Smith supported the prosecution's contention that there weren't three actual profiles to submit, McGee said the judge was oversimplifying and "confusing the way the interpretation is done between humans and computers."

Referring to Perlin's testimony, Smith acknowledged Cybergenetics did provide "a format suitable for a one-time keyboard search of CODIS-style allele database of DNA-referenced genotypes."

But, Smith said, the motion was coming too late to act upon. If it had come shortly after Cybergenetics issued its report in January, or even after its CEO testified in April, he would have had time to schedule a hearing so that the DA, the state attorney general, and the county's CODIS administrator could determine "if that was appropriate or not." But doing so now would mean continuing the trial for another thirty days.

"We are not going to do that," Smith said, because that would put us "into June, and we would lose all of our jurors."

Still, McGee wouldn't let it go, even as Daugherty pointed out the futility. The CODIS administrator, Susan Anderson, had already said she couldn't run the profiles, because she didn't have the "format suitable to run in CODIS," Daugherty said. "Dr. Perlin called this antiquated. Well, this is what the rest of the well-established DNA community uses."

McGee retorted that this was a problem of asking the wrong question. This would be a manual "single-target" search to see if two specific alleles were at a particular loci in a person's DNA. "I tried to explain it to them before, you are reading the wrong section [of the law]. They don't want to listen."

"The problem is, then that leaves a defendant barred from access to information that could be exculpatory and lead to an acquittal," McGee said. "Under the due process clause, that requirement is unconstitutional," and if the court agreed, they could move forward. "That's our request."

Daugherty accused the defense of making a tactical decision not to seek "relief earlier," and announcing they were ready for trial several months before the Cybergenetics report came back.

McGee called that "unfair and untrue. When I finally came to my cognitive senses to inform Mr. Maline of what should be done on this, he did it as soon as he could. This wasn't an intentional delay."

Smith denied the defense's motion as well as McGee's request to continue the trial to meet the hearing dates Smith had outlined.

The next morning, photogrammetry expert Leonard Rudin testified that he'd been a prosecution witness at one time but was never asked to write a report. He'd only submitted "images with measurements on them that were sort of self-explanatory."

As McGee had him run through his method of analysis, Rudin explained how he'd superimposed images to identify key fixed points of comparison between Merritt's truck and the one in the Mitchley video. But the only way the respective points would have matched up was if Merritt's wheels were underground.

So, Merritt's truck "should be excluded, yes," he said, a conclusion he'd reached a week after testifying at the 402 hearing in February. "I just realized what—mathematics don't lie."

"And did you inform the prosecution of this?" McGee asked, eliciting an objection from Imes. "Were you told to stop working?" Another objection.

Rudin recounted listening to Eugene Liscio's testimony on YouTube, then calling McGee to ask if he would allow Rudin to do the same "live reprojection" experiment the prosecution had rejected.

"You said you wanted to do that to be thorough and accurate and complete and you were told no?" McGee asked.

"Well, in slightly different words: 'We don't have time,' this kind of thing."

Rudin said he also called McGee because he disagreed with Liscio's conclusion that the two trucks were consistent. "It's not his fault, he used some software that was not specifically for that," he said.

Noting he'd invented one of the software programs Liscio

had used, Rudin said Liscio's methods and conclusions were simply wrong.

At a 402 hearing that same day, with the jury absent, Rudin was asked to discuss the circumstances surrounding his change of opinion and the resulting alleged Brady violation, which Imes denied committing.

Rudin described the "stand down" email from Imes, and showed his phone to the court to prove he still had the text he'd sent to Imes afterward. Then he was excused.

"I think at this point, there's been an allegation of misconduct, or at least sniffing around for misconduct," Sean Daugherty said. "I find it hard to believe that this wasn't discussed."

The prosecution claimed they'd sent an email about Rudin's text to the defense, but the defense said they never received it. Because they didn't have a complete picture of what happened, McGee said, "we are going to tread very lightly here," but the jury should be informed regardless.

Asked why this was relevant to Merritt's case, McGee referred back to the defense's opening statement, claiming "there was been a confirmation bias on the part of this government prosecution of Mr. Merritt. They ignore information that does not fit their theory. Now we know that information was presented to the government saying, 'Our original theory is gone.' And instead of giving that over and the details, they intentionally made it vague and then said, 'Let's not call him. Call somebody else.' They didn't tell the defense as to why that happened."

Smith said he didn't think the evidence supported "the so-called confirmation bias argument." Deeming the whole Rudin text-disclosure issue "a collateral matter" that had nothing to do with "whether or not Mr. Merritt is the perpetrator," Smith declined to disclose it to the jury.

He agreed, however, that Rudin's follow-up text should have been given to the defense at the time. "If it was intentionally withheld, that would be a violation of prosecution's Brady responsibility. But at this point, there is no prejudice, because the defense now has it."

That said, Smith said he needed more time to make a formal ruling to incorporate a response to the brief, denying any Brady violation, just filed by Deputy District Attorney Mark Vos.

Back on the stand, Rudin reiterated for the jury that he was only offering a qualified opinion that it wasn't Merritt's truck in the video. He couldn't be more definitive without collecting more data, and he still couldn't understand why he'd been told not to do so.

Excusing the jury, the judge questioned Rudin again about his conversations and emails with McGee about Liscio's testimony, and Rudin's problems with Liscio's methodology. Rudin emphasized that the defense had subpoenaed him to testify, which terrified his wife, and that he wasn't working with the defense's expert. Nor was he a defense expert.

At that point, Maline revisited the Brady allegations, noting the defense would never have seen Rudin's text to Britt Imes if he hadn't showed them to the court on his phone the day before.

"The conduct of not only Mr. Imes, but all the prosecutors in this case, because we believe they all know what was going on, can only be described as reprehensible," Maline said. The defense's cross-examination of Liscio would have "gone a whole heck of a lot different if we had had this information at that time."

Maline requested Smith dismiss all charges against Merritt, or, alternatively, declare a mistrial. He also requested that Imes be removed from the case, "if not all [three] prosecutors," and Eugene Liscio's testimony be stricken.

Daugherty argued that the defense received the basic information on February 15 that Rudin's opinion had changed, so recusal and dismissal weren't the proper remedies. He suggested, rather, that Liscio be recalled for further cross-examination.

"I don't believe at this point there is prejudice," Daugherty said. "I certainly don't think there was suppression."

Ultimately, Smith ruled there was no basis for a Brady violation. Although he reiterated that Rudin's text to Imes was exculpatory and should have been provided to the defense, the defense was "free to contact Dr. Rudin. In fact, there was contact. The reality is, they obviously did obtain all of that information and have Dr. Rudin testifying to it. So, in terms of, is there any prejudice? I don't see any prejudice. Was any evidence suppressed? No, the evidence was not suppressed."

As a result, he said, he was denying all three of Maline's motions.

McGee objected, saying the prosecution used "shell game" tactics to deprive the defense of crucial information. "You have to look at the whole thing, the totality of circumstances and prosecutorial misconduct." He pointed out that Rudin initially refused to provide more information, because he was worried he'd get sued for sharing his opinion as a prosecution witness.

Maline accused the judge of serving as an advocate for the prosecution. "There is zero sanction for this prosecutor not turning over [the text] in light of the history," he said. "They said they were going to provide proof they sent it. Of course, they haven't, because we never got it."

When Daugherty and his colleague, Mark Vos, requested that Smith hold a formal hearing on the misconduct allegations, Smith said, "We're not going to interrupt Dr. Rudin's testimony. But I am certainly willing to do that."

Despite the number of times these allegations were made during this trial, no such hearing was ever conducted.

Back in front of the jury, Imes tried to regroup while attempting to impeach his former expert's testimony. He did this by targeting Rudin's proprietary methods and criticism of Liscio's approach, which Rudin did not take lightly.

Their exchanges became increasingly combative as Imes made veiled implications that Rudin's memory was flawed, while Rudin called the prosecutor "a little confused" and implied that he lacked the necessary technical understanding.

"Isn't it true you're upset he didn't use your software?" Imes asked.

"That's ridiculous," Rudin retorted.

After a brief recess, Imes tried a new avenue of attack. "When the judge asked you a question at the break on the record, you said, quote, 'It's a new method I dreamed up.' Isn't that what you said?"

"That's the way mathematicians talk," Rudin said.

"There is no way to validate or test to ensure that your measurements are accurate, correct?"

"Yes, there is, because point-per-point is exactly the same method people use for human height, and that was validated."

Still, Imes tried to portray Rudin's methodology as invalid, saying "no one has reviewed your work in this case to judge its accuracy."

"I just spoke to a number of people in the forensic community, and they think it's beautiful and it's right," Rudin countered.

"Your goal that you testified to yesterday was if you could make this work, you could retire, correct?" Imes asked.

"You see, sir, what you are doing is impugning my character and my motives instead of arguing my methods and mathematics," Rudin said, clearly agitated. "That is called ad hominem. It is a very dirty trick, used way back in Roman history."

"Did you not testify yesterday, quote, 'If I could make this work, I can retire'?"

"I may have said something like this, but it's not the reason I am developing the methods," Rudin said.

On May 17, a few days before Kavanaugh's ex-girlfriend, Lauren Forest-Knowles, was set to testify as a prosecution rebuttal witness, defense investigator Gary Robertson spoke to the man she and Kavanaugh had reportedly stayed with on Oahu.

Larry Haynes, who had previously told the prosecution's investigator that he didn't remember meeting Forest-Knowles and that Kavanaugh hadn't stayed at his place in 2010, wanted to change his statement.

Haynes said he'd since found a photograph on his iPhone of dirty dishes in the sink and an ant trail, which he'd sent Kavanaugh as proof of the mess he'd left. Haynes sent Robertson a screenshot of the message, which was dated February 10, 2010.

Haynes admitted he'd spoken with Kavanaugh two weeks earlier. "They are trying to pin it on [me]," Kavanaugh told him, saying the defense was trying to "use him as a scapegoat."

Haynes gave Robertson two recent phone numbers in San Diego he'd used to speak with Kavanaugh. So, if Robertson genuinely wanted to get a hold of Kavanaugh, he now had the chance to do so.

Because the defense hadn't finished its case yet, Forest-Knowles was called out of order on May 22 because she'd been flown in from Northern California to testify.

Questioned briefly by Daugherty, Forest-Knowles confirmed her previous statements that she was with Kavanaugh in Hawaii when the McStays disappeared, and that her boarding pass showed she returned on February 17. Her presence also allowed the prosecution to enter into evidence the Facebook photos she'd posted on February 4, 2010, allegedly featuring Kavanaugh.

Asked if they'd been taken that day, she said, "That's when I uploaded. Might have been that day or, I don't recall."

She said they were together in Hawaii for their entire vacation; he didn't leave for one day or "an extended period of time."

However, the document she called a boarding pass was actually labeled "receipt, not valid for transportation," and it was issued to her on February 15, 2010, for a return flight on February 17.

"Did Mr. Kavanaugh sit next to you on that flight on the way back?"

"Yes."

She said she dated Kavanaugh from March 2009 until November 2011. The last time she saw him in person was on a visit to San Diego in 2012 after she'd moved home to Santa Rosa. He'd messaged her on Facebook about eighteen months ago, she said, but "I blocked him so that he can't message me. Like, unwanted contact."

On cross, Maline questioned her about Kavanaugh's spending habits while in Hawaii, and read aloud her previous statements to detectives, which she said she couldn't recall. For example, when asked if he had any liquid cash, she said, "Oh, God, not at all. We had, like, no money when we lived out there." But once they returned from Hawaii, she said, Kavanaugh started spending money "frivolously."

"You guys were going out a lot, is that correct?" Maline asked.

"Yes."

"Nightclubs? All the time, bottle service?"

"Yes."

Kavanaugh told her he was making money selling water features, she said, and that he "was currently being bought out by Joey."

Asked if she used texts or emails to communicate with Kavanaugh while they were in Hawaii, she replied, "Text or calling."

Maline showed her an email she'd sent Kavanaugh on January 28, 2010, asking, "When are you coming back?"

She said she couldn't remember where Kavanaugh was when she sent it, "but it was probably something like the store."

Maline pointed out that her next email to him wasn't until March 5, which supported her previous testimony that they rarely communicated by email when they were in the same locale.

Asked whether she'd told her mom she was afraid of Kavanaugh, the prosecution objected, and again to Maline's next question: "Are you afraid of Dan Kavanaugh?"

Smith overruled the objection, saying she could reply "yes" or "no." But she chose not to answer directly.

"Um, he makes me uncomfortable," she said.

The jury never learned about the restraining order she obtained against Kavanaugh or his subsequent conviction. Forest-Knowles didn't respond to a request to be interviewed for this book.

The next morning, May 23, the defense recalled Sergeant Bachman, who acknowledged that his department had received an award from the International Association of Chiefs of Police in 2015, after nominating itself for its work on this case.

The prosecution objected to this as irrelevant. Although the judge initially didn't want to let this information in, he agreed due to Maline's persistence in a sidebar.

Because the department received the award before the case was over and went to trial, Maline contended, "We want to be able to argue that when you nominate yourself for an award and hold yourself as a hero" for solving a case, "it's very hard to then say, 'we were wrong.'"

Once the prosecution's last rebuttal witness had stepped down, it was time for Merritt to decide whether to take the stand.

Merritt had wanted to testify, an urge the prosecution attributed to "narcissism." But to Merritt, this was his final chance to dispute the prosecution's false accusations and to tell the jury the facts he believed his attorneys hadn't delivered effectively.

"I realized how little my attorneys knew about the case and

how well they were going to bring out the facts," he said in 2022, recalling that he'd thought, *I'm screwed*, as soon as Taylor and Cathy Jarvis had finished testifying.

"Mr. Merritt, you understand you, number one, have an absolute right not to testify if you do not want to? Nobody can force you to testify," Smith said. "Do you understand that?"

"Yes," Merritt replied.

"You also have an absolute right to testify if you want to. Nobody can stop you from testifying, if you want to testify, including your lawyers. Even if their advice is that you should not testify, you still have that right. Do you understand that?"

After Merritt said yes, the judge asked if he wanted to do so. But before he could answer, McGee jumped in to ask about "the use of which priors or any priors that would come in during cross-examination. We would object to any."

As Imes proceeded to list Merritt's criminal convictions out loud, Smith said he didn't see any connection between Merritt's history of theft and the current murder charges, but he would allow in "something very specific that would be impeachment to a specific bit of testimony." Then he gave Merritt one hour to speak privately with his attorneys and make a decision.

In the back room, Merritt's attorneys tried to talk him out of taking the stand, just as his daughter had.

"We're at a good place, we're at reasonable doubt," Maline told him, warning that if he testified, prosecutors would run through his whole life, ask leading questions that, regardless of his answers, would cast him and his past in a negative light, and make him look like a liar. "It's not going to be pretty. The jury doesn't know anything about your cons right now, and I want to keep it that way."

Merritt believed his attorneys just wanted the trial to end so they could move on. Looking back later, he said, "They knew it was going to take days and they wanted the trial over. McGee told court a couple of times, 'We're literally trying to eliminate witnesses, Your Honor.' Well, I was one of them. They wanted to finish the trial, nothing more nothing less."

Back in court, Merritt appeared somber and dejected.

"So, Mr. Merritt, you've had a chance to have some additional discussion with your attorneys?" Smith asked.

"Yes."

"What's your decision? Do you want to testify or not?"

Merritt, who had been staring down at the table, glanced up briefly to answer. "No," he said quietly before lowering his gaze again. Tearing up, he wiped his eyes with a tissue.

And with that, the defense rested.

Chapter 43

Closing arguments lasted three days, as both sides battled to persuade the jury that their opponents were not only unethical, but that their interpretation of the evidence was wrong.

When a second male juror came down with a medical issue, Judge Smith replaced him with an alternate rather than delay the closings for two days as the juror's doctor suggested.

Britt Imes's argument, which took most of one day, served as a bookend to Sean Daugherty's opening statement. It even started off with the same question: "How does a family of four disappear off the face of the earth?"

But after the prosecution had promised to answer important questions about this case, Imes said the law didn't require him to prove when or where the murders were committed, arguing, conveniently, that the specifics weren't important.

"Despite what precipitated the killing of whoever went first— whether it was an argument with Joseph over finances, whether it was Summer because of hatred over how he was treated and the disagreements over raising the kids, the fact that he believed she was a bitch—whatever precipitated the first killing ultimately won't matter. Because what will matter is, you intentionally then killed three other people."

Because, again, it all boiled down to the sledgehammer. Theatrically pounding repeatedly on the podium to emphasize each impact, he said, "It was blow, after blow, after blow to a child's skull."

"That is an intentional killing, that is willful, deliberate, and premeditated, when you kill a three- and four-year-old who know who you are, by this man, the defendant, Charles Merritt."

Citing the jury instruction that direct and circumstantial evidence are "of equal weight," Imes said, "you can't just look at one thing in isolation. It is one big piece of collective evidence. You must look to the totality of the circumstances surrounding the murders to understand the defendant's means, motive, and opportunity."

Rather than providing answers, Imes spent most of his argument raising more questions for the jury. Common sense, he said, would lead them to accept the prosecution's "reasonable interpretations" of the evidence. Such as the timing and location of cell phone calls. Merritt's long periods "off the grid." The truck in the Mitchley video, Merritt's truck. Merritt referring to Joseph in the past tense. All that suspicious activity with the QuickBooks checks and ledger.

"Even if there is an innocent explanation for this, there is no evidence that Joe's business practice was to create, backdate checks, and then delete them from his QuickBooks accounts," he said. Instead, it was Merritt's "failed attempt to cover his tracks."

Discounting Joseph's well-established efforts to push out Kavanaugh, Imes claimed Joseph was actually sidelining Merritt due to "project failures" and "sloppy" workmanship. Aware of the "problems" Merritt's former assistant conveyed, Joseph was looking for other fabricators and cutting Merritt's percentage by diverting more money to Metro Sheet Metal.

Imes took the jury through the timeline again, starting on February 1—when Joseph told Merritt he owed him $42,845, McGyver McCargar sensed the tension between Summer and

Merritt, Merritt was added as a vendor to QuickBooks, and checks started being written in lowercase letters, printed, and deleted.

Then on February 4, amid calls Joseph made to his bank, Imes said, Joseph also called Walker Welding, implying this was part of his search for new fabricators.

What Imes didn't tell the jury was that when his investigator, Jesse Moon, interviewed the owner, Warren Walker, a month earlier, he said he'd never talked with Joseph. It was only after he disappeared that Merritt came by and said they were looking for a fabricator to do some work, so Walker did "a few small jobs" *for Merritt.*

Imes alleged that Merritt made nineteen calls to Cathy Jarvis throughout the lunch he claimed to have had with Joseph, which would have been "rude."

But in fact, Merritt's phone records showed those nineteen calls were over the course of the entire day, ten of which were during a seven-minute period before Joseph arrived in Rancho Cucamonga, and didn't even connect.

Although those records also showed that Joseph stayed in Rancho Cucamonga for ninety minutes before heading south, Imes claimed, "There's no credible evidence of a meeting either," only the "self-serving" defendant's word, in the absence of any receipt, credit card, or bank activity proving Joseph paid for their meal at Chick-fil-A.

But if there was a meeting, Imes said, playing it both ways, it was only long enough for Joseph to say, "I know you forged checks, I know you cashed that twenty-five-hundred-dollar check, I am done with you." Because why would Joseph drive all the way there to give him checks when he'd given him a couple of checks two days before? And why would he give Merritt a blank check when his checkbook was in the car?

Imes tried to make Eugene Liscio's testimony sound more convincing than Leonard Rudin's, the expert he'd replaced, claiming that Rudin had his own agenda to make money and retire, his "explanations were blurry and fuzzy," and he "introduced his own error that, ultimately, could not be validated."

Cathy Jarvis was on the chopping block next. He painted her as "a failed alibi witness," who couldn't offer any "corroborative evidence" that Merritt was home the night of February 4. Who "clearly has a bias, a witness who potentially profits off the defense documentary film if her story is believed and he's acquitted." And who was "coached by the defendant."

"You did not even hear evidence from Cathy or Taylor that he was sitting in the clubhouse watching a movie or having dinner with them," he said.

Imes reminded jurors of their trip to the gravesite and the Quartzite cell tower on the mountain above. "Within eyesight of those graves, the defendant's phone is pinging" on February 6, he said. Merritt denied that he was in the desert, even with "his phone records logging six cell-site hits" there.

Imes used this chance to offer alternative scenarios to the prosecution's original narrative: "Maybe he is checking on the condition of the bodies he buried there to make sure they weren't washed up. Maybe he's burying them that day. Is there conclusive proof? No. In that circumstance, when you put it together with all the rest, what's the explanation? It all comes back to the defendant."

He then called attention to the defense's unfulfilled promise to call their "fancy Russian cell expert named Vlad," who "was going to come and debunk all of this evidence." All they had was the defendant's claim that the only reason he would have been in the desert was to visit his sister or brother. But the defense didn't call his brother, and although Merritt's sister did testify, she couldn't "put him in the desert on the sixth."

"So why would the defendant be there on the sixth?"

On February 8, he said, the defendant was off the grid again until more QuickBooks checks were written that afternoon, when Merritt also called the company. "The only reasonable interpretation of that is he tried to cancel it online, realized, 'Oh, crud, it didn't work, it doesn't delete the information, the account is still there,' because as you were told, it stays in the cloud. So, he called QuickBooks, 'Hey, I need to cancel this.'"

Adjusting the prosecution's timeline again, he said, Merritt's phone went dark, this time for thirteen hours overnight. "It's during that time, ladies and gentlemen, that the Trooper was noted at 9:18 p.m." in the parking lot in San Ysidro, which left "a lot of time on February 8 for the defendant to move evidence, clean evidence, hide evidence."

Imes told the jury it didn't matter that the security guards couldn't say when the Trooper had been left there, because Merritt's whereabouts were known earlier that day "while he's forging checks to profit off the disappearance of Mr. McStay."

Then came February 15, the day Joseph's brother reported the family missing, which Imes used as a segue to counter the defense's "line of questioning with various witnesses about an incomplete, unthorough investigation" by the SDSD.

"You have to remember, we are not talking about what we know today. We are talking about what they were confronted with in 2010."

Jumping ahead to the discovery of the family's remains in the desert in 2013, Imes disputed the defense's theory that "a team of two" killers drove them there, by turning their own argument against them.

"That ignores the conditions that were present in the desert at that time," he said. "That would be confirmation bias."

Although the jury instructions said he didn't have to prove where the murders occurred, "to ignore the evidence connecting the graves to the house, and to claim that you can't prove that a murder happened in that house, is not an honest representation of the evidence that was found there."

DuGal had testified that he could still smell fresh paint nine days after the family went missing. No towels were found in the house, a terry cloth robe was missing, and towel remnants and a bra were found in the grave with Summer's remains.

"It is a reasonable interpretation that something happened in that house. Something disabled the McStays, rendered them unable to fight back, allowed them to be secreted from that residence," and got them to the graves, where they were found "dead of multiple blunt-force trauma."

But what? "Only the killer knows."

Just as he'd dismissed Rudin as an expert without outside research validation, Imes did the same with Mark Perlin's probabilistic genotyping technology, calling it "fringe."

"His testing is unreliable. It gets into the weeds of the machine noise. And all of it based on inferences based on assumptions. It even excludes the victims, despite the conditions."

As Imes riffed along, he made a number of factual errors and misrepresentations that conflicted with previous testimony, such as his comment that there was more of Merritt's DNA in the graves than Summer's or the boys'.

"Misstates the testimony," said McGee, who voiced objections to only a few of these errors. Sustained.

Imes continued on as if nothing had happened, though he gave himself an excuse that afternoon. "When you have a case this big that drags on for so long, some innocent misstatements of evidence can occur."

Despite the scientific expert testimony that bacteria from decomposing bodies eats DNA, Imes still claimed the victims' DNA should have been there, because to say otherwise "flies in the face of all logic, flies in the face of the science."

"Dr. Rudin, Dr. Perlin, Cathy Jarvis, Sara Taylor," he said, misstating the name of Merritt's daughter, "the whole defense case was nothing more than smoke and mirrors. The whole defense case was, don't look at Charles Merritt."

Then he attacked forensic accountant Dennis Shogren, who, he said, "ignored the whole Hawaii evidence, all the transactions in the PayPal records from Hawaii."

"Clearly, it can be inferred from their testimony that they were hoping to gain notoriety and business from the publicity," Imes said of the defense experts. "That is a factor of bias that you can consider in evaluating their testimony."

And finally, he got to the "elephant in the room": Dan Kavanaugh, the man vilified by the defense "from opening statement forward," whose phone records reflect his call to the SDSD on February 10 from the 808 area code, and "are indicative of that totality of evidence that Dan was, in fact, calling from Hawaii."

"There is no credible reliable evidence that Dan Kavanaugh was involved in this crime at any time," he said. "In fact, their own PayPal records, their own bank records, show he continued to attempt to operate that business from the internet side. He even went the extra mile to help try and complete custom projects. There is no evidence, no credible, reliable corroborated evidence to justify pointing the finger at Dan Kavanaugh, let alone Susan Blake and Mike McStay."

The only person who benefited from these crimes, had the opportunity to commit them, and the motive "to erase the debt," was the defendant.

"This is a man who is selfish and self-centered and self-interested and motivated by greed," a man who makes "false statements" about "his injury to his hand being done at Metro Sheet Metal, where there is no evidence of that." Who coaches witnesses. Who originally told DuGal he was "changing up how QuickBooks was to hide it from Summer, not Dan Kavanaugh."

"How can you assertively tell someone, 'I was definitely the last person to see them alive' unless you are the killer?" "Ladies and gentlemen, would it have been nice to have a bloody crime scene? Sure. Would it have been nice for Detective DuGal to seize a piece of evidence, kick in a door, explode a Bluestar bomb? Sure. That's not the state of what the evidence is."

All he had to prove was that Merritt was the killer, he said.

"What you have, is an overwhelming convincing set of circumstantial evidence that no matter which way you turn the wheel, it always comes back to that center point being the defendant."

Because it was late afternoon, Judge Smith offered the defense a chance to start fresh in the morning. But James McGee wanted jurors to leave with his voice in their heads.

"I didn't want to wait," McGee told them. "I've been wanting to give this since October twenty-ninth, when you showed up here."

After expressing sympathy to the McStay family, McGee reintroduced himself to the jury as a former prosecutor, then proceeded to accuse his former colleagues of wrongly targeting Merritt's character and failing to answer important questions about the murders as they'd promised.

"Justice will not be given when you convict an innocent man," he said, highlighting the jury instruction dictating that if an innocent explanation is reasonable, then jurors must accept it over the one that points to guilt. "They don't want the law applied here, because it would require that acquittal. They want you to focus on hatred and emotion. Hate Mr. Merritt and have sympathy for the family."

But worse, McGee said, the prosecution was lying to the jury. "Do you like being lied to?" he asked, turning his back to the jury as Imes had done. "It's easier to lie when my back's to you."

Describing their entire case as "a fraud," he said, "When they gave their closing, they even misrepresented the facts and the evidence you heard. I will go through all of that."

First, they claimed there was no evidence Joseph had lunch with Merritt that day, then they claimed he fired Merritt at that same lunch to replace him with other welders.

"Let's recount the witnesses that the government called to the stand to discuss how they are taking over Chase's spot," he said. "Okay, we are done. There is none. They have nobody set up to replace him, because he wasn't getting replaced."

In fact, it was Kavanaugh who was out. McGyver McCargar had testified that Joseph said he'd bought Kavanaugh out of the business, and he saw Merritt and Joseph trying out LED lights for future fountains in the living room.

"Joseph is the one that figured out you can write checks and delete them so Dan couldn't see them. We know that by the time it was happening in his house," he said. "When they drove up and met for lunch, part of the reason was that Joseph was bringing him blank checks. The meeting was for that, not to fire him."

Joseph also called Merritt seven times after the meeting. "When you fire an employee, do you call them afterward to see how they are doing? No."

"If Joseph did not fire Chase on the fourth, Chase is done. There is no motive. This case is over. Everything else is fluff. Everything else is misdirection."

With that, McGee stopped to let that sink in overnight.

The next morning, McGee resumed by highlighting factual errors and omissions Imes made during his closing, starting with the actual number of calls Merritt rudely made to Cathy Jarvis during lunch on February 4. It was not nineteen, as Imes said, but six. "Only one connected, and it was four minutes long," he said.

In fact, neither attorney was correct. Merritt's phone records show Jarvis made a four-minute call to him at 1:23 p.m., which was followed by a two-minute return call to her.

McGee said the prosecution also contended Merritt was "able to corral four people and kill them without leaving any evidence in the house," and to do that "with no noise, no screams, no signs of violence."

But if Merritt disposed of the bodies on February 6, "where were the bodies during this time? If they're in the house, you are going to have pooling of blood. You will have blood everywhere. Were they in his truck? He's going to have him driving all over town with four dead bodies in the back. None of their theory makes sense." Especially if he pulled his truck out of the driveway at 7:47 p.m. and "we have computer activity at 8:05, and a phone call from Joseph's cell from the area of the house at 8:28."

McGee raised the issue of the dueling photogrammetry experts, who disagreed over whose truck was on the Mitchley video, underscoring that one of them testified during the defense's case only after being fired by Imes.

"Mr. Liscio was retained four days later. 'We have a problem. Our whole theory that we've sold this whole time is wrong. Mr. Liscio, how much would it cost you to say a light is not a light?' 'Fourteen grand.' 'Okay, well, that's what I need you to come in and say.'" McGee even accused the prosecution of "doctor[ing] evidence to sell their story. That's desperate."

But if that's not Merritt's truck, "you are done. We don't have him driving down there. We don't have him fired. There's no motive and no opportunity."

Based on the clothing the family was wearing, the coffee and the breakfast food out on the counter, McGee said the family was taken the morning of February 5.

"We know where Mr. Merritt is [at that time], he's in Upland on his phone at 7 a.m. He's on his way to LA" when he called his voicemail, Jarvis three times, and Joseph twice.

"What day were they killed? We don't know. No evidence can tell you that. We can tell you when they were killed *by*: approximately noon on February 12. The prosecution says, 'Well, they were buried on the sixth.' Why? 'Well, because Mr. Merritt's phone is in Victorville on the sixth.'"

And yet, even "their own expert, FBI Agent Boles, who had no reason to help the defense, says, 'yeah, it's reasonable that he wasn't at the grave.' 'Can you say with any certainty where the phone was?' 'Not with this type of analysis, no.'"

But based on the 11:52 a.m. call on the sixth, Merritt's phone was "moving, driving, not staying still, digging holes, killing people," and his calls were pinging off two elevated antennae that pick "up all the calls throughout the desert."

The prosecution's logic wasn't even consistent, he said. It was "circular reason[ing]" to claim Merritt turned off his phone to kill the family but left it on to bury their bodies. "Their theories contradict themselves."

The other problem with the prosecution's timeline, he said, was that it rained an inch on February 6. "You ever try digging a hole in the rain? You never do. Why? Because the mud and the water keep sloshing in." It made more sense if they were buried a day or two later, when the ground had dried, but "is still wet where the tracks were made."

McGee repeated the more likely scenario, which he'd proposed in his opening statement, even before he received Cybergenetics' test results showing DNA from three unidentified people at the gravesite: the killings and burial were done by three people in two separate vehicles, "one to drive, one to control."

Even if the government accepted this scenario, he said, they might still argue Merritt was involved. Yet, when they tapped his phone, he never called anybody to say, "Hey, we need to meet." There was "no coordinating with anybody."

The fact that Joseph's body was wrapped in a blanket, with cords tied around his neck, showed he was killed somewhere else, whereas Summer's broken jaw, and the position of her panties and pants above her head in the grave, indicate she was raped and fought for her life in the desert.

"She had a bra on, so they had a knife there because they cut it off," he said, and when they were taken from the house, they were bound with blue painter's tape.

"So, this all happened to the McStay family. Who did it? We all feel for what the family went through. I said, 'Let's give this family answers. So, let's do DNA analysis of the grave.'" Yet Imes argued the DNA evidence should be excluded, saying it "flies in the face of science. He said Bode said there were no results. Again, misrepresentation."

But Mark Perlin does "knows the science," McGee said, and he testifies for the government 90 percent of the time. "The DNA suggests that we have the three people that were involved."

The prosecution's own witness, Carmen Garcia, threw them a "curveball," because they had that "perfect window" of six hours on February 8, when they thought Merritt drove the Trooper to the border. Garcia "shattered" their timeline by placing Merritt at her office in Asuza mid-morning, when she also didn't see any injuries on his hand.

"Their case was falling apart right there, and they knew it, because their window now is gone."

They also purposely ignored the Trooper key in Joseph's pocket, he said. "So, they have had the keys in the pocket of the victim to a vehicle of interest and they never see if it worked on it. That is intentional blindness. Why are they playing games like this? Why are they trying to convince you with facts they haven't proven or thought up? Trying to pull one over on you."

The day the family was reported missing, Deputy Tingley took photos of the house, "showing you the drawers, the paper, stuff all laying out. Trash on the floor, you can see the dirt on the floor here. It's just dirty. Of course, a murder happened here, right? And they cleaned up and then they made it dirty again. The bedrooms, there's no blood anywhere."

The prosecution asked Tingley, "'When you went in, did you smell anything?' 'No, I didn't really smell or notice anything.'" They also asked Susan Blake, "'Did you smell paint?' 'No, I didn't smell paint. I smelled rotten food and diapers.'" Same with Michael McStay. "Nobody said paint but DuGal. Why? Because DuGal is part of the prosecution team. He knows what theory they need him to say. There's paint. There's cleaning up."

"These arguments are ridiculous. And then, what do they do in the middle of the trial? Let's get good ol' DuGal. 'What do you see on this table?' 'Oh, my God, I was devastated when I saw the blood. It looks like blood.' So, I had to have Mr. Beasley go through the whole thing, explaining why it's not blood. Remember, the whole detective team sat around that table. They didn't see anything."

The prosecution also overlooked the fact that Merritt was upfront with investigators since his first interview with DuGal. "Did they even bother listening to the interviews? Because since day one, he said, 'Yeah, Joseph gave me the checks, told me when to write them,'" used a credit card to purchase Quick-Books Pro, then threw the credit card number away. "What all this does is say the detectives weren't brilliant in finding all of this stuff about QuickBooks."

The prosecution, he said, hasn't "proved any of those points, let alone one of them. And why is this going on? Because of confirmation bias. They want it to be him, so they are going to make up stories, twist facts. We're going to say whatever we want because we arrested this guy, we got awards for arresting this guy. We got promotions. They're all sergeants now. If they admit they made a mistake and arrested the wrong guy, how is that going to look? This is a national case. They have made promises to the family. Don't worry, we got him. If they're wrong, they don't go to jail. Nothing happens to them. There's no risk."

McGee brought up Dan Kavanaugh only briefly, saying Maline would talk more about him. "They should have called Dan, but they called his girlfriend instead." They didn't want to "open that can of worms. Let's hide what is really going on here. Dan, why did you sell a company that McGyver said you were bought out of? Why isn't he charged?"

Daugherty objected, and Judge Smith sustained it, instructing the jury to "disregard the last comments."

Then there was the mysterious deletion of the voicemail messages from Joseph's T-Mobile account. When McGee called the records custodian to testify, he asked if one T-Mobile customer could call into another customer's voicemail, and the answer was "yes, if they know the code."

"Joseph had T-Mobile. Dan had T-Mobile. The only person that had the opportunity to do that attached to this case is Dan Kavanaugh."

"This case screams for not guilty. This case screams for Mr. Merritt to be acquitted. Justice demands it, so maybe San Diego can pick this case up again and get that family justice. Because what we have here in this trial, since October, has not been justice. It's been a fraud."

After the jury was excused, the prosecution complained to the judge about McGee's closing.

When Melissa Rodriguez accused Smith of failing to uphold his previous ruling prohibiting either side from criticizing the other for not calling Kavanaugh as a witness, McGee pointed out that he was out sick and knew nothing of this or he wouldn't have mentioned it.

Still, Britt Imes contended the defense had intentionally violated the rules of professional conduct, "ascribing conversations to people, including prosecutors, eliciting false testimony," engaging "in unlawful activity, and manufacturing evidence. That is misconduct. That is reportable to the state bar by Your Honor, who sat here and listened to it."

Smith said he didn't think it was "an unusual defense argument," and told Imes the matter was "better dealt with in your rebuttal argument." But he agreed to tell the jury to disregard McGee's comment that the prosecution should have called Kavanaugh.

After lunch, Raj Maline delivered the second half of the defense's closing argument from the podium, facing the jury. Meanwhile, the cameras caught Sean Daugherty texting repeatedly, laughing to himself, and showing his phone to Sergeant

Smith, who smiled. Imes also turned around and made a comment to Daugherty, which prompted grins all around.

Maline started by replaying Detective DuGal's testimony about the surveillance footage he collected from the San Ysidro mall, which started at 5 p.m. because the security guard had said the Trooper wasn't there before then.

Four years later, Maline said, that became "a problem" for investigators. So, Detective Hanke drove down to talk to the lot owner, and that's when the story changed. Mistakenly thinking February 8 was a Sunday, the lot owner agreed the car could conceivably have been parked as early as 7 or 8 a.m.

By the time the trial started, the guard whom DuGal had interviewed was dead, "but there was really nothing to be clarified. It was Detective Hanke going down there to get a statement to keep them in the game on that issue."

As McGee had stated, Merritt was upfront with DuGal from the start, when he handed over Joseph's spreadsheet and explained "the overpayment situation," how it related to Joseph's email about the $42,845 and their new projects, and how Joseph gave him some blank checks on February 4.

Based on the $297,954 that Merritt and Joseph earned together in 2009, Maline said, "the idea that these six checks, two of which went to Metro Sheet Metal for whatever amounts, somehow provide some type of motive is ludicrous."

"DuGal didn't really pay a lot of attention to it. Neither did Detective Fiske." That's because it didn't become an issue until the case got to San Bernardino, "and all of a sudden they wanted to use this QuickBooks and the financial motive."

Although the spreadsheet was on Joseph's computer the whole time, backing up what Merritt had told DuGal, the SBCSD's computer expert didn't even notice it. The new investigators "didn't really have a clear grasp of what the business was or what the history was. Nor did they care, because, remember, once they locked sights on Chase Merritt, this stuff didn't matter."

The defense's forensic accountant explained all of this to the jury, Maline said, and "I know it was tedious." But Dennis Shogren explained what was on the spreadsheet, which Maline encouraged the jury to study. In contrast, the prosecution's accounting expert simply put up graphs about Merritt's cash withdrawals at casinos.

"How does that help anything?"

Shogren contended that Provecho's credit card default, listed as $19,000 in the email, "has nothing to do with Chase. That's a credit risk that Joseph took. He's a separate company. So, for the prosecution to just add that in when it's clearly not a part of the calculation," and claim there is a "debt of forty-two-thousand dollars, is misleading."

He also noted that prosecutors never mentioned Joseph hadn't updated the spreadsheet to include the $26,000 credit coming to Merritt for the deposits Joseph had received in January. "Close your eyes."

Moving on to Cathy Jarvis, Maline said she told investigators Merritt got home while it was still light on February 4, and that she saw Joseph's call come in at 8:28 p.m. "They told her that she was lying. That call never came in. You are wrong." For the investigators, that call was a "big problem" for their case, "because eight thirty, if Chase is at home, he ain't in Fallbrook killing anyone."

But when they confronted her, they only showed her Merritt's phone records, which didn't reflect that call. "Later on, she is vindicated," he said, because it was on Joseph's records. "Lo and behold, there was the call at eight thirty."

"This relationship that Cathy describes is not a relationship where Joseph is going to fire Chase. He can't fire Chase. They're in the middle of Paul Mitchell and Saudi Arabia. Plus, they are on the cusp of some very big projects, million-dollar projects. They are only expanding. And, quite frankly, ladies and gentlemen, Joseph needed Chase."

Maline pointed out that it was the defense, not the detectives, that requested Kavanaugh's PayPal and bank records, which the jury could also review to see how much Kavanaugh was "dipping into [Joseph's] PayPal accounts and stealing Joseph's money," starting on February 10.

As Shogren testified, "Never one time before that day, not once, had Dan ever helped himself to Joseph's account. Mr. Kavanaugh had to have known when he was dipping into that account and swiping $13,000 right off the bat that there is going to be a problem when Joseph gets back, unless you know he is not coming back."

After the prosecution suggested Kavanaugh had used a VPN to mask his IP address in Hawaii, the defense's expert, Bryan La Rock, said no, because his previous IP address showed he was in Hawaii, so he would have been using one then, as well. That testimony, he said, "remains uncontroverted, untested by the prosecution. They didn't call a witness to say he is wrong."

But what was "mind-boggling," Maline said, was that investigators "haven't been able to get a ticket or a boarding pass or verify that [Kavanaugh] was in Hawaii. How is that possible? Shut Maline up and get the dang ticket."

The fact was, "law enforcement didn't care about Dan Kavanaugh. If they talk about financial issues being a motive in this case, Dan Kavanaugh took in $206,000 from the online account in a ten-month period from February to December 2010, money that should have gone to the McStay family."

Sure, Kavanaugh bought "a few waterfalls," but "he kept a hundred and fifty-plus thousand dollars that he stole. That's why he had to sell the company. By the way, how do you sell a company that ain't yours? Did anybody ask him?"

The prosecution claimed Merritt's motive was greed or forgery, but "those are not the human emotions that cause you to bash four skulls in. Doesn't work that way." Not for "$42,000 or $20,000, to forge four checks for $10,000, $15,000, whatever those checks came to."

The prosecution's case all boils down to six checks, he said, "and if he stole those checks, two of them he gave to Metro Sheet Metal. What a weird thing to do when you are stealing checks to commit a mass murder."

There are emotions that "can cause us to act in a way that can amplify our anger, can make [us] uncontrollable," he said. "I would subscribe to you, ladies and gentlemen, that betrayal is one of those human emotions," and Dan Kavanaugh was the one who felt "betrayed by Joseph by cutting him out when he was doing all of the business with Chase."

When Detectives Hanke and Bachman interviewed Merritt for eight hours, they claimed to have surveillance video showing his truck at the McStay house the night of February 4. They expected to come away with a confession, Maline said.

"That's why it lasted eight hours. It's only because they believe they can crack him. And even at the end of the interview when they are still pounding on him, he still says, politely, no."

Maline recalled asking Bachman what changed in the two weeks between that interview and the day they arrested him. "He said, 'Nothing, not that he can recall.' They were unsure on the twenty-second. They were unsure on the fifth when they arrested him. And I subscribe to you today, they are even more unsure because of what we have come up with. These prosecutors are unsure as well. You have seen the behavior in court. You see the way they laugh and scoff at us."

Daugherty and Imes both objected. Sustained.

"This family deserves justice, I believe that, and the prosecution has put you in a position that's unfair, without giving you everything and asking you guys to make that decision." Referring to the three DNA profiles that had yet to be run through CODIS, he said, "We are this close to completing this investigation. But it's not complete yet."

Melissa Rodriguez got the last word on rebuttal as she tried to realign the jury's focus.

"This is the case of the People versus Charles Merritt, and I think after listening to the closing arguments by both defense counsel, that's been forgotten a little bit. This is not the People versus Dan Kavanaugh," she said. It isn't "a case against Sean Daugherty, Britt Imes, or Melissa Rodriguez, despite the fact that we have been attacked constantly throughout."

Rodriguez asked the jury to "focus on the evidence, the evidence that you actually heard come from that witness stand." She also brought up the principle of Occam's Razor, which dictates "that simpler solutions are more likely to be correct."

While Imes raised doubt that Joseph and Merritt had lunch on February 4, she stated flatly that they never even met that day, piling more doubt on the claim that Merritt "received blank checks from Joe on that date. Why in the world is Joe going to give financial responsibility to a convicted felon with a gambling problem?"

McGee objected to that statement and her next one as well: "We know from Susan Blake's testimony that Joe had bailed the defendant out of a gambling debt for about twenty thousand dollars."

"Objection, Your Honor, that violates the court's ruling and assumes facts not in evidence," McGee said, referring to her conflation of two statements. Overruled.

Rodriguez accused Merritt and his attorneys of coaching the defense's "two star witnesses," Cathy and Taylor Jarvis, whom she called biased. McGee objected again, alleging prosecutorial misconduct. Overruled.

"How can she distinctly remember a phone call on that date that was never received by the defendant's phone? Never happened, that's why," she said.

After McGee had disputed Imes's remark that the jury shouldn't ignore evidence indicating something nefarious happened in the house, Rodriguez claimed that McGee had pulled his comments from thin air.

"Nobody from the prosecution team has stood up here and

said to you, all four of those people were murdered in that house. But what happened in that house? I wish we could tell you that. We know somehow the defendant got control of that family and got them out of that house."

She also dismissed the defense's theory that Summer had been raped, citing the pathologist's testimony that vaginal tissue was needed to make such a determination. Similarly, she picked apart McGee's scenario that had three intruders abducting the family and wrapping them up in blue tape without the neighbors noticing.

"The only one who had blue painter's tape around him was Joseph," she said.

Negating the defense's suggestion that Merritt's DNA was transferred to the Trooper through a handshake with Joseph, she mocked the study their expert cited, which involved people shaking hands for two minutes. "First of all, who shakes somebody's hand for two minutes? That's almost ridiculous. You have zero evidence that the defendant and Joseph shook hands that day."

When she tried to claim the defense presented an assumption that "DNA recovered from items in the grave was representative of at least three up to eleven individuals," McGee objected, citing "misstates the testimony."

After Daugherty objected to McGee's objection, Smith let Rodriguez's interpretation of Mark Perlin's arcane statements stand, though the prosecutor seemed to be confusing her terminology.

"It's up to the jury to determine precisely what Dr. Perlin's testimony was on those issues," Smith said.

Moving on to the cell tower testimony, Rodriguez claimed the "flyer" call to which Kevin Boles referred actually occurred on February 10, not February 4, and suggested the jury go back and check. In fact, McGee was comparing the two calls while cross-examining Boles.

"I can't cover all of the misrepresentations that were made to you yesterday, because we would be here all day again," she said, turning the defense's accusation against them.

Rodriguez tried to change the prosecution's timeline yet again, saying, "Nobody has ever sat here and told you the bodies were buried on February sixth. What we said is that the defendant's phone pinged off of a tower next to the graves on February sixth. If you buried them before, and we have these heavy rains, maybe he needed to go check and make sure that they were still buried."

But to claim Merritt "would have been driving all over the place with these bodies and blood pouring out of the back, we know that's not true, because Dr. Changsri said as soon as the heart stops pumping, the blood stops," she said.

Then, mocking the defense's claim of confirmation bias, she said, "The prosecution witnesses all have confirmation bias. Family members, Sequeida, Garcia, Geis, Fonseca, all have confirmation bias. Ryan Baker, he didn't even know he wasn't talking to Joseph McStay. He just made notes. He's got confirmation bias for sure. San Diego police officers, they have confirmation bias. Oh, wait, they never went and arrested the defendant. The defense witnesses are the ones that actually had confirmation bias."

She encouraged the jury to review Merritt's bank and phone records, the time he spent at casinos, and the ATM withdrawals he made there. "The simple explanation is that the defendant dug himself into a financial hole. We have the email from Joseph on February 1. We knew that his gambling was out of control."

Rodriguez claimed Merritt didn't call 911 or go to Joseph's house to check on him until Carmen Garcia started asking where he was on February 8. Then, after his "best friend in the whole world is gone, you can't find him, [he says] let me go work that out at a casino table, because that's where he was the night of February ninth."

As for the DNA, she said, "The defendant's DNA was on the

steering wheel of the car because he drove it to the border. And the defendant's DNA wasn't on the items in the grave because none of those items would have retained reliable DNA evidence, which is why the defense didn't want to run that DNA [through CODIS]."

In closing, she said, "You don't get to murder an entire family and get away with it because you left behind no witnesses, and that's the reason those two children were killed, because they could identify the person that did this to them. Justice has been delayed. There is no doubt about that. But ladies and gentlemen, when you go back into that jury room, justice does not have to be denied for the McStay family."

Chapter 44

After eighty-five days of trial, the jury began deliberating late Thursday morning, May 30. Due to one juror's job as a summer-school teacher and football coach, the court tried to accommodate an afternoon-only schedule, but ultimately decided to excuse him and replace him with an alternate.

Britt Imes waited until this point to file his declaration denying the Brady violation allegation. McGee objected, arguing that Imes should be forced to testify and be cross-examined rather than "sneaking" in the statement "at the eleventh hour."

Denying it was "snuck in," Imes said, "Counsel was provided a copy, and they were given notice that it would be filed in a day or two at that hearing."

Smith rejected McGee's request.

Once that was settled, Merritt waited with his attorneys in a back room. While he was skeptical about his chances for acquittal, his attorneys were optimistic.

"We were in a positive [place]," Maline said. "Momentum had shifted in our favor. Jim and I felt good, not great. We got enough in front of the jury [about Imes deleting Rudin's text] that we thought it was helpful."

Soon after the deliberations began, word came back that Robert Wallace—the defense team's author and "media liaison," who had been assisting the documentary crew—had approached the remaining two alternate jurors.

All the attorneys were called back to court the next morning, where Rodriguez threatened to seek sanctions against the defense.

McGee and Maline said they'd instructed Wallace not to contact or film jurors, and had further discussions with him after he spoke with the alternates. Professional journalists are trained not to approach jurors until after a verdict is reached, because it violates court rules and can get them thrown out of the courtroom.

The following Monday, Smith called a formal hearing to find out what happened.

"Right at the end of the proceedings, I saw the two in the hallway and I mentioned to them that, when the trial was over, we would like to extend a voluntary invitation to talk with us," Wallace said. "I understood that things weren't concluded, that they may or may not be on the jury."

Smith said that was no excuse. "That's still improper contact with a juror. That's really serious," he said. If Wallace had said anything to influence a juror, he could be prosecuted for jury tampering. If that resulted in a mistrial, Wallace could be charged for all trial costs and expert witness fees, "and that's, I'm guessing, hundreds of thousands of dollars."

Smith said that Wallace, as a member of the defense team, should be held to the same standard as an attorney. Smith questioned the two alternates individually, then banned Wallace from the courthouse for the remainder of the trial.

Wallace invoked the Fifth Amendment in a subsequent declaration, citing "the expressed potential threat of contempt court proceedings and of potential criminal prosecution." Smith ultimately decided not to take further action against him or the documentary crew.

* * *

After six days of deliberations, the jury announced it had reached a verdict on Friday morning, June 7. However, the court delayed the reading and sealed the jury voting forms over the weekend, because two panelists were unavailable due to a graduation and a trip out of town and McStay family members needed time to travel to court to hear the verdict.

On Monday morning, June 10, the media and curious observers crowded into the courtroom with members of the McStay and Merritt families.

Before bringing in the jurors, Judge Smith cautioned the family members that if any of them became "so emotional that it's going to be disrupting the proceedings," they should step out until they regained their composure.

Once the jurors were seated, the clerk began reading the verdict: "We the jury in the above-entitled action, find the defendant, Charles Ray Merritt, guilty of the offense of murder in the first degree, in violation of Penal Code Section 187(a), of Joseph McStay."

Hearing this, Merritt closed his eyes as Michael McStay called out, "Yes!" Many in the courtroom, including the defense staff, teared up or began crying. Several members of Merritt's family scurried out, sobbing, as the McStays hugged each other with relief, and the clerk read the remaining "guilty" verdicts on the other three counts. The jury also confirmed the special circumstance allegation of multiple murders.

After jurors reaffirmed their votes by nodding their heads and by individual polling at McGee's request, Smith told them to return the next morning for the penalty phase of the trial. Their next task was to determine whether Merritt should be sentenced to life without the possibility of parole or sent to death row.

At a news conference afterward, Maline said the defense team was "shell-shocked."

"Based on the evidence, we did not expect this. From our standpoint, our client is innocent," he said. "How the jury can come up with a guilty verdict today, knowing there are still three profiles from the gravesite, from our standpoint, just [defies] logic. They didn't get the whole picture."

Later, he added, "We felt we had a good jury. We didn't know they would disregard evidence like they did. These jurors wanted to believe Merritt did it."

The verdict also surprised some legal observers who believed the prosecution failed to meet the "reasonable doubt" standard and prove Merritt was the killer. Yes, he was a gambler and a thief, they said, but that didn't make him a murderer. Because of Merritt's lack of violent history, some court-watchers were still convinced that such a horrific bludgeoning was the work of drug traffickers or a cartel.

Chapter 45

The penalty phase began the next morning, June 11, as Melissa Rodriguez delivered the prosecution's opening statement with tear-jerking video and photos of the McStay family on the overhead screen.

"Those are the voices that you did not get to hear from," she said. "And at the end of the evidence in this case, the People believe that there's one penalty that is appropriate, and that is the death penalty."

The defense chose to wait until the prosecution finished its case to deliver its opening, and also to forego any cross-examination.

Testimony began with Susan Blake, followed by Michael McStay.

"What does it make you feel when you hear their voices and see the video?" Rodriguez asked Susan.

"I miss them all," Susan said. "They were little boys in a fantasy world. They did everything with their parents and us, parks and Legoland. They didn't know fear. They didn't know to be scared. They didn't know hurt. We'll never get to see them grow up or talk to them."

The following week, Kenneth Aranda and Tracy Russell testified remotely by Skype and FaceTime.

Tracy and Summer "were very, very strong-minded people,

and it's definitely taken a part of [Tracy]," Kenneth said. "My sister and her were very close. Her best friend's gone. There's a hole in her heart. She has a husband and a son, but when you miss your sister, if you have a sibling, it's hard to explain."

Tracy kept breaking into tears as her voice dropped off, leaving long silences in her testimony while everyone waited patiently for her to regain her composure.

"I have a lump in my throat," she said. "I can't even talk. Sorry."

Although Kenneth said Summer's murder had changed his entire outlook on life, he and Tracy both said their mother had been hit the hardest, both mentally and physically.

"She just hasn't been able to gather all the pieces," Tracy said. "It has been too much for her. She's definitely not the same person. She's lost all her strength. She cries constantly," and when she isn't, she's having conversations with her dead daughter.

Britt Imes gave the first half of the prosecution's closing argument, urging the jury to vote unanimously for death.

With no signs of forced entry, "that pointed to someone who came into the house willingly, knowingly, acceptingly. Who would have known that that night, February 4, the McStay family was letting a killer in their front door or in through the garage? Who could have seen that coming? That is someone that they have had a business and a friendship relationship with for a number of years. This is more personal. This isn't a stranger who kicked in the door. This is someone who walked in. That is a circumstance that makes this crime even more horrific."

"What possible motive can a human being have to murder a four-year-old and a three-year-old? Are they the only people left in that house, after killing Joseph and Summer, that could identify him? If we are talking that, it's cold, callous, collateral damage, then it's evil."

Imes blamed Merritt for the "lack of forensic evidence" that forced the prosecution to present only circumstantial evidence, which admittedly "leaves a lot of unanswered questions" that "neither us, nor the defense, not law enforcement, not even a psychic" could resolve.

The family wasn't reported missing until they'd been gone for eleven days, leaving no evidence in the house, and allowing their bodies to decompose in shallow graves in the desert for three years, nine months, and seven days—all circumstances "orchestrated" by the defendant to escape accountability.

"A monster of destruction," he said, Merritt must have felt great rage and anger to break Summer's jaw in two places, to fracture Joseph's leg, and to shatter the skull of this "forgiving, generous individual."

Sean Daugherty, who delivered the second half of the argument, anticipated correctly that the defense would try to appeal to any "lingering doubt" among the jurors.

The defense was essentially saying the panel "got it wrong," he said, but that wasn't true. "You are not in this position because of bad prosecutors, bad police, the DA's ego, or the police's ego or pride, or anything else. You are here because he murdered four people. Because of his actions, his greed, his choices." To suggest otherwise, would be "irresponsible." In fact, he said, it would be "an injustice" not to vote for a death verdict in this case, which would give "meaning and dignity" to the victims and their surviving loved ones. "You didn't get this wrong. You got this right."

The defense started its case the next morning, June 20. Rather than present character witnesses, they revisited the evidence that contradicted the prosecution's narrative, hoping to persuade at least one juror to save Chase Merritt's life.

Raj Maline reminded the jury of his comment during voir dire: "My biggest fear in this case was the human emotion part of it, that when you have a family that is killed in the brutal way that this family was killed, it's going to be very difficult to set that aside and say this family doesn't deserve some type of closure, some type of justice that pulls on everybody to somehow make it right for them."

But as much as the anger about this tragedy may be justified, "the law isn't revenge." With so many unanswered questions, three unidentified DNA profiles, and evidence that contradicts the prosecution's timeline, it doesn't change the fact—no matter how loud prosecutors shout that Merritt is a greedy liar during their closing arguments—that "we are no closer today to finding out what happened than we were in February 2010."

"There's not one single shred, speck, molecule—you name it—of evidence, blood or otherwise, that ties Mr. Merritt to this crime," he said. "Not one. That's the state of the evidence in February of 2010 and that's the state of the evidence today."

Maline ran through all the flaws in the prosecutors' timeline, replaying clips of them changing their stories mid-trial about certain pieces of evidence after the defense had made Swiss cheese of their scenarios.

"These prosecutors sold you a bill of goods," he said. "This family is not getting justice."

After lunch, the jury began deliberating for the second time and sent a question to the judge soon afterward: "What happens if we can't agree on our decision, verdict in this phase of the trial?"

Judge Smith came to the jury room to respond. "I discussed this with the attorneys," he said. "The answer is, don't worry about it. Not your concern. You try to reach a verdict if you can. If you get to a point where you say we just can't, let me know."

"Thanks for joining us," one juror said.

"That was clear as mud," another one said.

*   *   *

The jury reached a verdict the next day, but the announcement was delayed overnight. When it came on the morning of June 22, it was more bad news for Merritt: jurors voted for a penalty of death on three of the murder counts for Summer, Gianni, and Joseph Jr., and life without the penalty of parole for killing Merritt's best friend, Joseph McStay.

Chapter 46

The following week, Merritt met with his attorneys to discuss a motion for a new trial, still upset at McGee's decision not to call their cell phone expert, Vlad Jovanovic.

"Don't you think we should have called Vlad?" he asked.

McGee said no, and stood by his decision. When Merritt kept arguing, McGee said, essentially, "If you're saying I did something wrong, that's fine, but that does raise what we call a conflict of interest. I can't represent you."

Maline, who was willing to do whatever it took to help Merritt's case, said he would "be the first to tell the judge I made a mistake."

Maline was willing to "fall on his sword," Merritt said. "That's why I let him stay on, which [turned out to be] the worst idea in the world, and let him argue the motion for a new trial."

But it took several months for the attorneys to inform the judge of this decision, while Maline made repeated jail visits to discuss the motion with Merritt.

"Chase was almost universally focused on the cell towers, nothing else," Maline said.

Ten days before the scheduled sentencing date in late September, McGee filed a motion for a continuance, requesting permission for him and his associate, Jacob Guerard, to withdraw from the case due to a conflict that had developed with their client. Merritt needed time "to seek other representation," the motion stated.

On September 27, Judge Smith met with the defense in chambers to discuss the undisclosed conflict. Afterward, he announced publicly only that the defense attorneys needed more time to determine whether McGee could participate in the filing of post-conviction motions.

Clearly parsing his words, Maline said those motions deal "with a lot of the work that was done by Mr. McGee, and since he has taken this position and filed the motion, the exchange of information has not been the same."

Smith said he would meet with the attorneys in chambers again on November 1 to determine whether "Mr. McGee should be relieved." The motions hearing and sentencing would follow in mid-December.

Britt Imes opposed the delay, characterizing it as "excessive and unnecessary," coming three months after the verdict. He also contended the People should have input into whether Merritt "is entitled to a completely conflict-free counsel. The way this is playing out in open court, you have a position of potentially pitting one trial counsel against another," he said.

Smith said the defense attorneys were no longer law partners or housed in the same office, so "that might not be as much of a problem."

But Imes's characterization seemed apt. McGee sat at the table behind Maline and Merritt, neither lawyer looking or talking to the other.

During the November meeting in chambers, Smith allowed McGee and Guerard to withdraw, but the root cause of the conflict was still withheld from the public.

"I recused myself," McGee told TSG later. "I cannot defend myself and my client at the same time."

This decision rendered Maline as Merritt's sole defense attorney to draft the post-conviction motions about witnesses he'd never prepared to question at trial. When Maline asked for more time to compile them, Smith granted it over the prosecution's objections, which delayed sentencing for ten more weeks.

McGee declined to be interviewed for this book.

On January 17, 2020, Smith called the courtroom to order at 9:15 a.m., only to call an immediate recess to review two motions Maline had just filed, one of which was ninety-one pages long.

Meanwhile, about twenty people waited in the courtroom, including four jurors from the trial. Subpoenaed to testify, McGee and Guerard were also there, along with the cell phone experts from both sides, Vlad Jovanovic and Special Agent Kevin Boles. Once the hearing started again, Smith asked McGee and Guerard to wait outside.

Maline's new-trial motion argued there was insufficient evidence to support the verdicts, citing newly discovered evidence that McGee should have elicited during his cross-examination of Boles and by calling Jovanovic. Also alleging prosecutorial misconduct, Maline faulted the judge for not disclosing the constant bad behavior, including the Brady violation allegation, to the jury.

Maline told Smith that Jovanovic was in court to give a PowerPoint presentation and explain the technical details of why the phone records couldn't prove Merritt and his cell phone were where Boles said they were.

However, Smith said he wasn't going to allow that or consider Jovanovic's written materials, though he would enter them into the record for Merritt's appeal.

Jovanovic's materials basically deemed AT&T's service, towers, and records to be flawed on so many levels that the records "cannot be used for geolocation purposes under normal evidentiary standards." The expert said, "AT&T network problems from 2009 to 2011 were known widely enough within the cellular industry" to be documented in the *New York Times* and *Wall Street Journal* and to become the butt of jokes by late-night talk-show hosts David Letterman and Jon Stewart.

Jovanovic said the Quartzite cell tower "could easily cover over twenty miles," while other towers could cover more than twenty-two miles, meaning the caller could be standing or driving anywhere within that area. He also said it was "impossible to corroborate" the prosecution's assertion that Merritt had been on Interstate 15, let alone driving north, when he made the 9:32 p.m. call on February 4.

But without Jovanovic's expert testimony, Maline had to summarize this highly technical data—*and* argue the main points of his motion—by himself. The case was no longer in the jury's hands, so it was solely up to the judge to evaluate the value of this information.

Maline said Boles had testified only about the starting tower information for Merritt's 11:52 a.m. call on February 6, "intentionally" omitting the ending tower information. Still, according to those records, Merritt would have had to travel 8.5 miles in thirty-five seconds for that call to have registered as it did.

"That's an impossibility, and Vlad's original report indicated that that's an impossibility. It could never happen," Maline said. "So, obviously, there's a problem with the [Quartzite] antennae, and this was the issue that came up in trial that Mr. Merritt wanted to be brought forward."

After Maline had talked for a while, Smith began growing impatient and asked how much longer Maline intended to go on. Told thirty more minutes, Smith said no. He'd already heard this information at trial, and a new-trial motion hearing wasn't the time to have experts or witnesses testifying for days.

Smith said Maline should have filed a writ of habeas corpus with declarations so a judge could decide if an evidentiary hearing was warranted. In fact, Smith indicated Maline could still do that, after the case was over.

"We believe that Mr. Merritt should have a new trial, Your

Honor," Maline said, "especially considering the cell tower evidence, that we believe would have had a tremendous impact on what the outcome would have been in this case."

Smith wasn't moved by Maline's arguments or by the motion itself, which contended the prosecution had "manipulated the evidence" to a point that even Maline didn't fully understand until studying it after the verdict, when he realized that McGee had failed to present crucial evidence to the jury.

"For unknown reasons that caused significant prejudicial harm to the defendant, Mr. McGee did not use this exculpatory evidence," Maline's motion stated.

Smith complained that Maline had waited to file his motion until fifteen minutes before the hearing. "You still had seven months since verdict in the case, and this is all information that you and Mr. Merritt had [previously]," he said.

Maline pushed back, arguing that "certain critical evidence was either misrepresented by the prosecution or outright lied about, and I think the court should pay attention to that. I would go as far as to say that nothing, not one thing that they argued [in their closing] was correct."

"You don't need to repeat your closing arguments," Smith said.

Maline said he also wanted to discuss the pattern of prosecutorial misconduct during the trial, and he would keep talking until the judge shut him down. Smith agreed to give him fifteen more minutes on the cell towers.

But the longer Maline talked, the more Merritt thought his attorney was muddying the waters, jumping from point to point, and lacking a clear understanding of Jovanovic's analysis, which had originally been McGee's responsibility.

"He was literally all over the place with his arguments, he was arguing crazy shit, misquoting the evidence," Merritt recalled. "He did argue for a while, and then the court kept saying, 'Are you done yet, are you done yet?' It was ridiculous."

In his view, Maline "should have looked at [Smith] and said, 'If you're not going to let me argue this, then I'm done, and have a good day,' because that would have automatically given me another motion for a new trial."

Before things got any worse, Merritt tried to appeal directly to the judge. "Your Honor—"

"You can't talk," Maline snapped.

After leaning down to hear what Merritt had to say, Maline said, "Okay, he wants to take a few minutes to talk with me, if that's okay."

Smith agreed, and called the lunch recess, during which Merritt said he laid into Maline. They were talking at the defense table when Jovanovic approached them to say he didn't understand why the judge wouldn't let him testify.

"I've never seen a court do this," he said, then left.

Back in session, Judge Smith invited Maline to talk about the misconduct, but the attorney said he couldn't proceed after his discussion with his client.

"He informed me, during the break, that he does not want me to continue as his lawyer, and also some other issues that would necessitate me declaring a conflict. I don't feel in good conscience, based on what I have been told, that I could go forward," Maline said, eliciting audible responses of shock and dismay throughout the courtroom.

Smith broke for another recess to speak to Merritt and Maline in chambers for what is known as a Marsden hearing. Merritt believed that if he could go back to representing himself, he could get another chance at making a few salient points his attorneys had failed to present.

Smith listened, but as he'd warned at the outset, he said Merritt had to stick with Maline as his attorney. So back to the courtroom they went.

* * *

Starting again, Maline recounted that "emotions [had run] high" since the start of the trial, "with both sides making allegations against each other of misconduct."

"Which continued throughout the trial," Smith interjected.

But the defense didn't get the judge's protection, Maline said, because Smith abdicated his responsibility to arbitrate that behavior, and let the prosecution's "constant snickering, the constant eye rolling [go] on almost daily."

"It was addressed," Smith said.

"But it didn't stop, and that does create an atmosphere that we felt was prejudicial to our client."

In a veiled reference to the Colonies trial, Smith replied that "prosecutors were acting similarly, at least the defense alleged that they were, that had an extremely negative impact on the jury, and was one of the reasons that jurors indicated they voted 'not guilty' on all defendants. When counsel are not respectful and not professional, I think that's detrimental to those attorneys, at least that's been my experience, that jurors generally do not reward such conduct."

Even so, Maline said, factual errors were allowed into the record. Cybergenetics was, in fact, accredited by the FBI, yet the prosecution claimed the opposite in their closing argument.

The three DNA profiles also could be run through CODIS in minutes, he said. "That's real DNA, those are real results, and those are three people that don't match the family, and they don't match Mr. Merritt, and it's a shame that they have been able to hoodwink everyone, including the victim's family. All I can say is only time will tell, and I'm not going to stop fighting."

Asked to respond, Britt Imes said they could "sit here today and argue until we are blue in the face, rehearing testimony and rehashing exhibits, [but] a reinterpretation of the evidence is not new evidence."

Imes objected to the video clips Maline submitted to support the prosecutorial misconduct claims, alleging they were "taken in violation of a court order." He also argued there had been no showing of such misconduct, or any evidence these alleged behaviors "had any effect, whatsoever, before this court."

As for the DNA evidence, Sean Daugherty said, the memorandum of understanding with an outside lab needed for the CODIS administrator "to accept that evidence to put it into CODIS is missing."

"Mr. Maline wants to paint this as the government has biological evidence and they are refusing to test it, and he's known better since January," Daugherty said, reiterating that the defense chose at the outset not to ask for its DNA evidence to be run through CODIS.

Finally, Imes argued, "Nothing before this court" backed up the accusation "that McGee was ineffective in his representations."

At this point, the hearing moved into the surreal, as Maline called his former partner to the stand to respond to the allegations of ineffective counsel.

Merritt expected Maline to call out McGee for his failures during the trial concerning the cell tower evidence, "to put him on the stand and say basically, 'You didn't do this, did you? You didn't do that, did you?' But it didn't happen." Instead, Merritt said, Maline questioned McGee for about thirty minutes, but never challenged any of his answers that Merritt believed were partial or outright falsehoods.

For example, when McGee was asked if he'd found any anomalies or discrepancies with the Quartzite tower, he replied, "Anything major that I remember? No."

That "was an absolute lie," Merritt said later, because Jovanovic's report was full of analysis about discrepancies and anomalies. In fact, the expert told McGee that they were "the worst records that I have ever seen in my career."

But McGee and Maline did address the moment during

Boles's testimony when they learned the prosecution had been relying not only on AT&T records for cell site location and data, but also on the FBI lists they had refused to share with the defense.

"We kept asking for [them] even before trial, and they said, 'We weren't using it.' But we knew they were, because they were showing locations of towers that weren't contained within the records that we had," McGee said.

However, even after the judge issued the court order to turn them over to the defense, the FBI only released records for February 6, 2010, which showed the signal for Merritt's call was bouncing between two antennae on the Quartzite tower.

"With that kind of movement and that kind of direction," McGee said, "that's evidence to show that he actually wasn't or couldn't have been at the gravesite during that time."

McGee claimed he'd consulted with Jovanovic in preparing to cross-examine Boles, but made a "tactical decision" not to call the expert witness, because they both agreed his testimony would be "counterproductive."

"The main reason is, what we were trying to establish in the defense perspective, we achieved better than we had ever hoped with Boles," McGee said.

However, Merritt and Maline both said later that Jovanovic still wanted to testify regardless.

After McGee was excused, Smith delivered his point-by-point ruling on Maline's motions, starting with the ineffective-counsel allegation.

Based on McGee's explanation that day, Smith said he saw no problem with McGee's decision not to call Jovanovic. It wasn't that McGee didn't understand, or ignored, the cell tower information and analysis. He made a strategic decision—in concert with that witness—that he believed was in his client's best interest."

In Smith's view, McGee actually did cover the points that Maline claimed he didn't raise during his cross-examination of Boles, which illustrated to the judge that McGee had a "commanding knowledge" of the technical data.

"The court finds, number one, there was not ineffective assistance of counsel. To the contrary, Mr. McGee's representation on that issue—on all of the issues—was at the higher end of representation," he said.

The judge also found no discovery or due-process violation concerning the FBI tower records, because defense attorneys obtained the "information for the critical date of February sixth" and were able to discuss it with their expert.

As for the insufficient-evidence claim, Smith did agree that two "significant questions" remained unanswered: one, where had the murder occurred, if it wasn't in the house? And two, where were the McStay family's bodies between February 4 and 6 if they were buried on the latter date?

"Those could be considered significant holes in the prosecution's case," he said. "Without knowing that, a jury could say that was sufficient for reasonable doubt and vote not guilty, or the court, sitting as the thirteenth juror, could say that raises a reasonable doubt."

But the jury had found Merritt guilty, and as the judge summarized the prosecution's case, Smith indicated that he, too, was convinced by the government's interpretation of the evidence.

Although "the defense did present a very vigorous defense and did challenge all of the issues that I have just discussed," Smith concluded that the evidence was in fact "sufficient to prove guilt beyond a reasonable doubt." So, he denied that portion of the motion as well.

As for Dan Kavanaugh, Smith said, "a compelling case was made that Mr. Kavanaugh had at least the same motivations [to murder the McStays] and was at least in the same position as

Mr. Merritt. However, there was no credible evidence connecting Mr. Kavanaugh to the commission of the crimes," to the McStay house on February 4 or 5, to the gravesite, or to the Trooper left at the border. Although the defense made a case that Kavanaugh had a motive for murder, that alone "isn't sufficient to prove guilt."

By this point, the hearing had dragged on past 5 p.m., and they were nowhere near done. Because the following Monday was Martin Luther King Day, Smith said they would have to finish up on Tuesday, January 21.

The courtroom erupted with dissension as Michael McStay called out that he would stay until 10 p.m. if necessary. Informed that some family members had traveled long distances to deliver their impact statements, Smith said he couldn't keep his staff there all night, but he allowed Patrick McStay to speak, since he was flying home to Texas the next day.

"My son did nothing but help you and your family," Patrick told Merritt, claiming Joseph had taken care of Merritt's family's bills and groceries while he was in jail. "How did you repay him? By brutally killing him, his wife, and his defenseless infant sons." Calling Merritt "a ruthless mass murderer," he said, "I hope you burn in hell."

It felt like Groundhog Day on Tuesday morning, when Judge Smith opened the proceedings simply to call another recess, because Maline had filed yet another last-minute motion. This time, Maline wanted Smith to disqualify himself for showing bias the previous Friday and also seven months earlier, when he mingled with jurors, prosecutors, and the victims' family in the jury room after the final verdict in the penalty phase.

After reviewing the motion, Smith cited a procedural rule allowing him to reject it as untimely. If it had been filed sooner, he said, a more complicated process, involving a judicial council, could have been triggered. He also rejected the motion for a new trial based on "cumulative" prosecutorial misconduct and prejudice.

Smith noted that he'd already ruled on the defense's individual complaints during the trial, which never rose to the level of misconduct or prejudice. He said he wasn't going to consider the six CDs of video clips of the prosecution's antics, either, though he agreed to enter them into the record.

Finally, Smith denied Maline's motion to reduce Merritt's penalty to life without parole, saying the "extreme violence and savagery of the killings" far outweighed the mitigating evidence.

Ten years of trauma to Joseph and Summer's families colored the victim impact statements they delivered that morning, which were peppered with religious references. Merritt turned to face the speakers, but he listened stone-faced.

Summer's sister, Tracy Russell, stood at the microphone, sighing as she struggled to get the necessary volume to describe how "excruciatingly painful" Summer's death had been for the Aranda family. Her mother, Blanche Almanza, who had been hospitalized numerous times since Summer had gone missing— twice this past summer—couldn't endure the pain of attending the entire trial.

"It's almost been ten years. The pain hasn't subsided," Tracy said, and yet, Merritt "still hasn't admitted what he's done."

Susan Blake was next, calling Merritt a "despicable, evil monster."

"How could you beat two precious little babies? How scared were they, crying for Mommy and Daddy? You had a choice. Chase, you are a low-life coward and baby killer," she said.

Susan said her only consolation was that her son, wife, and grandsons were "all together in Heaven. The boys are sliding down rainbows, Joey's surfing the clouds, and poor Summer is chasing after them." With a photo of her family's headstone on the screen, she said anyone was welcome to visit and say a prayer for them.

Summer's ex-husband, Albert Vergara, recounted a conversation they'd once had about what they wanted if one died before the other. Summer asked Vergara to play Norman Greenbaum's "Spirit in the Sky" at her funeral.

Vergara agreed, "never thinking that I would outlive her." As the song started to play in the courtroom, family members cried and dabbed their eyes with tissues.

Vergara told Merritt he wanted to "kill [him] with kindness," but he was unable to. "I don't forgive you," he said, adding that he hoped Merritt would be haunted by the memory of the sounds of murdering the family.

"Come on, Chase!" he said, banging on the lectern. "Aren't you tired, man? Just stop all the appeals, all the shenanigans."

Michael McStay said the discovery of the family's remains in the desert had "left on a mark" on his life, and on his mother's, nephew's, and children's, too.

"I'm not a gambler, but this is a pretty horrible exchange rate. Lose four beautiful souls for one to remain," he said, describing Merritt as "unrepentant" and "conscience-deprived."

Michael recited the poem Joseph had written for him when they were young, which read in part: "I led you down a dark road of death and decay, a place our souls were anchored, a place of angels' shame. Then the heavens opened up and brought us into the light, freeing us from blindness, grace restoring sight."

In closing, Elijah said he had "lived in the shadow of losing my father, stepmom, [and] two little brothers. Sometimes just seeing another boy with their dad reminds me of the tremendous loss I have endured. I fight each and every day to mend the wounds left by someone who, instead of healing, sought to destroy others, my family, for their own personal gain."

Once the family members had spoken, Chase Merritt stood up to say his piece, shedding light on why he lacked remorse for the murders. This was among the aggravating factors Judge Smith cited and was echoed in the impact statements.

It wasn't due to a lack of sympathy for Joseph's surviving family, Merritt said, but because he was innocent. He "was so very sorry" Joseph and his family had to "bear this horrific tragedy," because none of them should have to lose loved ones this way. But he felt conflicted.

Part of him wanted to remain silent, knowing Joseph's relatives found solace in the prospect of "ending my life for a crime that I did not commit. I loved Joseph. I never would have hurt him in any way. I did not do this thing. I know you do not believe this. That's what kills me."

Then he went on the offensive, calling prosecutors "professional liars," and accusing them of manipulating evidence and misleading witnesses to make Joseph's mother and others give false statements, "all to simply get a win."

"Their theories throughout trial have been a target that moves opportunistically when confronted by contrary evidence," he said.

Merritt also criticized the judge for abdicating responsibility, saying he didn't want to stop the trial for a misconduct hearing, but rather "let the next court deal" with the allegations. He condemned Smith for entering the jury room with prosecutors and family members after the verdict, where there were "high-fives, hugs, and congratulatory remarks," reminiscent of the days of lynchings.

"What's happening here is wrong," Merritt said, crying. "I may deserve a lot of things. I don't deserve this. I did not do this. And as God is my witness, I will be back here and prove to everyone that is true."

After Maline made one last effort to save Merritt's life based on the judicial-bias allegations, Smith issued his decision to send him to death row.

Chase Merritt arrived at San Quentin State Prison nine days later, on January 30, 2020.

* * *

As a gesture of closure, the three prosecutors, Sergeant Smith, and several jurors met up with Michael McStay at the desert memorial to take down the crosses and scatter the white rocks.

"Mike wanted the memorial site removed, because he did not want to think of their final resting place in the desert, but rather at the beach, where they were happy," Smith said later. "The family has a memorial bench overlooking the ocean in San Clemente."

Chapter 47

Over the next month or two, Raj Maline tried to help Merritt get the three DNA profiles from Cybergenetics run through CODIS by preparing a "pro per" request for a new defense attorney to be appointed to file a motion for DNA testing under Penal Code Section 1405.

"I am making this request because I am not the perpetrator of the crimes in this case, and DNA testing and comparison is relevant to my assertion of innocence," Merritt stated in the motion, dated February 2021.

Merritt said he thought this move was misguided, because the evidence items had already been tested.

A public defender was assigned to help, but Merritt was correct, so the matter was taken off the court calendar eight months later.

"There is no basis to file a PC1405 testing motion," the minutes state.

But Merritt doesn't believe the DNA profiles will be the thing that frees him, anyway.

"Personally, I don't give a flying rat's tail about the DNA in the grave, because it would be the slowest means of getting exonerated," he said. "Number one, it's almost certain that the DNA will never get [run], because my attorneys screwed up."

The SBCSD didn't respond to several requests to interview the county's CODIS administrator about why the profiles couldn't be run through the database when Mark Perlin testified that they could.

"There isn't an actual rule that says they can't," Taylor Jarvis said. "The judge could order the prosecution to do it. It's a push of the button for them."

Taylor, who was twenty when her father was arrested, said this case inspired her to become a lawyer. She tries to give him guidance, but she's not involved in his appeal, because she's focusing on her burgeoning career. But, like her mother, she believes her father is innocent. Why?

"Because I've seen the evidence. I haven't seen him ever be violent. I feel he was the more reasonable parent. His version of punishment was, if us kids did anything wrong, 'go stand against the wall for an hour and think about what you've done.' It was never any physical punishment."

Although she acknowledged she may be biased, she said she'd like to think she's capable of stepping back to evaluate "what was there and what wasn't there and draw my conclusions. He's never been a huge, huge part of my life, but I just don't see it. The prosecution's case was so circumstantial, it would have taken just one thing to prove my dad's innocence, like a fingerprint."

Apart from the theories about Mexican mafia and "drug people" being involved, she still doesn't see a solid suspect or scenario for the murders.

Because the SDSD's initial investigation was so "botched," potentially exculpatory evidence was destroyed, and the agency "missed a lot of opportunities to investigate things that they didn't," she said, "we just don't have that smoking gun for anybody. There's so many answers that no one will ever have."

Even if her father can get his conviction overturned, she wonders if it will ever be known for sure who killed the McStays.

"It's been too long. Memories fade, evidence deteriorates. And that's the sad part about this case," she said.

Lieutenant Ryan Smith, however, said he believes Merritt is exactly where he should be.

"The guy pretends that he's some saint, it's never his fault, he's always got a reason for everything," he said. "You're either the most unlucky guy in the world, or how do all these things happen to you? He absolutely did it and would have been convicted, but when you look at his personality, the sociopath he is, he can't accept fault for anything."

The documentary production company, TSG Documentary, eventually entered into a joint venture with Red Marble Media, which sold the *Two Shallow Graves* project to the Discovery Network as a seven-part series. After Warner Bros. acquired Discovery, the series aired on Investigation Discovery and discovery+ in May 2022.

According to Merritt, Discovery paid $4.7 million for the first six episodes and $600,000 to $900,000 for the seventh, but those numbers couldn't be confirmed.

Maline said he didn't know the sale price, "because we're not allowed to have that information," but estimated it was "maybe half that much."

"What we got was pennies," he said. "If it was $4.7 million, I'm going to be pissed."

Jim Nelson of TSG Documentary laughed when he heard Merritt's figures, but said he couldn't talk about money other than to say that his company didn't pay Merritt or his family members for participating in the project.

"Chase is misinformed on a lot of things, so I have no comment," he said.

Cathy Jarvis said she ultimately did receive Merritt's share of the money, but the check came from Robert Wallace, not Nelson or TSG. "Maybe for a lawyer it is [pennies]," she said in late

2024. "I paid off a little bit of debt, but most of the money goes to pay for Chase's care packages and things that he needs, and that money is almost gone."

Some of the original TSG interviews were woven into new footage featuring Patrick McStay, several detectives, and prosecutors Britt Imes and Melissa Rodriguez, who agreed to participate once they were promised the end-product would be balanced.

Dan Kavanaugh, wearing a knit cap and a blazer, was featured in the seventh episode, dismissing Tracey Riccobene and her claim that he'd confessed to killing the McStays.

"Oh, the Tracey girl? What a joke, huh?" he said, describing her as "just a friend who kind of lost her mind," and her story of his confession as "creative." After watching a video clip of her interview with investigators, he laughed and said, "That's next-level psycho."

Asked point-blank if he had anything to do with the murder of the McStay family, Kavanaugh said, "Not only did I not, but I have no knowledge of anybody that did."

Nonetheless, when asked if he was "100 percent convinced that the right man is in jail," he said, "Yeah."

Kavanaugh claimed detectives told him to "stay out of Dodge" so he didn't have to testify, quoting them as saying, "If they can't find you, we're just going to take care of this." So, he said he changed his lifestyle to avoid detection, because he didn't want Merritt to "gaslight more people."

Lieutenant Smith vehemently denied saying any such thing. "No! I was like, that's bullcrap," he said. "That's just a straight-out lie. We didn't tell him to hide. We didn't freaking care. We weren't worried about Dan."

It's unclear what Kavanaugh meant by "changing his lifestyle," because he was in and out of jail before and after the trial. He was arrested in 2017 for possession of methamphetamine in a Best Buy parking lot in Orange County, although the charge was later dismissed. He violated his probation with an arrest in August 2019 for possession of cocaine while driving a Land Rover that didn't belong to him, without the owner's consent, and with a suspended or revoked license. The two felonies were later reduced to misdemeanors, for a total of four. In June 2020, he was arrested on a DUI in San Diego County, which he pleaded down to reckless driving. After he failed to comply with his one-year summary probation, a bench warrant was ordered for his arrest in April 2021.

Once Merritt was convicted of murder, he wasn't allowed to profit off his crime, so he asked that Cathy Jarvis receive his percentage of the documentary proceeds. However, he wasn't apprised of the negotiations and never got a straight answer about how much his attorney's share, or Jarvis's, would be.

"I have no idea," Merritt said. "I was never kept in the loop."

Maline and Merritt said that any ethical concerns of a potential conflict created by his entering into the "media rights exploitation" agreement with his attorneys and letting them participate in, and financially benefit from, the documentary, were addressed in court, when Merritt agreed to waive those concerns. Maline noted the defense even hired outside counsel to ensure the arrangement was ethical, and the judge looked over the contract.

When the prosecution issued a mid-trial subpoena for footage of the interviews Taylor and Cathy Jarvis had done prior to testifying in court—to see if their answers changed or if they were guided to modify their statements—Judge Smith granted a motion to quash it.

After the series aired, a notable number of viewers posted on Twitter and in Facebook discussion groups that they thought Merritt was innocent or didn't receive a fair trial. Others said they thought Merritt was a sociopath, who was definitely guilty.

Merritt said he was personally disappointed with the outcome of the series.

"A guilty verdict makes me more valuable," he said. "Had I been found not guilty, do you think this documentary would have actually even happened? People just stop caring once a 'not guilty' verdict happens. These people, meaning my attorneys and the people doing the video, aren't stupid."

Maline wasn't thrilled, either. "I never would have agreed to this nonsense they put out," he said.

Merritt has since worked with an outside party to create a website to post parts of his book, along with various transcripts and documents from the case.

Although prosecutors successfully fought claims of misconduct throughout the trial, the allegation was levelled so many times that Maline believes it will likely be part of Merritt's appeal.

"There's no question," he said.

Cases involving prosecutorial misconduct are on the rise nationally, according to a Reuters article by Hassan Kanu from June 2022, which states, "The number of criminal exonerations in the U.S. has been growing for years, and official misconduct is consistently a top reason for those false convictions."

As of 2023, the National Registry of Exonerations (NRE), which tracks these cases, had documented 3,307 exonerations since 1989. Of the latest batch reported, 70 percent involved defendants "convicted in part because of official misconduct," 48 percent were homicide convictions, and nineteen of them involved DNA evidence. California ranked third nationally with eleven exonerations. Illinois was first with thirty-eight, and New York second with eighteen.

But as Kanu pointed out, "Prosecutors are rarely disciplined for even plainly corrupt behavior, and civil lawsuits are almost never successful because of court-created legal immunities."

So, has this been happening all along, or are prosecutors less ethical these days? Is this an outgrowth of the general trend of aggressive and sometimes violent partisan divisiveness and political attacks featured 24/7 on cable TV, or is more attention being focused on these types of allegations in the legal system?

Whatever the reason, none of these allegations seemed to affect the race for an open judicial seat in San Bernardino County Superior Court for which James McGee vied against Melissa Rodriguez, one of his opponents in this case.

In early 2022, McGee's campaign signs were posted all over the streets and fences of San Bernardino, especially near the courthouse. Yet, come June, Rodriguez beat McGee by a landslide in the primary election, garnering 71 percent of the vote.

The voters of that county also make up the jury pool, which sends more defendants to death row per capita than all but three other California counties. As of December 2022, thirty-nine of these 674 condemned inmates were convicted in San Bernardino.

The county is so conservative that its electorate passed a ballot measure to study seceding from California in the 2022 general election.

If Merritt's conviction stands, he will more than likely die a natural death, as will most of his fellow death row inmates in California, which has the nation's largest condemned population by far.

Although California voters have historically supported the death penalty, the state has had a moratorium on executions since 2006, due to the controversial cocktail of drugs used in the injections. As public debate was closing on a new single-injection method, Governor Newsom extended the moratorium for as long as he is in office. (He terms out in 2026.) Newsom said he couldn't, in good conscience, allow executions to restart when the system unfairly targets people of color and those with mental disabilities or low IQs, and when so many executed inmates turn out to be innocent after it's too late.

"Ending up on death row has more to do with your wealth and race than it does your guilt or innocence," he said.

This position didn't stop Newsom from beating a recall attempt with a vote of 62 percent in 2021, or from handily winning re-election in 2022, when he also announced he was going to dismantle death row at San Quentin and turn the space into a rehabilitation facility with a "positive, healing environment." Merritt and other inmates were to be distributed into the general population at other maximum-security prisons, where they would participate in rehabilitation and work programs, with 70 percent of their wages going toward restitution to victims' families.

"I think premeditated murder is wrong, in all its forms and manifestation, including government-sponsored murder," Newsom said.

In 2024, Merritt was moved, as planned, to the Richard J. Donovan Correctional Facility in San Diego County, where he was busy working on a detailed petition for a writ of habeas corpus, reasserting ineffective assistance of counsel. He said he intends to file it without an attorney in 2025.

Acknowledgments and Author's Note

I'd like to thank these people, and others who will go unnamed for various reasons, for helping me obtain documents, photos, and other information for this book: Michael Smith, Raj Maline, Britt Imes, Ryan Smith, Jeff Allison, Jacob Guerard, Jimmy Dorantes, David Gotfredson, Taylor and Cathy Jarvis, Diana Klay, Gina Watson, Tricia Arrington Griffith, Mary Ellen Attridge, Sam Hodgson, Merrie Monteagudo, Eric Vilchis, John McCutchen, Tracey Riccobene, Amanda Frolio, Lyndene Aman, Debra Storch, Kat Dean, Paula Rogers, Teri Perez, Mark Gutglueck, and Tess Tallman.

I'd also like to thank my partner, Géza Keller, who lived through the research and writing of this project; my agent, Joe Veltre and his team; Michaela Hamilton, my editor at Kensington/Citadel; and my beta readers, Géza, Alana Albertson, Mary Wotanis, Mark Stalnaker, and Carole Scott.

Some dialogue, court testimony, and quotes have been edited—by deletion, not addition—only for storytelling purposes and ease of reading, never to change the meaning. Nothing was created, embellished, or exaggerated. Any errors are completely unintentional. A limited number of pseudonyms were used to protect people's privacy.

I've followed this case from the very beginning, when it was all over the news. I read all 300-plus pages of search warrant affidavits the judges unsealed, attended the preliminary hearing, and scoured public records and media reports about every possible suspect and key witness in this case. I followed the livestreamed trial and rewatched parts of it on YouTube, reviewed trial transcripts, tracked news and reactions on social media, and read through the 1,200 trial exhibits and four-volume court file, the latter of which took five days to manually copy. I also interviewed everyone who would talk to me, including one of the prosecutors, the lead detective from San Bernardino County, Chase Merritt, his ex-partner and their eldest daughter, and his longest-lasting attorney.

But I didn't really see this case unfold until a few months before my deadline, when I was, at long last, able to obtain thousands of pages of coveted discovery materials, including investigative reports and witness interviews from both sheriff's agencies, most of which have never been made public. There lay the compelling story behind the story, which I've done my best to tell in these pages.

Although I often quote directly from these investigative reports, I can't guarantee their factual accuracy. I present them for their content and wording only, because they sometimes differ or directly conflict with other statements or evidence. This will allow readers, just like the jurors, to decide the truth of the matter for themselves.

Given the extensive and protracted media coverage of this case, the unwelcome criticism and scrutinization of the victims' extended families—and their understandable desires for privacy and to move on with their lives—my attempts to gain their cooperation with this book were unsuccessful. I reached out through the prosecution and victim's advocate office, through friends on social media, by email and even snail mail, and most either communicated their lack of interest through third parties or didn't reply at all. So, I tried to convey their thoughts and experiences with sensitivity and compassion through comments they made in the media, to investigators, or on the witness stand.

As usual, I'm not taking a position on anyone's guilt or innocence in the murders of this family, I'm just the messenger, laying out the evidence and the sometimes ugly truth of how this case came together. But I hope this book opens readers' eyes on the workings and flaws of our criminal justice system and also changes preconceived notions about this case in particular.